A

INSIDE THE FRONT PAGE

From copy boy to managing editor: My life in the newspaper business

BY RUSSELL W. FREEBURG

To Kay,
a great and old
friend. With my best
wishes!
Russ

AMP&RSAND, INC.
Chicago • New Orleans

ISBN 978-099947753-3

Design
David Robson, Robson Design, Inc.

Published by
AMPERSAND, INC.
515 Madison Street
New Orleans, Louisiana 70116
www.ampersandworks.com

Printed in U.S.A.

A Note From the Author
Throughout the text, the names Chicago Tribune, Tribune, and City
News Bureau of Chicago have been set in body type and not italic as is
customary. The names appear so often in the narrative that setting them in
italic would have been distracting.

To my fellow newspaper

men and women

The life of a person is not what happened,

but what he remembers and how he remembers it.

Gabriel Garcia Marquez

PROLOGUE

It is said that nothing is forever. Certainly, I've lived long enough, and experienced enough, to understand that there is truth in the saying since I was a print journalist in a disruptive and changing media world. The strong and powerful newspaper industry that I knew and loved is fading away. What is left of it, after decades of erosion, still has faithful staffs that carry on, but financial distress is common as advertising revenues and readerships shrink.

I have a melancholy feeling every time a paper folds because something important is at stake: it is the protection a free, unfettered paper press provides for us all. There is something solid and lasting about a printed word. It doesn't float away into the ether like the spoken word. So many of the words used over the airwaves and cable, all those modifying adjectives and adverbs, the polarizing interchanges among talking heads, are often useless, even detrimental, to reporting the news. They create emotions and opinions that rob a listener of independent thought, a power to think events through.

Give me a hard-hitting verb in 10 point roman type any time to make an impression.

There have been many changes in media in my lifetime. Newspapers have had a tough slough of it in the last half of the 20th and into the beginning of the 21st-century. According to the Bureau of Labor Statistics, daily and weekly newspaper publishers employed 455,000 reporters, clerks, salespeople, editors, designers, photographers and the like in 1990. By January, 2017 that workforce had been more than halved to 173,000 and the slide continues.

The decline is ominous. In a 2018 article in the *Washington Post*, Margaret Sullivan wrote that research shows newspapers still produce 85% of accountability journalism—journalism that unearths corruption and exposes abuse of power.

New technology has given us the internet, Twitter, Facebook, and thousands of other sites to communicate with each other on the World Wide Web. Everybody, more or less, has become neighbors. In cyberspace, we share thoughts and, maybe, dreams with others. But, do we get hard facts that are crucial to wise decisions? Or, is it mostly idle chatter? Is it nothing more in the end than constituency journalism? I'm not a Luddite. I enjoy and use modern technology. But, I refuse to let it enslave me. I'll leave it to Father Time to referee the future, to determine whether the tools of cyberspace lend themselves to introspection and the serious thoughts that come with the power of the printed word.

I'm not the Young Turk of yesteryear; I'm less of a participant in events and more of an observer. It's not my working world anymore. But, no one can take from me the experiences I had from starting as a copy boy at the City News Bureau of Chicago to become managing editor of the Chicago Tribune, a renowned and storied newspaper. I keep up with things going on, who's doing what. But, I'm not in the actionable crucible anymore, no longer in the hustle and bustle of a journalist's daily life. I muse and read more. I comprehend a changed world, even encourage it. Still, I stay loyal to my time, and that's where my story lies in the pages ahead as I mix my own career with the decline of the newspaper industry.

Everybody has constants as they move through life, season after season, year after year, boundaries that anchor and shape thoughts and actions. A philosophy is developed by which to live, a tenacity to absorb blows, grace under pressure, and forgiveness in victory. Growing old, as I have, I've become a linchpin with the past. I remember people and events I saw as a journalist, earlier titans of politics and giants of business, who may be unknown to younger people. These recollections mean something to me, the part I played. They create an intimacy, a comforting solitude, which comes with putting my thoughts down on paper at the end of my era.

Memories and afterthoughts whisper the life I've lived back to me in my old age. They're fortified by random notes jotted down from time-to-time through the years, old memos and letters, and scrapbooks that my dad pasted up with clippings of stories I covered as a reporter and editor. Everybody has their yesterdays: for me there was my boyhood in the Midwest, soldiering on the battlefields of Europe, covering the White House in our nation's capital, fighting to bring a staid and stationary Chicago Tribune kicking and screaming into the last half of the twentieth century.

God knows, I wasn't perfect. But, I tried to give the best that was in me.

Russell W. Freeburg
January 2019
DeLand, Florida

CHAPTER ONE

THE BEGINNING

I t was autumn 1948. The City News Bureau of Chicago was connected to newspaper city rooms around town by pneumatic tubes that ran through freight tunnels under the city. Reporters would telephone in stories to rewriters wearing headphones. The rewrite people would type the stories onto thin wax stencils. The stories would be edited with a stylus by editors, mimeographed and stuffed by copy boys, like me, into brass and leather cartridges which the pneumatic tubes whisked through the tunnels to their destination.

It was a mechanical world then, not the digital one that was to come.

The City News Bureau was a cooperative news agency that ran around the clock and all year long. It was started by newspapers in Chicago to provide a common, frugal source for police and court stories and as a training ground for young reporters, who either stood shoulder to shoulder with experienced counterparts on the dailies in gathering the news or perished. My own hope, of course, was to survive when my time came. Meanwhile, I would bide my days as a copy boy until I could get out on the street and into the skirmish.

I'll always have warm feelings for the time I worked at the City News Bureau. Its colorful past will always be a part of media folklore. But, like many of the newspapers it once served, City News, too, is gone, another casualty in the revolutionary changes in communications. In the end, its operational financial losses could not be sustained.

The City News Bureau of Chicago, 1890–1999, may it rest in peace.

I've sometimes wondered how close I came to not being hired at all to work for the City News Bureau.

Here is what happened. In late August, 1948, I met with Isaac Gersh-man, the bureau's general manager. I had graduated from Washington University in St. Louis that June and I'd been accepted to the graduate school of the Medill School of Journalism at Northwestern University for entrance in the fall of 1949. I needed something to do for the next year. At Washington, I attended classes for two straight years, summers and winters, to make up for time lost in the military in World War II. I'd fallen in love with the school years earlier as a youth when I visited it while my uncle, Axel Carlson, underwent exploratory lung surgery in its medical school hospital. I gave serious thought to being a doctor, but when I took organic chemistry I knew the curriculum necessary for a medical career was not for me, whereas journalism came naturally.

A chain of events, rather mystic in its way, led me to Gershman. It began a few weeks after my graduation while my wife, Sally, and I visited with my parents in my home town of Galesburg, a prairie grove crisscrossed by railroads on fertile, but windswept, Illinois farm land 180 miles southwest of Chicago. One sunny morning I stopped by the city hall to see another uncle, Leo "Curly" Morrison. He was city treasurer then. Later, he would become mayor. A big ceiling fan slowly rotated high above us as we chatted back and forth in his high walled office about my hope to become a journalist. Bob Jordan, the assistant treasurer, also took part in the conversation. My heart jumped when Jordan mentioned that his cousin, J. Loy (Pat) Maloney, was managing editor of the Chicago Tribune.

"I'll write a letter of introduction for you," Jordan volunteered. I still remember how casual the conversation was with never a thought that two decades later I would sit in Maloney's chair.

Curly and Bob Jordan were both sons of Ireland. Curly was married to my mother's youngest sister, Jeanette. You can guess by his nick-name what his head of thick black hair was like. The Irish population in Galesburg, with its own schools and hospital, had settled over the years on the south side of Main Street with established Swedes to the north. That didn't stop biology from taking its natural course. My best man at my wedding, Ray Nelson, a Swede like me, married an Irish girl. So did other friends and another uncle, Pete. After a century long line of Protestant Swedish mayors, my Irish uncle Curly became the first Roman Catholic to head the city government. Galesburg's 30,000 citizens, in a rough and tumble election, chose him by 106 votes.

Maloney was friendly and informal when I met him. As we talked in his fourth floor corner office in Tribune Tower, I could see traffic below on Michigan Avenue and the bridge over the Chicago River as the waterway zigzagged among the skyscrapers hugging its banks. Maloney sat facing me behind his highly polished mahogany desk with his legs pulled up and crossed under him in his chair, yoga style. To be brief, he liked my education and military background, but he thought I needed street experience.

"Go over to the City News Bureau for 17 months," Maloney advised me. "Work there. Don't worry about anything." He picked up a pen on his desk and quickly wrote a letter of introduction to Gershman on Tribune stationary.

I thought Maloney's backing would be a sure fire ticket to a job since the Tribune owned a piece of the City News Bureau. It turned out to be harder. Gershman was a lean man who wore thick glasses and moved cautiously. Clearly, he wasn't an easy conversationalist. After we stumbled along for a few minutes, he said that he had nothing for me. We sat and looked at each other for what seemed to me an eternity.

"I do have an opening for a copy boy," he said finally in a quiet voice, his owlish eyes peering over his spectacles.

It seemed like a throw-away line. My mind churned. I was 25 years old with a university degree. I was married. I'd traveled Europe, granted at times on my belly, with the United States Army. Okay, I thought, forget all that. The chain of letters from Jordan to Maloney to Gershman, seemed like a fateful pathway to bring me to this spot, a road traveled for a reason. Why hesitate?

"I'll take it," I said.

Gershman seemed surprised at my reply, but he agreed to hire me. So, I became a copy boy the day after Labor Day in September, 1948.

Over the late fall and winter I spent an occasional day with a beat reporter. I learned how the City News Bureau functioned. When I came to work one morning in early spring, Larry Mulay, the bureau's editor-in-chief, motioned me to his desk. A big smile broke out on his face as he spoke.

"Russ, we're promoting you," he said. "Beginning today, you'll be covering the north police beat. Are you ready?"

I replied, "You bet I am." Of course, the truth was that I was filled with apprehension. I had seen others fail the challenge in this bit of journalistic Darwinism. Mulay looked up at the bureau's big wall clock. "I guess you'd better get going then," My time had come to survive or perish. As I moved toward the door, he yelled, "Good luck."

I hopped on a streetcar to the Chicago Avenue police station, heard some routine police court cases with no news in them, then headed for the Hudson Avenue police district, where I looked over the arrest book and gabbed a little with the desk sergeant. Later, as I sat alone on the Fullerton Avenue elevated platform, I felt isolated. I looked at my watch and realized I was behind schedule. Court at the Town Hall police district farther north would be over before I got there.

It's a spooky experience to be alone, and unprotected, on an El platform with no train in sight, just empty space in both directions along cold, unending stretches of steel tracks. Since it was my first day on a beat, I was on edge. Wind whipped scraps of paper around: an empty gum wrapper, a discarded crossword puzzle. A dust eddy whirled skyward. A squeaky door to the stairs to the street swung menacing back and forth. Paranoia set in.

"I'll get fired," I muttered. I'd been out of contact with Mulay for more than an hour. "I'll just never go back." This was in the days long before cell phones. I couldn't just whip one out of my pocket and punch out the news desk's numbers. That convenience didn't exist. I looked around for a telephone booth, but there was none.

Far down the tracks a train rumbled into view. My anxiety lessened. When a car rolled to a stop in front of me and its doors slid open, I hopped aboard. A hope of success sprang anew. But, those isolated moments, the helpless feeling I had, haunted me. I turned in a couple of routine police stories that first day along with an obituary late in the afternoon. One of the duties of City News Bureau reporters was to check out all deaths on his beat that were reported to the Cook County coroner's office. I turned the obit in to Selma Friend, who was working rewrite. As she ripped the stencil out of her typewriter, I heard her yell over to the copy desk: "He's doing O.K." I had prepared some for my first day on the street. During my months as a copy boy, I made notes on the content of the various stories that came through the mimeograph room, and I arranged the notes by categories — robberies, fires, murders, obituaries — in a small pocket notebook that I carried with me. For routine stories it amounted to just filling in the blanks — name, place, age, address — so on and so on.

In his book *Slaughterhouse-Five,* Kurt Vonnegut Jr. recalled his first day on the street for the City News Bureau. He worked there a year or so and had moved on before I arrived. His story involved a WWII veteran who'd taken a job running an office building elevator with an ornamental iron lace door on the first floor. The veteran decided to take his elevator into the basement. As he started down, his wedding ring caught in the ornaments. The floor of the car dropped out from under him and the top of the car squashed him to death as it went by. When he returned to the office that afternoon, the woman rewrite (whom he didn't identify) asked Vonnegut how the squashed man looked hanging by his wedding ring. "Did it bother you?"[1] she inquired, as she munched on a Three Musketeers candy bar. That sounded to me like Selma Friend. She loved Three Musketeers candy bars and she was forever probing for gory and salacious details. One late afternoon when I returned to the office, Selma cornered me.

"What really happened in that sexual assault case you turned into me earlier?" she asked, a conspiratorial gleam in her eyes.

"Come on, Selma, not now," I replied. "I've got to pick up my paycheck."

"No, tell me." She laughed mockingly with delight. "The intimate details, please?"

The hell with it! Wasn't the motto of the original three musketeers all for one and one for all? I told her every gory and salacious detail of the court testimony, the attack, the struggle, the perversion. Selma never blushed.

"Very good," she said, her voice strong. A smile crossed her broad face. Everyone liked Selma. She'd come aboard during WWII, when civilian men were scarce. "I'll make a reporter out of you yet."

Vonnegut said in his book that he had a telephone habit of calling people late at night to talk. I guess I should have called Kurt late some evening to ask if he was writing about Selma.

After I had worked for the City News Bureau for 17 months, as Maloney suggested, I wrote him a letter to inquire what I should do now. I received a letter from him in reply that said in its entirety: "I am keeping you in mind." Phyllis Theroux in her memoir *The Journal Keeper* tells of opening Gary Zukav's *The Seat of the Soul* one morning. Her eyes fell upon these lines:

As you face your deepest struggles, you reach for your highest goal....

This is the work of evolution. It is the work you were born to do.[2]

By trial and error, you become what you are. My mother-in-law, Frances Woodford, insisted I had a good angel that sat on my shoulder and took care of me. I believe otherwise, that I was born to be a journalist. Maybe, it was a process of elimination; I wasn't cut out to be anything else. Maybe, there are "naturals" in other crafts besides baseball. I've always been inquisitive. I've always wanted to know how things work. I believe that when corruption is found in this world it needs to be righted. A journalist has always to be in search of facts. It is facts, of course, that reporters, good reporters, deal in. I've always believed that "good getting" is more important than "good writing" for journalists. There is nothing to write if there are no facts. The turn of a beautiful phrase is more attuned to literature. Hard factual copy is the name of the game in reporting.

A repulsive phase like "fake news" used so often nowadays didn't exist in my journalism years.

As I settled in, Sally went to work for Ma Bell again, this time with Illinois Bell, as a service representative, just as in St. Louis at Southwestern Bell. Again, she came through with housing for us; an apartment in a lakefront high-rise on Chicago's far north side. We could afford the location because WWII rent controls were still in place. The building was owned by the mother of B.J. Barker, one of Sally's college roommates. It was a lucky break. Or maybe not. Everyone liked Sally. A friend told me once that to know Sally was to like me.

We weren't exactly newlyweds, but this was our first real home, and we liked buying furnishings, little by little as our money allowed. Our first priority was the bedroom since sleeping on the floor had no appeal. Next came a dining room set to replace four borrowed chairs and a card table. Sally liked early American maple for both rooms, so early American maple it was. We furnished the living room last, but once it was done we spent many pleasant evenings there, sometimes alone, sometimes playing bridge with friends. In the summertime, breezes off Lake Michigan kept us cool. Like so many things now taken for granted, universal air conditioning was still to come.

CHAPTER TWO

TV, WHAT'S THAT?

An aura of *The Front Page* still existed when I went to work for the City News Bureau of Chicago. The famous play about journalism in the city was 20 years old by then. More or less, however, its brashness lingered among the news people. It wasn't anything a person could put a finger on. It was a feeling. Newspapers were king and I seldom gave a thought to the possibility this would change.

As I learned my craft, I didn't foresee the enormity of changes to come. Very few news people, if any, did. It crossed my mind that newspaper owners were busy acquiring federal licenses for television channels. But, that seemed no different than owing radio stations, which augmented rather than competed with newspapers. Looking back, it's clear that I had a front row seat to earth-shaking shifts in media power. Just as I went forth, a pivot took place that marked the beginning of the end of newspaper invincibility. Something called TV had invaded our realm. But, now, the ascendancy of TV is being challenged in turn by the internet. I'm tapping this out on a laptop computer. I began typing copy at the City News Bureau on its thin, wax stencils.

I've come to view the fate of newspapers as the second extinction in the world of communications. The first extinction was the printed word replacing hand written manuscripts. There was a long period of tranquility after the first extinction. The second extinction, with the visual world of television replacing newspapers, may be shorter. As the century progresses, a third extinction—the digital world of websites, iPhones and streaming—may be much faster at demolishing cable and over-the-air television.

I hoped, as the years passed, that I had fought a good battle even as I came to understand that use of the printed word to tell the news, the thrill to be first on the street with the day's headlines, the excitement of a newsboy calling out "extra!" "extra!" was slipping away. It's been an agonizing death. There were occasions I tossed and turned as managing editor of the Tribune as I tussled with how to give freshness to big events that everyone already had seen live on TV. In my old age, I've realized it was a fool's errand. But, in 1948, all of that was in the future as viewers gazed at TV test patterns for hours. That should have told me something. But, I was more interested in the newsmen upon whom characters in *The Front Page* were based. They were known intimately by the playwrights, Ben Hecht and Charles MacArthur, their colleagues in Chicago.

I was the new generation of what they were.

Walter Howey, the prototype of the play's colorful editor, Walter Burns, was a former Tribune city editor. Hildy Johnson, the intrepid reporter of the play, was dead, but in the Cook County Criminal Courts building, where I worked one thrill-filled summer for the City News Bureau, Hildy's brass name plate, polished and revered, still adorned his old cubicle in the pressroom. To my delight, Roy Benzinger was alive. Eventually, I met him.

Benzinger was the original for the skittish, hygiene conscious reporter in the play. He was older now, heavier, with ailments, some real, others doubtful, a little temperamental. His name was spelled with an "s" instead of a "z" in the play, but everything else was on target. I watched him in the mornings, in that summer of 1949, take a rag and cleaning fluid to wipe away any germs that had arrived overnight on his desk and telephone in the Criminal Courts pressroom. He worked for Hearst's *Herald American* after an earlier stint at the Tribune. Once in a while, Buddy McHugh would show up in the Criminal Courts pressroom. In the play, he was McCue of City Press, a takeoff on the City News Bureau. He also worked for the *Herald American* when I met him. He was a police reporter whose black fedora reeked of smoke from covering too many fires. McHugh had a habit of cupping his hand around the mouth piece of any telephone he used as though he were revealing great secrets. Other reporters told me not to worry about being scooped. They said McHugh played the horses and he talked to bookies that way.

Benzinger made it plain that I was not to call in any story I ran across in the building until I'd given him a chance to tell his city desk about it first. Every afternoon, after the last *Herald American* edition of the day had gone to press, he took a nap on the pressroom's big leather couch. Only then was I on my own without him. Being a young cub reporter, that was all okay by me.

Except, one morning I'd been back in the Felony Court holding pen for arrestees talking to Ruth Ann Steinhagen, a pretty 19-year-old Chicagoan, who the night before had shot and wounded Eddie Waitkus, an all-star first baseman for the Philadelphia Phillies. The team was in town to play the Cubs. I chatted with Ruth Ann as she was waiting to appear in her preliminary hearing. As we talked, she expressed remorse. She began to cry, and sobbed how sorry she was about shooting Eddie. She told me that the only way she could relieve the nervous tension of her infatuation with Waitkus was to shoot him.

The incident was one of the first examples of what has become known as stalker crimes. Elements of the Steinhagen case paralleled the plot of *The Natural*, Bernard Malamud's best-selling 1952 baseball novel. Later a motion picture, as authors say.

Benzinger was late to arrive that day. I waited for half an hour, or more, for him. Finally, not knowing if, or when, he would appear, I called in my story, which moved on the City News wire to the *Herald American*. Benzinger was more than a little peeved with me when he finally showed up and was asked immediately by his city desk about my story. Eventually, he claimed he couldn't find anyone who'd seen Steinhagen actually crying. It was the word of a veteran newsman against that of a young reporter. His editors contacted my editors and I spent the rest of the day defending what I'd seen and heard. Sometimes there's a little chaff with the wheat.

Ruth Ann was a brunette, rather tall, approaching six feet, who worked as a typist for Continental Casualty Company in Chicago's loop. She'd become obsessed with Waitkus when he played for the Cubs. It came out that she had spent the preceding fall just roaming the streets of Chicago hoping to see him. When the Cubs traded Waitkus to Philadelphia she became more unhinged. On the afternoon of June 14, 1949, she watched the Phillies beat the Cubs 9 to 2 at Wrigley Field. The Phillies were staying at the Edgewater Beach Hotel where Ruth Ann had a room on the 12th floor. That evening she sent a note to Eddie's room, saying she had something important to discuss with him. When he went to her room, Ruth Ann told him the woman who wrote the note had stepped out for a minute. As he waited, she walked into a closet. "I have a surprise for you," she said from behind the closet door. She stepped out and shot him with a .22 rifle she had purchased in a pawn shop. She then called the hotel desk, a belated move of compassion that probably saved his life.

I never talked to Ruth Ann again after the interview in Felony Court, but I followed her story through the years. She was declared legally insane by a later court and sent to a state mental hospital for three years of psychiatric treatment. Waitkus recovered to help the Phillies win the National League pennant a year later. Upon her release in 1952, the charge of assault with intent to commit murder against her was dropped at his request.

Ruth Ann lived in anonymity on the northwest side of Chicago after her release from the state hospital, first with her parents, then with a sister. I've always questioned the insanity ruling. But, she certainly was a troubled young woman, with a romantic crush on a man she could never have, and she behaved foolishly. Her obsession with Waitkus faded with the years, and she lived a long life, dying on December 29, 2012, in Chicago's Swedish Covenant hospital, where she'd been taken after a fall at the age of 83.

Gordon "Spike" Martin, who married Sally's older sister, Marilyn, played with Waitkus for Moline in the Three Eye League, so named because its teams were spread across the prairies of Indiana, Illinois and Iowa. Spike played third base. When big league scouts were around, Waitkus encouraged Spike to make his throws across the infield low into the dirt or high and wide so Waitkus would look good catching them. Waitkus made it to the majors, Spike didn't. I asked Spike once if he thought there was a lesson here.

I left the Criminal Courts in the fall to cover the Civil Courts in the County building downtown. By then, I had decided to forgo graduate studies at Northwestern. It was a tough decision for me. Should I become a student again or should I continue working for City News, always hoping to hear from Maloney? I thought of the years lost in WWII. Another year of schooling would delay a career even further. I decided to take my chances with Maloney.

As the spring rains came I was brought into the bureau newsroom to do rewrite, always hoping that I would hear from Maloney again. Then, one day a call came from the Tribune. Gershman informed me that Paul Hubbard, the paper's metropolitan editor, wished to interview me for an opening on his staff. It was April, 1950, 19 months after I had started at the City News Bureau. Maloney was true to his word.

He had kept me in mind. The following letter, dated March 15, 1950, was found in my file at the City News Bureau:

Dear Gersh,

How is this fellow coming along? I would appreciate a little note. Somebody told me he was a trifle slow in the writing game—perhaps it was you. Have you anyone you would prefer to recommend? Any information would be appreciated.

Pat

Any slowness on my part "in the writing game" was due to my typing. I had no trouble constructing a story, but I'd no experience typing at the rate necessary for a fast moving wire service. I made a start to correct the discrepancy when I enrolled in a nighttime typing course, but after two weeks I had to drop out when I was shifted from a daytime to a nighttime beat. It was a big surprise to City News Bureau editors when Hubbard told them I was a good writer. At the Tribune, with less pressure for speed, a bit slower typing pace didn't matter.

My final assignment at the City News Bureau was on a Sunday, a week after I was hired by Hubbard. In early evening, I was sent to Henrotin Hospital outside of the loop on the city's near north side, where injured passengers in an automobile accident were being treated. Undoubtedly, police would be there to question.

I went to the first floor emergency room, where a doctor in scrubs was attending a slim, youthful man lying on an examining table. A powerful, bright light shined down upon them. I stood in the shadows. I saw no lacerations. I saw no blood. The man was fully dressed, but his breathing was difficult. Suddenly, he became still. The doctor, who had been gently probing the man, turned away. How easily death can come, I thought. An hour earlier, this man must have had no thought of dying. Police told me he was not responsible for the accident. Nevertheless, he didn't beat the dealer. I called it all in to rewrite. As I exited the hospital into the night air, it occurred to me that it might be a long time, if ever, before I covered an automobile accident again.

The next morning I joined the Tribune.

CHAPTER THREE

GROWING UP, THE TRIBUNE IS THERE

I had a long romance with the Chicago Tribune. There wasn't a fairy tale ending, but in between its start as a toddler, and my exit in middle age, it was a wonderful affair. The newspaper was already a fixture in my parents' home when I was born, and I grew up hearing its stories and editorials quoted, and reading it myself as a boy. The turbulence that would later overtake the newspaper industry, even the Tribune itself, couldn't be imagined.

That day I joined the paper in the spring of 1950, its daily circulation was 1,022,000. It said so in a little box on the front page. Only its sister paper, the tabloid *New York Daily News*, had a greater readership—2,500,000. Neither paper would reach those figures ever again. Through the years, I had watched the circulation grow. The competition then was other newspapers and the Tribune was just better than its opposition.

Newspapers and television existed together in sort of a no man's land in the first years of my journalism career with neither giving much attention to the other. In 1948, according to *Time* magazine, only one in 10 Americans had seen a TV broadcast, about 350,000 people owned a set. The CBS television network was founded early in the year, and that summer it joined three other fledgling TV networks to carry proceedings of the Republican and Democratic political conventions in Philadelphia to 13 eastern seaboard states. An estimated 10 million viewers may have watched. But, there was no correlated effort to cover the presidential election that fall. Newspapers, for the last time, had an Election Day to themselves.

Reading the Tribune was a daily experience in my youth. The names of byline writers, some well-known, some famous, were familiar to us all. There was Arch Ward on sports and Sigrid Schultz in Nazi Germany. Arthur Sears Henning in Washington was another. They were considered part of the family. There was an intimacy to the relationship. News of the day drawn from Tribune pages was discussed around the dinner table. Treasured articles were clipped and saved. The Tribune was in my hometown each morning before the sun rose, although Galesburg was 180 miles away from its printing presses. Copies arrived overnight in baggage cars of passenger trains traveling west over the Illinois prairie from Chicago on the Burlington Route. Dropped off in the railroad's cavernous depot, they were picked up each morning by newsboys, and delivered as dawn broke.

The world was different then. Information in my youth traveled at a slower pace. Television was still a laboratory dream. The internet wasn't even a dream. But, as they developed, like the sirens of Greek mythology, whose seductive songs drew sailors to their island shores, they lured away one reader, then another, one advertiser, then another, until few remained. Air travel was in its infancy. A network of rails was what bonded people together; its steel rods crisscrossed the nation to connect big cities and hamlets alike. It was easy for editions of the Tribune to be piled inside baggage cars and circulated throughout the Midwest as part of the paper's "Chicagoland," a phrase coined to bring the area for hundreds of miles around Chicago together under its political and spiritual influence.

"The Tribune is a pugnacious newspaper, son." my dad remarked once when I was a boy. I remember he chuckled. "There's never any question where it stands on the great issues of the day."

It's okay for adults to argue issues, to be glad or angry about stands taken, and the Tribune always has had readers in both camps, but I was in knee pants, and like many young boys, the sports section was my favorite part of the paper. Sometimes, I dreamed of becoming a major league baseball player.

Of course, that changed in my adulthood. I never covered sports; I was never a professional athlete. Instead, I covered police, I wrote about finance; then, as Washington bureau chief, I covered politics and the White House. Eventually, I was appointed managing editor and I returned to Chicago to be in charge of the day-to-day operations of the paper. But, even an editor is once a child, who must grow up.

I was born in the roaring '20s. For grownups, it was a decade of Prohibition and speakeasies, bathtub gin and bobbed haired flappers, the Charleston dance and jazz. As a youngster, of course, I experienced none of that. I wish only that I had. The period was so carefree, my parents so optimistic. The world was everyone's oyster. Alas, the euphoria didn't last. Instead, my birth put me on a path to be a child of the Great Depression with its sorrow and hardship. It was the stock market crash of October 29, 1929, not flappers and jazz, that defined my youth.

I came into the world on March 4, 1923, as the newest member of an immigrant Scandinavian family. All of my grandparents were from Sweden. In an unusual twist, for me fateful, my maternal grandmother, Christine Holmes, arrived in the United States in 1892 as a 17-year-old, indentured in servitude to my paternal grandparents, Nels and Anna Freeburg and their six young children—five boys and a girl. Their fourth son, Carl, my dad, later married one of Christine's daughters, Ethel Marie, my mom.

It was common among immigrants to advance money for passage in exchange for work until the fare was paid. Such an arrangement for my maternal grandmother was made by her older brother, who preceded her to America. Once together in their new country, they lived next door to each other with their families for the rest of their lives. I showed up in the second generation of family members born as Americans citizens. I've been told that my birth was early on a Sunday morning. The place was Cottage Hospital in that prairie grove in west central Illinois, the land of Lincoln. Galesburg was an old abolitionist stronghold. It was there in 1858, during one of the famous Lincoln-Douglas debates on slavery, that Lincoln, after stepping though a window of Knox College's Old Main building onto the debate platform, remarked, "At last, I have gone through college."

Immersion in that history in my youth, plus the reverence my parents held for Lincoln, certainly played a part in my life long belief in equality among races. Soon after I was out of the cradle I was told to judge a person by whom they are, not what they are.

I knew as a child that the Tribune, closely associated with the fledgling Republican Party, had backed Lincoln in his run for the presidency. Joseph Medill, then its editor, was instrumental in his nomination. Both were anti-slavery: that was their common ground. But, Medill and his paper were often at odds with Lincoln on government appointments and other policy matters, and their relationship was sometimes acrimonious. Medill certainly laid the groundwork for the Tribune's long tradition of hard charging journalism. Colonel Robert R. McCormick was owner and publisher of the Tribune as I grew up. Like his maternal grandfather Medill, he was also strong willed and tough to bend.

In the aftermath of Lincoln, Republicans dominated national politics for decades. Even Chicago had a Republican mayor the first eight years of my life. After Franklin Delano Roosevelt was elected president, Galesburg continued as a Republican town. The Tribune's influence remained strong, but there were exceptions. "Doc" Bower, who ran a corner drug store downtown, was a New Deal Democrat and a backer of President Roosevelt. FDR and McCormick were renowned political enemies of the era. "Doc" Bower never refused to sell the Chicago Tribune, but when he did sell it, he always put on gloves and picked up the paper with a pair of pliers. Townspeople would buy a paper from him just for the joy of watching his ritual.

"Doc" was a neighbor of ours. I went to school with his twin daughters. I grew up two blocks through shady backyards from Cottage Hospital. Now, the hospital owns the property. Our house is gone. Our shady lawn is a blacktop parking lot, testament to the exponential expansion of healthcare in modern America. As it turned out, I was the only child of Carl William Freeburg and Ethel Marie Ekwall, the second of four daughters and a son born to Christine Holmes and Gust Ekwall. The extended family reared me there on the prairie. I've been gone for many years. World War II took me away first, then college, and ultimately my career in journalism.

CHAPTER FOUR

BEING A BOY

My family genealogy doesn't stretch back to the years in America before our Republic was born, as my wife, Sally's does. Some might say that I was born below the salt. But all American families originally come from somewhere else. When I was 16 years old, the world famous African-American contralto, Marian Anderson, was denied the right to sing in Constitution Hall in the nation's capital because of her race. I read about it in the Tribune. Sometime thereafter, FDR addressed a convention there of the Daughters of the American Revolution, who owned the hall, opening with the barbed words "my fellow immigrants." I read that in the Tribune, too. I drew from the two incidents that we are all random immigrants on this whirling planet. Dust to dust! Ashes to ashes! From nowhere to somewhere, we become rich or poor, able or sickly, fortunate or unfortunate, famous or infamous, gentry or unwashed. It's all the luck of the draw. In the end, we all sink or swim, rise or fall, together.

None of my family remains in Galesburg except in the graveyard. They are all buried there, but I won't be. I've chosen another place dear to me among the woods and dunes of Northern Michigan where I and my family have spent many happy times in our summer cottage. But, I'll remember always the town of my youth. Cameos of my life in Galesburg still pop into my mind, as I recall first one person then another, what we did, what happened to us. It's been years since I returned there. But, on earlier visits I relished the old times. My heart beat faster when someone rekindled a bygone incident—the roar of the crowd when I scored a basket for my high school team, or my minute of agony on graduation

Even an editor is once a little boy

night. As I rose from my chair on the stage to give the class speech, my mind went blank for 40 seconds, or more, as I reached the microphone. I had no back-up text. I had been required to memorize what I would say. The speech was timed for 12 minutes. Just as I was about to give up and return to my seat all its words returned with a rush.

Always, remember to thank God for small favors.

I sigh when I remember the sorrow of a bad happening. There was the illness of my father. My old high school is gone with the waxy smell of its wooden floors. Abandoned first, then burned to the ground one winter night by vagrants. My first kiss missed its mark and hit Betty Bower's nose instead of her lips.* Obviously, we were amateurs at romance. We did much better together later.

Growing up, I seemed to live in two different worlds — the church related Swedish world of my grandparents, and a more secular place dominated by school and non-Lutheran friends. Ben Bjorling, a relative of Jussi Bjorling, the world famous Swedish tenor, lived in Galesburg. It was always a grand social occasion for Swedish friends of Ben, like my family, when Jussi came to visit while singing in America. Such events were part of my Swedish world. In my younger days, I some-times went with my grandparents to the Swedish service of the First Lutheran Evangelical Church. But, I was not encouraged, to my later regret, to learn Swedish. My grandmother Ekwall would often lapse into Swedish, and I understood her. But, she was encouraged by her children to speak only English. I recall one occasion when she fell back into Swedish and I heard my aunt Jeanette, her youngest child, say, "Mom, we are in America, you must talk in English; that is our language now."

My grandparents arrived in the United States separately between 1874 and 1892 and all of them quickly became part of Galesburg's growing Swedish population. Both of my paternal grandparents left their native land under similar circumstances after their mothers died. Neither liked their stepmothers. Both were approaching manhood, mus-cular and strong from work in the saw mills of Sweden's forests. They also wanted to avoid the compulsory military service Sweden required of its men. It seemed an opportune time for both to leave depressing

---

*Betty Bower and "Doc" Bower, the druggist
mentioned on page 23, were not related.

European ways for a freer and richer life. My paternal grandparents became naturalized American citizens but I have found no record of my grandmothers doing likewise.

When I was 14, I had catechism instruction at our church for three hours every Saturday morning during the school year. In the spring, my junior high school basketball team was to play for the city championship, and our coach called a special workout for the Saturday morning before the game. The practice was in my secular world. In my Swedish world, I rode my bicycle over to the parsonage of my pastor, Charles Bengston.

I addressed him haltingly once inside the house. Even there, he wore his authoritative cleric collar.

I said, "I wonder if just this one time I could be excused from catechism Saturday to practice basketball for the city championship game. My team is playing in it."

His response came swiftly with no time for contemplation. His face was stern, no sympathetic smile, no hint of compassion. His eyes flashed the fire and brimstone that was part of his nature. "No, Russell, you know how important your Saturday lessons are."

I felt low as I left him. But, as I pedaled my bike back home I rationalized that religion was forever and there would be only one championship game. On Saturday, I snuck away to practice.

I'm content with the mysteries of God. I don't believe our universe is a coincidence. I don't see a conflict between science and God. God must be steeped in science and a world class physicist. How else can there be an intelligent design to the universe? How else can one explain our cosmos? Is God omnipotent? I don't know. There is plenty of evil in the world. But, that doesn't belie God's existence. Is there life after death? I don't know. I don't have the wisdom to come to a definitive answer as to God's true nature. Eons from now God might be revealed in totality. Disclosure comes little by little. I'm sure that my death will be for me a very interesting day; then, either I will know the truth of heaven, or experience nothing for evermore. That day, the mystery of a hereafter will take care of itself in one way or another. But, the promise of life in a hereafter seems secondary to living a worthwhile life on earth.

There's always been a paradox with me and my home town. I loved growing up in Galesburg, but I knew very early that I would not remain there as an adult. It wasn't unhappiness. It seemed inborn that my destiny was elsewhere. Still, there was an easiness about its tree lined streets, and a town square that is round. Once, the streets were red bricks and towering elms provided majestic canopies over them and the big Victorian-style homes along them. There was softness to life as one walked its neighborhoods.

Galesburg is the county seat of Knox County. The courthouse, of gray stone surrounded by a park, has a clock tower whose bells rang the hours of the day in my youth. It was a pleasant sound whenever I caught myself scurrying through the park. Earlier travelers always knew when they entered Knox County because the concrete highway suddenly turned into those red bricks. The change was partly local pride, partly convenience, partly economics. Purington brickyard, with its hometown investors, was just outside the east end of town. There was something unique about the texture of the local clay. The yard is abandoned now, but once it was the largest producer of pavers in the world with its bricks laid as far away as the bazaar in old Bombay, India. My grandfather Ekwall worked at the yard as an inspector.

The patterns of my youth were so different in the early years of the 20th century than those that exist now. There were no SUVs for "soccer moms" to haul us kids around to events. Most of us had a little of Huck Finn in us with our pocketknives and marbles. All of us boys wore knickers. Changing into long pants was a ritual that usually took place as we entered junior high school. It was a serious moment for everyone, since long pants were symbolic of coming manhood. As a young boy, I either walked, or rode a bicycle, everywhere. Some days I would leave home in the morning, only to return in time for the evening meal. Some Saturdays my Mom would pack me a lunch, and with a couple of buddies, I would hike four or five miles over a country road, and across farm fields, to a stream called Second North to spend the day. I was 11 years old. It was my first experience with stiff and aching muscles. I remember how good a hot bath felt when I got home. In the winter at that age, and even younger, I had a set Saturday routine. The temperature might hover below freezing, it might be snowing, but I would walk eight blocks to downtown, first to the YMCA for gym and swimming from nine o'clock in the morning until noon, then to a nearby "buy 'em by the sack" hamburger emporium, where I would sit at the counter for a hamburger and soft drink for 15 cents. From there, I would be off across downtown to the matinee cowboy movie at the

Colonial Theater, which always erupted in wild cheers when the hero in his white hat routed the bad guys, saved the ranch, and won the heroine.

The 10 cent admittance included the weekly chapter of a long-running adventure serial and a cartoon.

Cartoons were the movie industry's answer to newspaper comics. Everyone in town followed the Tribune's comics in my youth. We called them "funnies." *Dick Tracy* debuted in 1931; *Terry and the Pirates* in 1934. Even before those two, there was *Gasoline Alley*, which began in 1920. Its main character was Uncle Walt. The father of my life-long friend, Walter Howland, was so taken by Uncle Walt that he named his son after him. In the internet age, Walter used "UncleWalt@..." as part of his e-mail address. A well-known broadcaster of the time, Quinn Ryan, read the Tribune comics every Sunday on WGN, the Tribune's radio station that went on the air a year after my birth. *Little Orphan Annie* first appeared in 1924. Her adventures became a radio show in 1930 broadcast daily from Chicago. Chicago, strategically located in Middle America, in the 1930s was the point of origination for much of the nation's radio.

The way I grew up might seems archaic now with children's television programming, complicated computer games, and Pop Warner football, but for me it was the stuff of life. I learned how to maneuver in a world outside of home and family. By the time I was 13, to have spending money of my own, I peddled bags of popcorn along downtown Main Street from a small stand next to the Colonial Theater. That was in addition to mowing lawns. It was a great feeling to jingle a few quarters together in my pocket that were truly mine. I went from peddling popcorn to detasseling hybrid seed corn in farm fields stretching mile after mile outside of town. Almost every teenager in Galesburg must have detasseled seed corn at one time or another. It was hot, boring work to walk among the so-called "female rows" pulling tassels all day long, and heaven help a detasseler, who, by mistake, got into a "bull row," where the tassels were to stay for cross-pollination. But, the pay was good. It was even better when I worked two summers in the steel plant of the Butler Manufacturing Company.

The wage I made then was "real money," not the inflated currency of the first years of the 21st century. A dollar in my youth, and my early working years, went a long way. Anyone who left an estate of $100,000 was considered wealthy and newsworthy by the Tribune well into the late 1950s.

We weren't rich. We weren't poor. We were better off than some, worse off than some. We didn't live day to day. Before the Great Depression, my dad was manager of a Shell Oil bulk gasoline plant, which then closed. During the Depression and thereafter, he was the shipping clerk for three different companies. But, I don't think my parents ever wanted to be bothered with accumulating wealth. Their first priority was a comfortable home.

And, so, I grew up. Ballroom dancing came along. It was no longer sissy stuff to me. Every Friday night, as an eighth grader, I attended class for an hour at Maude Alma Main's School of Dance above Nyman's jewelry store downtown. I learned the fox trot and the waltz, maybe a slide step or two. The price was a quarter. There were always more girls present than boys, including some of the best lookers in town. It was one way to learn social graces and hold a girl close. Also, every now and then, a parent would have a dinner party for us in hopes that we would learn to sit upright, use silverware properly, and keep our arms and hands off the table.

We learned small talk. We learned how to catch the eye of a favorite girl. We learned how to cope with rejection. The clumsiness of adolescence faded away. Armed conflict dominated parts of the world. Japanese military was on the march in Asia. Europe was clouded in battle. England was on its knees. Hitler had invaded Russia. I enrolled in Knox College in my hometown to await my call to military duty. One tranquil Sunday afternoon, I was stretched out on a couch in our living room listening to a WGN radio broadcast of a Chicago Bears football game. Suddenly, there was silence. Then, a male announcer's voice said:

"Flash—White House says Japan attacks Pearl Harbor."

It was 1:27 p.m. CST December 7, 1941.

The next morning's Chicago Tribune eight column banner headline pronounced in big bold black letters:

"U.S. AND JAPS AT WAR"

CHAPTER FIVE

THE GIRL I MARRY

Without a doubt, WWII changed the direction of my life. Once the war was underway, I faced a future of uncertainty. I might survive, I might not. The peace I'd grown up in was gone. Events happened that altered how my later life would unfold. The timing of a person's birth is obviously a factor in life's journey. The world you are born into isn't fresh and new. The woes of earlier generations are yours to inherit. Your destiny is controlled to some extent by what already exists; the options you have, what fate holds for you. In my case, the war altered the vision I'd had of how my life would be in the years ahead. If I'd been 10 years older and already a working newsman, I might have become a war correspondent. But, I was too young. In later years, I came to believe there was a place, as an older journalist, I would have prized as an assignment: the Berlin of pre-WWII days to cover Nazi leaders, see their evil, and write about it.

Although I wasn't there at the beginning like Sigrid Schultz in her coverage of Nazi Germany for the Tribune, I was there at the end as a conquering soldier. But, first I had to decide how to vie with a world at war. Soon after the Japanese attack, Hitler also declared war on the United States. After some time, I determined the best way to make my wartime journey was to be on my own and footloose — no commitments, nothing unfinished left behind. I would turn myself into a soldier-tourist: besides soldiering, I would visit cultural and educational sites wherever the military sent me, bars and dance halls as well. The war would be my own Grand Tour at government expense. I've never regretted my decision. It left me unanchored to one person or place.

Still, that decision made certain that the world I came home to, if I came home, wouldn't be the one I left.

But, I did come home. And, all in good time, the girl I would marry came along. Years had passed since my rites of passage began. In the army, I'd been many places. I'd seen and done many things. And, I'd become rather libertine concerning women, somewhat of a free soul — a girl here, a girl there. Then, I saw Sally Woodford. I've never been able to decide whether our meeting was accidental or fate. Such things are not easy to self-analyze. All I know is that it happened and I'm not sorry for it. It was the spring of 1946. I'd survived the war and I was taking a couple of courses at Knox College while I waited to enter Washington University in St. Louis. That first spark of romance came when we passed each other in a stairwell of Old Main on the school's campus. I was going up, she was coming down. We both turned for a second glance. It was my first glimpse of her brown eyes, so quick and alluring. Throw in that I'd always been a sucker for brown eyes. But even more, I felt the tug of chemistry between us. I sensed the thrill of mutual attraction.

I knew I had to meet her, so I described her to friends: her wavy brown hair that fell soft over her shoulders, those brown eyes, the pretty face, the trim figure. I kept hoping I would see her again strolling across campus in that same yellow dress she wore when I first saw her. When finally I was introduced to her a few days later, I told her I was glad to meet her at last.

She said quietly with a smile, "It's about time."

I laughed. "Maybe, now that we've met, you won't get rid of me."

"Maybe, I won't want to," she replied calmly in an even voice.

And that's how our romance began. I wanted to take her in my arms right then. I could travel a long way with her, I thought. She would be nice to come home to. We took a slow walk around the campus together. She seemed to be my other self, I hers. For fun I gave her a teddy bear, then seriously a ring. Eight months later, on December 21, we were married in the First Lutheran Evangelical Church in Galesburg so her collage classmates could attend the wedding before departing for their holiday vacations. Her family came down from Chicago, and I was home for Christmas from Washington University in St. Louis. She was stunning at the altar in her white, floor length wedding dress, a long train trailing behind. It was the same dress her maternal grandmother,

Daisy Wimer, had worn at her wedding. Now, her grandmother sat in the church watching Sally's marriage ceremony. Her father gave her away. But his participation was a close call. A storm during the night had blanketed northern Illinois with a deep snow, making travel difficult. He arrived shortly before the organist began the wedding march.

I sighed with relief when I heard her say, "I do."

My mom said she knew the first time I brought Sally home for a Sunday dinner that she'd just met her future daughter-in-law. Beyond desire, there was affinity between us on politics and sports. Like me, she loved to read. I was comfortable with her family. She was straightforward. She was witty. There was a lot to this woman to love and admire.

After the Christmas holidays, we returned to St. Louis and Washington University for me. Sally went to work as a service representative for Southwestern Bell. Initially, we lived in one room in an old mansion several miles from the Washington campus and ate most of our meals in a nearby boarding house. We looked upon it as an adventure and we were not alone. There were other married couples just like us — a student husband who'd fought in WWII and a working wife. But, we kept an eye out for more living space and scoured newspaper rental ads.

There were three newspapers in St. Louis when we lived there — the *Star Times*, the *Globe Democrat* and the *Post Dispatch*. Now, like most others, it's a one paper town. Only the *Post Dispatch* survives. The *Star Times* went first, then the *Globe Democrat*. The *Post Dispatch* eventually gave up being an afternoon paper as its circulation dwindled and it now limps along with morning delivery plus an online edition. We mostly read the *Post Dispatch*, especially the Sunday edition, which we picked up as we walked home from Saturday evenings in the nearby Chase Hotel bar.

The newspapers didn't help our housing quest. But, in early fall, we upgraded to a small apartment Sally discovered through a coworker. True, the apartment was another renovation project in a nondescript, out-of-date house whose main attribute was it was big. But, here we had a living room, a bedroom, a Pullman kitchen and a bath of our own.

It wasn't New York's Park Avenue or the swank dwellings along Chicago's lake front. Housing was hard to come by after WWII. It took years for a pent up demand to be worked off. We considered ourselves lucky and to a certain degree financially secure with my income from the G. I. Bill and Sally's wages. We thought if I could ever make

$10,000 a year we would be on easy street. Again, such was the worth of money then. St. Louis was a sophisticated place but it wasn't the largest of America's cities so everyone pretty much did everything at the same time. When the Metropolitan Opera Company came to town everyone went to the opera. With only one legitimate theater, everyone attended the same Broadway plays. It was similar with hotel cocktail lounges and bars. Forest Park, with its outdoor summer musicals and light opera, was a few blocks from our first place of residence. No matter where we went, we always saw friends. But all those activities were confined to weekends. On week nights, I studied. I devoured psychology. Sally read and on occasion took in a movie. Our sex life came easily. We enjoyed pleasing each other.

As my graduation neared, Sally and I decided we would leave St. Louis for Chicago. Mainly, the decision was based on St. Louis weather. As all river towns along the Mississippi, St. Louis was unbearably hot and humid in the summer. Every July, the papers printed a picture of a policeman frying an egg on the pavement while walking his beat. Air conditioning was rare then. It would not become common for another decade or more. A happy mom and dad came to my graduation. It was a new experience for them, since neither had been to college. Maybe, that's why they never tried to possess me, that they always let me seek my own level. With degrees in hand, my classmates scattered to find their destiny. A few days later, with a couple of suitcases, Sally and I boarded a Wabash Railroad passenger train at its Delmar Street station near Washington University and headed north to Chicago, our future unknown.

CHAPTER SIX

THE TRIBUNE BECOMES MY WORKPLACE

When I joined the metropolitan staff, it was located off of the city room in its own private quarters on the fourth floor. It had its own copy desk and team of photographers. It dealt with the soft side of journalism—features about people and community events. I was assigned to the Sunday west section, where I united with Betty Jane Merrill, a lively transplant from Bryan, Ohio. She covered Chicago's west side and Oak Park. The other western suburbs as far out as Elgin were my beat. We handled no spot news, although I recall covering a trial daily in which early environmentalists had sued the village of Glen Ellyn west of Chicago for using DDT in its mosquito abatement program. One day a big cockroach appeared on the courtroom floor in front of the bench and listened to the testimony for a while.

I could write pretty much about anything I wanted as a metro reporter. It was up to me to dig up stories and photo layouts in the territory I covered. It wasn't difficult. There was plenty of interesting material and personalities available. People were always calling in with tips or asking for coverage of events dear to them. I began thinking more about the structure of newspaper feature stories. There had been little opportunity for me to do that at the City News Bureau. It takes a feel for human pathos to write a good feature story no matter if it's funny or sad. It takes a light touch to do a feature story right; to engage in a little whimsy from time to time.

I began to think about what makes a really good reporter, one who would stand out from the crowd, a work ethic that would separate excellence from the ordinary. I assumed competition would be tough among members of the Tribune staff, many of whom had been with the paper for years. I thought I had an instinct to recognize what made news, an instant recognition of the newsworthiness of events and personalities I encountered. I also knew that I had not yet developed a mind like a steel trap to see me through tough assignments.

One day it came to me bluntly that Colonel McCormick's farm west of Chicago was on my beat. I'd never thought about the farm that way. I thought of it as his home. But, in my second or third week on the metro staff, Hubbard called me into his office.

"The colonel has been hiking in the fields of Cantigny," Hubbard informed me. He glanced at the memo on his desk. "He's spotted two highway bridges in the distance, completed, but unconnected to any roads. He wants to know what they're doing there." I nodded. "Drop whatever you're working on and get up a story."

That evening Sally and I drove out to find the lonely bridges. If I didn't give the colonel the information he wanted, my Tribune career might indeed be short. One bridge spanned a single track of the Aurora & Elgin interurban railroad, the other the DuPage River. They were part of a highway planned to run west from Chicago into the Fox River valley. I prepared a long story for publication with photographs, a map from the art department, and every detail I could wring out of the Illinois highway department.

Cantigny was named for a World War I battle in France in which the colonel fought. It was an experimental farm. My friend, Dick Orr, wrote a column called *Day by Day on the Farm*, unusual for a big city daily. But, that's the advantage of owning a newspaper. You put whatever you want in it. You have reporters to answer questions you might have and they write a story about them, as I did on the bridges. I was somewhat in awe of the colonel and the empire he'd built with its vast timberlands and paper mills in Canada plus large lake cargo boats to haul newsprint down to Chicago. The closest I came to speaking to him was one morning when he entered an elevator where I was alone. But, the major domo in charge of the bank of elevators quickly motioned for me to step back out into the lobby so the colonel could be swiftly taken to his office atop the tower. The colonel, in addition to the farm, had a house on Astor Street adjoining the mansions and high-rise, luxury apartments of the so-called Gold Coast along Lake Michigan north of the loop. One morning he awoke to find the house without heat. He did what any cold publisher with a broken furnace would do: he called his city desk. Stanley Armstrong, the day city editor, was already at work and he took the call. Armstrong knew it would take time to find repair men, so he sent two Tribune photographers to clang on the basement pipes with wrenches until help arrived.

After I'd been at the Tribune for a year, Pat Maloney retired. I was disappointed to see him leave. The story around the city room was that Colonel McCormick was upset by a drop in circulation; probably the first caused by television, but not recognized at the time for what it was. I don't know why Maloney was blamed. Don Maxwell was moved up to managing editor from city editor to succeed him. I'd never met Maxwell, but the Tribune was a well-organized operation with a history of promoting from within. I was sure my future would be no different with Maxwell at the helm than it would have been under Maloney. And that is the way it went. In early 1952 I was transferred to the financial news department.

These were exciting times for Chicago's economic life. The city was moving away from wartime production and re-establishing its old self as a dynamic hub of the country's business and financial worlds. These would be the last years that were still symbolic of the ever pulsating commercial and industrial life quintessentially described in his *Chicago Poems* by Carl Sandburg.

> Hog butcher of the world,
> Tool maker, stacker of wheat,
> Player with railroads,
> And the nation's freight handler;
> Stormy, husky, brawling city
> Of the big shoulders.

Carl Sandburg was from my home town of Galesburg. Or, perhaps, I should say I'm from his, since he was the older one. He'd grown up a generation earlier in the same Swedish community so familiar to me. His family was right in there with mine. My mother was treasurer of the Carl Sandburg Association, a group of local women who raised money to buy and refurbish the small house in which the poet was born. Upon my re-entry into civilian life after World War II, she sent me down to the house to redo an uneven, weedy brick walk out to the privy, a return for a day or two to the Swedish world of my youth. When I revisited her legacy some 30 years later, the walk and outbuilding were gone. In their place was a pleasant flower garden with a large red granite boulder called Remembrance Rock, the title of a fictional family saga by the poet. His ashes, and those of his wife, Lillian, are buried there.

As Chicago separated itself from the war years, fierce struggles for power took shape. There were attempts to redo companies in a new image. Proxy fights happened. As a financial reporter, I felt that I was being paid to take economics 101. It was a heady experience to watch the energy unleashed in recharging a post-war Chicago. One sees and hears much as a journalist. You bounce from one story to another. Many of them are fleeting; others become part of the fabric you weave into your past. I met some of the business world's top personalities of the era while a financial reporter. I interviewed J. C. Penney on one of his visits to Chicago. He wore a Stetson hat and looked more like a corn farmer from downstate Illinois out on the town than a business tycoon. He told me that one reason for his success was that he avoided owning real estate. He said he always leased his store locations, explaining that the practice made it easier to close down non-performing outlets.

While covering financial news, I became witness to the sad end of an iconic American merchant of the first half of the 20th century: Sewell Avery, chairman and CEO of Montgomery Ward & Company. While I thought Penney was down to earth, I thought Avery was patrician. Montgomery Ward and Sears were locked in competition for retail dominance in post-World War II. Both of the renowned mail order houses were headquartered in Chicago,

The world is a cruel place. Avery's misjudgment began Ward's demise. His mistake surfaced publicly when his company was targeted in a hostile takeover attempt by the first corporate raider of the postwar years: Louis E. Wolfson, a flashy marauder who went after companies muscle bound with money. Avery had a big pile of cash. Wolfson came calling in late 1954 and the Homeric proxy fight captivated the business world until its climatic showdown the next spring.

The 42-year-old Wolfson was fresh from a raid on Capital Transit Company in Washington D. C., which was poorly managed, but which also had a huge cash reserve. When Wolfson distributed three million dollars in dividends to himself and other shareholders, the United

States government temporarily revoked the carrier's operating license. Wolfson sold his share in the Capital Transit for 13½ million dollars. He had bought it four years earlier for 2½ million.

Avery was silent at first, although pressed by shareholders, and the media, to speak out against Wolfson. Finally, he called a press conference one afternoon for 3:00 p.m. The time was the copy deadline for the Tribune's bulldog edition, a limited run for early street sales to homeward bound commuters. The press run began at 4:30. It was decided to hold the paper open until 3:35. Bill Clark, the assistant financial editor, and I went to the press conference. I was to duck out and call in on deadline what had already taken place. Bill would write a longer story for later editions.

The scene remains vivid in my memory more than a half a century later. It is rare to witness a merchant prince digging his own grave. Initially, the tall, gray haired Avery, 81 years old, sat erect at his large oak desk as reporters gathered around him. He was defiant and predicted victory. Then, he stood to open the highly polished double doors of a large built-in cabinet behind him. Inside was a series of big wooden framed panels that rotated on a steel rod.

Pointer in hand, he swung open the first panel. A paper graph was on it with up and down lines to show how the economy collapsed after the American Civil War. He turned other panels that displayed similar graphs of the Spanish American War and World War I. He explained that recession followed the fighting in every one of those wars and that was why it had been prudent for him to hoard the money.

He had a similar graph on the European economy after the Napoleonic War of 1812. That grabbed my attention.

When Avery displayed his World War II panel, however, he hesitated. He stared at the graph. He ran his pointer along the line soaring upward. Obviously confused, he shook his head.

"I don't know what has happened," he said. "There's been no downturn this time."

I peeked at my watch. It was 3:20. I looked at Bill Clark, He nodded. I rose from my chair with a pang of sorrow and slipped out to a telephone in the lobby.

As I dictated the story to Eddie Williamson on rewrite, the copy was rushed to the composing room, one or two paragraphs at a time. A different Linotype operator set each paragraph. A waiting printer placed the type, as it came to him paragraph by paragraph, in the empty column space waiting on page one. A headline was ready. Everything was done in a few minutes. But, my romance with "hot type" and the thrill of teamwork in breaking a story on deadline would soon change. Within two years the Tribune would have its first typesetting computers. The noise and bustle of the composing room, the seductive smell of ink and lead, would in time disappear to money-saving technological advances. Newspapers would be cleaner places, but, ironically, also slower in getting out the news.

Avery's poor performance left his executive ability in question. Other Ward officials took up the fight against the audacious and charismatic Wolfson. The young financier never got his hands on the money, but, at the annual stockholders meeting, he did win three seats on Ward's board of directors. Avery was befuddled and uncertain as he conducted the meeting, and soon after he retired. Wolfson had become nationally known, and he is credited with the invention of the modern hostile tender offer. Eventually, he served a year in prison for securities fraud. Upon his release, he became a philanthropist and stable owner. His horse, Affirmed, won the triple crown of racing in 1970.

During this time, I accompanied the board of directors of the Illinois Central Railroad on a trip down to the western tip of Kentucky, where three companies had built new plants side-by-side along the railroad. These were so-called feeder plants that interchanged materials for each other's operations. Robert E. Wood, chairman of Sears, was among the directors. One evening over dinner, he told me that he followed Montgomery Ward's problems closely. He said they would never happen at Sears. While Avery diddled, Wood had gambled. He'd taken Sears money after World War II to build new suburban stores with ample parking lots for young families he was sure would move from the cities.

"The migration has begun," he told me. "Our sales are climbing. Our debt is manageable. I feel secure about Sears' future."

Avery, meanwhile, stayed with his old downtown stores cramped for customer parking space. The opposite of Sears was happening with Ward, whose decline, and eventual ruin, had begun. Now, 18 years into the 21st century, the future of Sears, itself, seems doomed. It is closing its stores. It has filed for bankruptcy. Buying online in a computer generated economy is now making its brick and mortar outlets with the big parking lots obsolete.

Other proxy fights followed. I covered one over the North Western

Railroad. The North Western had long been held hostage by Wall Street bond houses when Ben Heineman waged his proxy war in 1956 for control of the storied line. When I was assigned to cover the battle, I arranged interviews with Heineman and railroad officials. While speaking to North Western's railroad president, I asked him what commodity produced the railroad's most revenue. He gave me a blank stare. It was one of those telling moments a reporter sometimes faces. I realized the North Western was under very bad management. The North Western ran out of Chicago into Wisconsin, the Upper Peninsula of Michigan, Minnesota and the Dakotas. It had feeder lines elsewhere. Heineman won the proxy fight, replaced the management, renegotiated the railroad's debt structure to give himself some financial breathing room, modernized equipment and increased revenues. He knew how to run a railroad.

New staff members in financial news were required to take part in what we called "Agate University." "Agate U" was responsible for all the securities and commodity tables that appeared in small agate type in the paper every morning. Every financial news reporter had to learn the routine of preparing the tables as back-ups to Adeline Gaynor, who ran the operation. Agate type financial tables have disappeared from newspapers. Now, markets are followed on financial news television networks, and stock quotes are available instantly on the internet and iPads. The change saves the cost of newsprint, but it gives the reader another reason not to buy a paper. Much has transformed since I covered the wheat and soybean pits on the floor of the Chicago Board of Trade and I visited the brokerage houses spread out along La Salle Street. Chicago's colorful Union Stock Yards immortalized by Sandburg are gone. Sometimes, a story came out of the yards that caught my imagination, like the one I wrote about Herman.

Mark Passing of Herman, Top Sheep at Stock Yards.

Last rites were observed yesterday in the Global Rendering company plant at 163d St. and Torrence av. for Herman, a pet sheep who died of old age late Friday at the stock yards. He was 13. Herman received the company's fitting treatment. He got the works.

It is said that every sheep trader that came to the

yards knew Herman. He was familiar to visitors at the International Live Stock Show each year as the leader of grand champion lambs and sheep from the sheep house to the amphitheater. All will mourn his passing.

Herman was reported to have spent his early years on a farm in downstate Illinois. He came to Chicago about nine years ago and rose to a position of leader in the stock yards.

He soon learned the ways of the city. Although his regular diet was hay, he liked an occasional nip now and then of beer or gin.

He was in trouble just once. Several years ago he took to opening gates to the sheep pens and releasing animals being held for slaughter. At times he would lead the other sheep to freedom after opening the gate.

For a time, his life was in the balance, but Herman survived the crisis. Friends said Herman was of mixed breed.

His family, which uses the Latin name, Bovidae, goes back many years. Before coming to the United States, they lived first on the high, treeless plateaus and mountains of central Asia.

Among relatives are oxen, goats, musk-oxen, chamois, and antelopes. There were no immediate Survivors, however.

An earlier headshot of Herman smoking a cigarette accompanied the story.

I talked to Charles "Boss" Kettering, one of America's foremost inventors, as a financial reporter. He came to town one day chipper and edgy. At one point, we were discussing inventions. He paused for a moment and laughed. "You realize a lot of people think inventors are nuts," he said. "No one ever asks inventors what they think of other people."

Women should be forever grateful to Kettering. His development of the self-starter for automobiles was a giant step forward in their liberation. Until the self-starter, automobiles were started with an iron hand crank that required great hand and arm strength. The crank also possessed a backward wallop that could break arms and even jaws. All that ended with the self-starter. Women could turn over an engine with the flip of an ignition key and go wherever they desired.

The "Boss" had large features and a ready smile. He was gregarious and humorous. His nickname "Boss" was an affectionate one. I could have talked to him for hours. He said everyone should be inquisitive and curious, always be willing to go for something new. I could tell he was taking my measure. He told me this story: Kettering worked out of his home town of Dayton, Ohio. Often, he drove to Detroit to General Motors headquarters, a 4½ hour trip over the main highway. Kettering told a skeptical colleague he beat that time. The bet was on and the pair drove off. Kettering soon left the highway to use back roads. When they arrived in Detroit under 4½ hours, the colleague acknowledged the faster time but insisted Kettering had done it only by not going the usual way. In the world today, Kettering would be described as someone who thinks outside the box.

Colonel McCormick became ill while I was in the financial news department, but he remained active, came to his office at the top of Tribune Tower, and continued to fire off his memos. One came down that involved me. The colonel wrote that he'd been watching the start of construction on the Prudential Insurance Company skyscraper across the Chicago River from his office window, a pair of field glasses in hand. He said that it looked to him like a new technique was being used for the caissons. Phil Hampson, our financial editor, told me to go over and check it out. I hoped to God that I wouldn't prove the colonel wrong. It was a pleasant spring day. I walked along the bank of the Chicago River and down into the construction site. I found the superintendent and showed him the memo. "You know, he's right," the super said. "We've run up against hard rock and we've had to deviate some." I asked him if he would write down what was being done since I strongly suspected that I would be asked to write a story when I returned to the tower. As he handed me the ragged and dirty sheet of paper he'd found for his explanation, he laughed. "Everyone, including me, has a boss to please," he said, "I hope this works for us." We both understood there was no margin for error.

McCormick died April 1, 1955 at Cantigny. He was 74. I caught the news when I saw the Tribune headline on my way to work. Maxwell became editor. He kept the paper running smoothly. But, I've always said that the colonel left everything so well-oiled that we all could have walked out of the tower and the paper would have kept coming out on its own every morning. Although Maxwell was an okay boss on a personal level, there was little change in the paper's format or ideas for almost two decades with him at the helm. The paper remained much like the colonel left it as the world, and media reporting on it, underwent cultural and political upheaval. Maxwell seemed willingly controlled by McCormick's ghost.

I enjoyed financial reporting. But, Maxwell and other editors wanted to switch me to the city desk several times. Hampson somehow always talked them out of it but when he retired as financial editor in 1957 my luck ran out. Within weeks I was working general assignment city side. I did that for a little more than a year. Meanwhile, Sally and I had bought the first of our six houses. We reluctantly gave up our apartment with its summer swimming and cool breezes off of the lake. Our son, Jon, was born while we lived there. But the Eisenhower administration had ended rent controls imposed during WWII, and we decided that instead of paying higher rent, it would be wiser to put the money into mortgage payments and begin building equity. I borrowed two thousand dollars from my dad and my uncle Pete for the down payment on a new subdivision ranch house in suburban Arlington Heights. The expanded living space came in handy, not only with Jon, but also when our daughters, Holly and Allison, were born. From there we moved to the nation's capital.

CHAPTER SEVEN

WASHINGTON BOUND

The royal blue Capitol Limited picked up speed as it pulled out of Chicago's Grand Central Station and moved through the south side of the city. It was on its nightly 772 mile run to the nation's capital and I was on board. It was late Sunday afternoon December 28, 1958. The next morning I would join the Washington bureau of the Chicago Tribune. I would be in a place I hadn't been before, and there would be people I hadn't known before. I don't recall any want of confidence, or anxious concern, as I settled into my compartment on the crack, all Pullman, train of the Baltimore & Ohio Railroad. I was full of thoughts of covering the nation's top politicians, their triumphs and their foibles.

It had been a century since the Tribune sent its first correspondent to Washington in 1859. He was Joseph Medill, then 36 years old, the same age I would be in three months. His dispatches, signed "Chicago" appeared under the headings "Our Washington Letter" and "From Washington." It was not the custom in those days to give by-lines to staff writers. An article marking the 100th anniversary of the paper's Washington bureau described Medill as no fancy Dan as a writer, but it said that he had courage, vigor, and common sense. His footsteps were still good ones to walk in. I was the first addition to the Washington bureau since World War II 15 years earlier. I would be one of 10 men in the bureau, one of the largest in the capital. Like me, all of them had first worked in Chicago.

It was during my Washington years that the media world turned upside down. Newspaper readership and influence declined while television viewership and influence increased. Politicians realized they could talk directly to the masses via television. More implicitly, they could control their message. As technology advanced, television networks steadily increased their news coverage. Television correspondents became popular and celebrities in their own right. In the summer of 1962, my fourth year in Washington, the first live transatlantic telecast took place, including part of a baseball game at Wrigley Field in Chicago between the Cubs and the Phillies, shown on the Tribune's TV station, WGN.

The pace of television's takeover was quickening.

My first thoughts about Washington came during the midterm elections in early November, 1958. Walter Trohan, the paper's tempestuous Washington bureau chief, was in Chicago, per custom, to write the lead story on election night. I was way down the ladder covering returns on municipal judges. I'd never met Trohan, but during the evening he took me aside and inquired if I had any interest in filling an opening in the bureau. I was thrilled and excited. Without hesitation, I told him I did. Weeks later, in a wonderfully crafted letter from Trohan, I learned that he had also talked to Bob Wiedrich and Tom Nuzum, both, like me, general assignment reporters in the city room. Wiedrich and I started at the City News Bureau the same day as copy boys. He became my closest friend and confidant in journalism. Like me, he was a WWII veteran getting a later start than usual in a civilian job because of years in military service. Trohan wrote the three of us that he felt like Paris, the prince of ancient Troy, who was called upon by Zeus in Greek mythology to decide the recipient of a prized golden apple. Inscribed on the apple was the word "kallisti," which meant "for the prettiest one." Eris, the Olympian god of discord, had fashioned the apple after not being invited to a party the gods were giving for the obvious reason that she turned parties into brawls. Only years later, as he neared retirement, would I realize how prophetic Trohan's letter was in that regard.

Things at the Tribune weren't that contentious. Wiedrich wanted to stay in Chicago. Nuzum, unmarried and living in a furnished apartment, was sent off to the Tribune's Paris bureau in France, a single suitcase in hand. Eventually, he married a French woman and faded away into her culture. But, 1958 was a down year for the economy so I still had problems with which to grapple. I would have to sell our house without Tribune help, and Sally was eight months pregnant. I agreed to the former and Sally and I decided it was best not to mention the latter.

Allison was born without complications three weeks before I stepped aboard the Capitol Limited.

For me, however, there was a scare in her birth. Sally and I left our home in Arlington Heights before dawn that morning for Sherman Hospital in nearby Elgin. I dropped Sally off at the entrance to park our car. When I returned to the hospital lobby, she was nowhere in sight. Over the loud speaker, I heard a call for a doctor to come to the delivery room. Minutes later, I heard the name of another doctor called. Then the voice over the loudspeaker pleaded for any doctor in the hospital to please come to the delivery room. I felt uneasy, the calls were unnerving, but soon I was told that Sally was fine and we had a new baby girl. Jon, now six years old, had been a breech birth with many hours of waiting. Holly, now three years old, wasn't far behind Allison in timing. She was also a quick and easy birth. Perhaps I was lucky that I didn't have to deliver both of them myself along the highway.

As the Capitol Limited traveled east in the growing darkness, I went to the dining car. I found it enriched with white linen table cloths, crystal glassware, and highly polished silver place settings. A table vase held a single rose. Once seated, a waiter quickly filled my glass with Deer Park Spring Water. He told me the special water was a prized staple of the Limited. As a luxury train, the Capitol Limited competed on the New York City to Chicago run with the New York Central's Twentieth Century Limited and the Pennsylvania road's Broadway Limited. The New York Central and Pennsylvania roads took a northern route hugging the Great Lakes between the two cities. The B&O took a southern route through Washington and Baltimore.

As I transferred to Washington, change was in the wind for America's taste in travel as well as communications. In late April, 1958, the B&O had cut the Capitol Limited service back to Baltimore, instead of New York, as the train's eastern terminus. When Sally and the children moved from Chicago two and a half months after I did to our new home in Virginia across the Potomac River from Washington, they left from O'Hare Field, newly opened to commercial aviation. The ticket terminal was in a leftover WWII quonset hut. In contrast, Grand Central Station, the smallest of Chicago's seven railroad terminals, was an architectural masterpiece of brownstone and granite rising along the south branch of the Chicago River southwest of the loop. I checked the time by its elegant 247 foot high clock tower as I entered graceful arched doorways into an ornate gold leafed interior with soaring Corinthian columns and marble floors. There was even a fireplace. As the railroad age faded away, Grand Central became just another old depot, torn down in 1971 when I was back in Chicago as managing editor. Meanwhile, O'Hare, with sleek modern terminals replacing the quonset hut, had grown into one of the busiest airports in the world.

When I dined that night, I wore a business suit with a white shirt and tie. Journeyers dressed up in those days. There was a certain elegance to travel, a feeling of adventure. There was pleasure in getting to a destination, not relief as there often is now, when arriving by air or auto with a "thank God, I made it." That night, after dinner and a nightcap in the club car, I climbed into my berth a book in hand. I was beyond the bustle of the two great cities that shaped my life, comfortable and alone. It was so different from later jet planes and the cattle herd atmosphere of congested cabins, unruly passengers and regimented terminals. Hardly anyone dresses up anymore to travel, the shabbier the better. I never wear a business suit and tie on an airplane with its cramped seating arrangements and chatter. Air travel has become even more tedious with the security checks put in place after the terrorism of 9/11.

Man's quest to race against time has a rough edge.

The porter woke me as we reached Martinsburg, West Virginia. That gave me time to dress and eat breakfast. My anticipation grew. When I walked out of Washington's Union Station and saw the Capitol dome, I thought this is my life at its best. I strolled a few blocks (weather records say it was a chilly 40 degrees) before hailing a taxi. As I climbed in, I instructed its driver to take me to the Albee Building. In those days in Washington, buildings were well known by name. Street addresses were seldom needed. The Tribune bureau sprawled through six rooms in suite 815. The building was old and its elevators ancient, but I noticed that the uniformed women operators wore white gloves. It housed a number of newspaper, radio, and magazine offices in addition to the Tribune. They dwelled there instead of the National Press building a couple of blocks away for a reason. It kept their staffs from easy access to the latter building's Press Club bar.

As twilight came, starlings stalked the eighth floor ledge outside the bureau's windows, back in the city after a day spent in the countryside. I soon accepted their evening return as part of the daily rhythm of the bureau.

CHAPTER EIGHT

I SETTLE IN TO COVER THE NATION'S CAPITAL

Three long running dramas took place during my years in the nation's capital: the Cold War, the Vietnam conflict, and the civil rights movement. The Cold War ended with the Soviet Union in history's dustbin. The deep wounds of Vietnam on the nation's psyche slowly healed. The civil rights movement is not over, and probably never will be. It will change in its aims, perhaps its racial makeup or ethnicity, but an individual's desires to be free from bondage will always rule the heart.

I covered parts of all three with an early look at the Cold War while still in the army in Europe in WWII. As a soldier on the demarcation line between East and West, Russian troops were a mile or so away from me. The stage was being set for the struggle still to come.

I arrived in Washington during the Christmas holidays and the capital was quiet. Bob Young, one of the few bureau members in the office that day, took me on a tour of the neighborhood late in the afternoon. The White House was a block away from the bureau. The Treasury Building was just across the street. So was Riggs Bank, where Secretary of State William Seward had borrowed money in 1867 to buy Alaska from the Russians. Nuggets of the nation's history were everywhere. We walked past Dolley Madison's house in Lafayette Square. I, and a dozen other journalists, met with Henry Kissinger in the Madison House for a briefing upon his return from his secret trip to China to arrange President Nixon's breakthrough visit to re-establish diplomatic relations with the long estranged Chinese.

The White House location confused and puzzled me. It seemed to face in the wrong direction. Only in time did I realize why. I'd grown up seeing the White House in news reels at the Orpheum Theater in Galesburg, where I faced east when I viewed the movie screen. In reality, the White House faces north. I adjusted in time, but the news reel image was hard to shake.

I wrote my first Washington story the next afternoon. How little times change.

At a press conference at the Department of Health, Education and Welfare, Arthur S. Flemming, the department secretary, said HEW would spend a record amount of money in the next fiscal year. Washington, of course, is a lot about money, who gets what and why. To understand Washington, a person must understand money. My 4½ years as a financial reporter were helpful. A quirk I remember from that day was that Flemming puffed on a pipe as he talked. I'd never run across that before at a press conference.

As my story moved over the bureau wire to Chicago, Trohan sent a note to Arvid Westling, the telegraph desk editor, directing that my byline be put on the story. Westling answered it would be his pleasure to do so then, and in the years to come. Westling had only one eye. He lost the other one when it was hit by an errant golf ball on a course in Florida. He feared his career was over, but Tribune management told him it was confident he would read copy with one eye better than some others did with two. Actually, Westling was one of three current staff members with only one eye. Larry Burd, the Tribune's main White House correspondent and my new colleague, was another. The third was Frank Winge, an old time police reporter. Winge was in a torrid poker game one night in the old Chicago Avenue police station when nature called. As he rose from his chair, he gave an amused look at the other players. Then, he casually popped out his glass eye, placed it on top of his cards, already face down on the table, and exclaimed, "Watch these bastards until I return." Of course, the most famous Tribune reporter ever with one eye was Floyd Gibbons. The trademark white patch he wore over his missing left eye established his identity to millions in person and in news reels. He'd lost the eye as a Tribune correspondent in WWI, when he was hit by German gunfire while trying to save a wounded American soldier in the Battle of Belleau Woods.

As the junior member of the bureau, it was my lot upon arrival in Washington to work weekends. I did this for several years. I covered any story that developed. That meant I needed a White House press pass. James Hagerty, President Eisenhower's press secretary, said that he would be glad to accredit me. The Secret Service interviewed me and took my photo. In due time, I received my White House press pass. My photo on it was a little more professional than the one on my new Virginia driver's license. With the press pass I could get into the White House on weekends when coverage required it, and to substitute occasionally for Larry Burd, who became a treasured friend.

I had a wonderful feeling of history and awe when I initially entered the Oval Office. My time came one day when I filled in for Larry. It was a photo shoot of Ike with a foreign diplomat. I'll never forget it. The president, in a dark business suit, stood behind his desk as the group of reporters and photographers entered. Sunshine filled the office through floor length windows and doors looking out on the Rose Garden. I felt I was in a political shrine. Protocol became paramount. The office was bigger than I anticipated with a fireplace and sitting area. It was beautifully furnished, and clean as a whistle. A quiet dignity filled the air. There was plenty of room to move around, but I had the feeling that nothing was ever really out of place. I didn't write a story. The Associated Press sent out a photo and a caption. That was enough if the Tribune wanted to use it back in Chicago.

I was in and out of the White House many times during my years in the capital. There's a puckish axiom, acknowledged with a wink and a smile, that presidents come and go but reporters remain forever. The Tribune was among a handful of news organizations that covered presidents full time, both in and outside of Washington. The paper had its own little cubicle in the pressroom with a direct telephone line to the bureau office. But, Henry Kissinger took over the pressroom for his office when he became President Nixon's national security advisor. He loved the beautiful view of the north lawn of the executive mansion. Nixon, a non-swimmer, built a larger and more modern pressroom over the White House swimming pool, which had been installed so FDR could undergo physiotherapy treatments for his polio, and where President Kennedy frolicked with women staffers.

The new pressroom, in a bow to the changing media world, had all of the accoutrements necessary for the age of television. It certainly wasn't designed with newspapers in mind. With the arrival of cable television, daily press briefings by the White House press secretary are sometimes carried in full over their channels. Not only can people read or hear about the news, they could now see it being made.

When Eisenhower held the first White House televised press conference in January, 1955, his opening remark was "Well, I see we're trying a new experiment this morning. I hope it doesn't prove to be a disturbing influence." A makeshift scaffold had been erected at the rear of the small and cramped Indian Treaty Room in the old State Department building adjacent to the White House, the site of Eisenhower's news conferences with reporters. A lone TV camera stood on the platform along with a camera for Fox Movietone News.

Little did Ike realize just how much of a disturbing influence the "experiment" would be for the newspaper industry. The irony of the event was that questioners who made the telecast a success were reporters representing the newspapers that television would put out of business. Without them, the telecast would have been impossible. TV news was a fledgling industry. But, the "experiment" quickly became the norm. Just two year earlier, in 1953, The Radio Correspondents' gallery on Capitol Hill had added the word "television" to its name to become the Radio and Television Correspondents' Gallery. Thirty-one names were listed as TV correspondents accredited to cover Congress. Two became famous—David Brinkley and Walter Cronkite. That same year, the Newspaper Correspondents' Gallery had some 450 accredited correspondents.

I rarely ran into a TV reporter on my beat in my early days in Washington.

The first story I covered in the nation's capital involved Cuba, which became such a big player in the Cold War clash between communism and capitalism. On my first weekend at work, Fulgencio Batista, the Caribbean island's dictator, fled into exile, and two days later rebels led by Fidel Castro entered the capital city of Havana. Castro became a thorn in the side of the United States for the rest of the 20th century, and beyond, as an ally of the Kremlin. A committed Marxist-Leninist, he turned Cuba into a one party communist state, and in concert with the Soviet Union, brought the world to the brink of nuclear war.

Castro came into my life again in April. By then, he was prime minister*

---

*Castro was prime minister from 1959 to 1976
and president from 1976 to 2008.

Castro, newly in power, tells the American Society of Newspaper Editors meeting in Washington that Cuba will always have a free press (AP Photo)

of his nation, but not yet an announced communist. This time, my involvement was different from reporting the reaction of Washington officials to his activities. The new Cuban leader was in the American capital partly because of Don Maxwell, the Tribune's editor. Maxwell wanted him to speak to the American Society of Newspaper Editors (ASNE) meeting in Washington.

He sent an invitation to Castro through Jules Dubois, the Tribune's Latin American correspondent, who had covered Castro when Castro was a guerilla fighter high in the island's Sierra Maestra mountain range. Castro arrived in Washington in mid-month for an 11 day visit that included, besides his talk to the editors, speeches at the National Press Club and Harvard University and a few days in New York City with the famous scenes there of his entourage killing, plucking and roasting chickens in its hotel.

During his two hour speech to the editors at the Statler Hilton Hotel, which included Q and A, he promised the editors there would be a free Cuban press. Willard Edwards wrote the Tribune's story. I listened to the speech, courtesy of Maxwell, but my main duty was to cover Castro as he strolled along the mall in his trademark olive green fatigues, laid a wreath at the Lincoln Memorial, and rode through the streets in an open Jeep with two armed bodyguards in the back. The relaxed atmosphere was possible because his visit was private, and not a state visit. I was never sure that the State Department was happy with the arrangement. Of course, a free press never came to Cuba and in due time Castro announced that his country would become the first communist state in the western hemisphere.

CHAPTER NINE

THE COLD WAR BEGINS

My initial encounter with the Cold War began shortly after Germany's surrender. In May, 1945, my Eighth Armored Division was moved from the Ninth Army in central Germany to Czechoslovakia. We were in General George Patton's Third Army again, but German troops were no longer out in front of us. Here, on the line of contact, we faced the Russians.

Patton's armor had rolled into Czechoslovakia from the west. The Soviets came from the east and they ended up with the bigger slice of land including Prague, the nation's capital, a key advantage to them in the long political struggle to follow in the last half of the 20th century between East and West, communism and capitalism.

My company took up positions southeast of Pilsen, the largest city of the region, in the village of Stary Plzenec. A little river ran along the village outskirts with farm fields and thick forests beyond. Russian forces were across a neutral zone from us. As part of occupying the area, the company manned a dusty and lonely roadside guard post a mile or two outside of the village limits on our side of the neutral zone. There wasn't much traffic, maybe a farm wagon or two each day. The Russians had a similar guard post a mile or so further up the road. We couldn't see each other. Often, we heard machine guns firing in the night. The Russians said they were just having their vodka and a good time.

The arrangement was a loose one although an undercurrent of political intrigue was there from the beginning. The ruins of an ancient fortress stood on a hilltop above our village. It was the highest spot for miles. One morning, we awoke to see the red Russian flag, with its yellow hammer and sickle insignia, flying above the ruins. It had been placed there overnight by persons sympathetic to Stalin and his communist regime. The flag was quickly torn down by villagers, but unease set in among them.

A farmer's wheat field bordered our tent encampment near our guard post. He harvested it alone, by hand, with the aid of a daughter. Sometimes, a few of us pitched in to help him. On occasion, I would visit his home among a cluster of houses just inside the area occupied by the Russians. Sometimes we discussed politics. He was an outspoken communist. He couldn't be shaken. His hope was that a communist government would come to Czechoslovakia.

I've often wondered what turns his life took after the communist coup in February, 1948, and eventually the invasion by Soviet led Warsaw Pact troops in 1968 to quash the reformist movement known as the Prague Spring. Did he become a communist official? Did he become disillusioned? What happened to his wheat field under collectivism? I'll never know what happened to the wheat field, or to him and his daughter, but I'll always be curious.

In the spring and summer of 1945, however, a feeling of freedom from tyranny prevailed. Pilsen was the birthplace a century earlier of its tasty Pilsner beer. It was easy to lift a stein or two in a pleasant evening with the famous brewery only a few kilometers away. Our cooks would often prepare warm and pulpy French fried potatoes for added pleasure. There might have been better places to be elsewhere, and better things to do, but it was a pleasing way to spend some lazy days now that the shooting war was over. Many of the young women of Stary Plzenec worked in Pilsen, to which they commuted by train. It became a daily ritual in late afternoon for us to watch them traipse down the hill from the railroad station, past the schoolhouse in which we lived, as they scattered to their homes. They were a lively bunch. After all, it was Bohemia.

At first, we could travel freely back and forth from Czechoslovakia into the neighboring area of Germany held by the Russians. We were having a book of our company's war time history printed there, and I and others made frequent border crossings. Some trips we would stay two or three days. That arrangement changed dramatically after the Potsdam conference of Western Allies and the Soviets ended on August 2. With President Truman and Stalin present, the conference officially

**Receiving the Bronze Star Medal during WWII
for capturing a German gun emplacement**

recognized the four zones of Hitler's former Third Reich to be occupied by the victors — The United States, Great Britain, Russia and France. East Germany was born. The Russians immediately closed the border. We now had to get written permission from Soviet officials to check on our book. The process was slow and cumbersome. Technically, each trip required new papers.

Fortunately, Russian border guards often returned the passes to us as we crossed back into Czechoslovakia from the new East Germany. That made it possible for us to sneak around the Russian border guards as we crossed into East Germany and then hand an old pass to the guards upon our return. We traveled by Jeep. If the guards questioned the passes, our plan was to just gun the Jeep's engine and speed across the border. But, that never happened. We sometimes saw Russian troops as we drove along East German roads. They waved and cheered. The police state wrapped in suspicion and despotism that became East Germany had not evolved yet. Still, it was a happy day when I crossed the border back into Czechoslovakia for the last time in a light truck with the books of our company's history stacked in the back.

I celebrated VJ Day on August 6 in Stary Plzenec. It was comforting to know that WWII was over. It had been a long slog. At times, it seemed that the conflict would never end, that I would be mustered out eventually as too old to fight. Then, with great suddenness, Japan surrendered after the United States dropped atom bombs on Hiroshima and Nagasaki.

I was grateful that I would never face redeployment to the Pacific theater and an invasion of Japan. I always considered myself lucky to have missed the jungle warfare of the Pacific. Europe at least had buildings and roads and a heritage with which I was somewhat familiar. I was duty officer the night of VJ Day. Stuck in company headquarters, I went to bed early. There was no demonstration in the village plaza like the wildness of Times Square in New York City and celebrations elsewhere in world capitals. We were far from the rejoicing crowds. It had been the same in the little German village we were in on VE day. The most poignant time for me then came at dusk when lights came on in homes and shops. Windows were open to the spring breeze, the nightly blackout and lockdown gone after years of darkness.

Little things like that, so expressive of the bigger picture, grabbed the emotions of war weary soldiers, like me, as peace came.

When the war ended, the plot changed. All those "Dear John" letters started coming home to roost. Life became the heartwarming tale of the men who fought and the women who waited. Stored away relationships sparked anew. Unfortunately, a romance bubble developed in WWII. In the uncertainty of the times, many made rash decisions. Marriage is a life bending ritual, once done lives change. With lasting regret, some folks went for a quick whirl of life in the excitement of war rather than travel a slower, surer road.

The Eighth Armored Division was deactivated shortly after Japan surrendered. Its personnel were scattered to units in Germany to await the homeward journey. I joined a unit of the 85th Infantry Division in Plattling, Bavaria with its large Bavarian Motor Works factory, maker of the sporty BMW so popular with modern drivers. We stayed in a line of row houses along a residential street. I was in Germany into the fall, including time out for a trip to England and Scotland. I rode the Flying Scot from London to Glasgow. As I and some companions settled in, we discovered the famous train had a dining car that night for the first time since the war's end. With our beer and dinner it was foamin' in the gloamin'. At a dance in Glasgow on a Saturday night, we heard an orchestra playing from a ballroom over a radio remote in Scotland, the first since the beginning of the war six years earlier. The crowd on the dance floor whistled and cheered as the orchestra's first musical notes went out over the airwaves.

Transatlantic telephone service had resumed. The USO in Glasgow had established an exchange for use by American service men. A call to the states had to be set up 24 hours in advance and was collect. The charge was $25 for three minutes. I talked to my parents at our specified time. The cost was worth it, especially for my mother. My aunt, Millie, told me that my mother went to church every day when I was overseas to say a prayer for me.

When I returned to Germany, after dallying for several days in Paris until I ran out of money, I found everyone in my outfit packed for transfer to Austria, where we guarded a hydroelectric dam on the Inn River. We were billeted in a little village along the shore. One weekend I drove to Salzburg with my cousin, Jim, who was stationed nearby. We went up into the Alps to Berchtesgaden to visit Hitler's Eagle's Nest retreat and the compound of homes of the top Nazi officials below it. I soon left Austria to return to Bavaria and a resort hotel on the shores of the Chiemsee that had been taken over by the U.S. Army. There, the paperwork began for me to leave Europe.

Meanwhile, Czechoslovakia was increasingly barren of American forces. Then, in December, 1945, all American and Russian troops withdrew under an agreement reached among the victorious powers. By that time, I was on my way to the States. On February 6, 1946, I was honorably discharged from military service at the army separation center at Camp Grant, Illinois, the same place I had gone on active duty in June, 1943.

I was a bit depressed by the landscape as I rode in a passenger train to Chicago that sunny but chilly Sunday over the flat, unending Midwest prairie after weeks of viewing the majesty of snow-capped Bavarian Alps. Still, there was sweetness in seeing the rich black soil. There was deliverance in the sight of familiar things now that I was only hours from home. In Chicago's Union Station I called my uncle and aunt, Harold and Ruth Olander, who lived on the city's north side. When they learned I had a two hour layover before boarding the Burlington route's Denver Zephyr to Galesburg they came along with my cousin, Bob, to see me. It was a comfort to be with blood relatives again. But, nothing surpassed the thrill of stepping from the Zephyr in Galesburg to catch the first glimpse of my mom and dad, uncles and aunts, and my grandmother waiting for me on the station platform beside the famous train. Sorrowfully, my grandfather had died while I was gone. I'd been away a long time. Those months that followed at home, before entering Washington University in June to continue my education, were the most carefree of my life. I had no obligations and no worries. It was a joyful time as I marked the end of army life.

The Europe I left behind continued to churn. On March 6, 1946, a mere month after my discharge, Winston Churchill gave his famous "Iron Curtain" speech at Westminster College in Fulton, Missouri. It questioned the very essence of postwar agreements. Included behind the imaginary screen was that little patch of Czech land that I had helped guard for a brief time in its bid for freedom. As I look back, it is difficult to believe how quickly the peace fought for in WWII deteriorated into the Cold War between the communist world and the west.

"From Stettin in the Baltic to Trieste in the Adriatic an iron curtain has descended across the continent," Churchill said. "Behind that line lie all the capitals of the ancient states of Central and Eastern Europe.

Warsaw, Berlin, Prague, Vienna, Budapest, Belgrade, Bucharest and Sofia, all these famous cities, and populations around them, lie in what I must call the Soviet sphere, and all are subject in one form or another not only to Soviet influence, but to a very high degree in some cases, increasing measure of control from Moscow. Athens, alone, with its immortal Greek glories, is free to decide its future at an election under American, British and French observation."

Churchill said that the communist parties, which were small in all Eastern European states, had been raised to preeminence and power far beyond their numbers. He referred to police governments in nearly every case. A communist government was being established in the Russian zone of Germany. After the Kremlin crushed the Prague spring, its troops remained until 1991. When Sally, our children and I, visited Czechoslovakia in 2002, our guide in Prague said that when the Russian troops finally left his country "we were happy to see them go."

Soviet soldiers straggling home from Czechoslovakia was anti-climactic after the collapse of communist East Germany three years earlier. The Berlin wall, the symbol of tyranny and subjugation, was gone. We saw only a few remaining pieces of it when we visited there. It seemed that the might of Moscow had passed away in the end with a whimper. But, the Stalinist state challenged the west with vigor in the aftermath of WWII. On June 24, 1948, a few weeks after I was graduated from Washington University, the Soviets cut off all road and rail access to Berlin in an effort to drive the United States, Britain and France from the old German capital 100 miles inside the Russian zone. The Cold War had begun in earnest. An airlift saved the parts of the city controlled by western allies from starvation and winter cold. Minute by minute, hour after hour, day after day, until the blockade was broken on May 12, 1949, cargo planes landed at Tempelhof airport. In the end, two million tons of food, coal and other supplies were flown in. There were 270,000 flights in all until the Russians admitted defeat and reopened the highway and rail line.

CHAPTER TEN

THE POSTMASTER GENERAL AND LADY CHATTERLEY

O n weekends, I covered any story that developed. On my three weekdays at work, I was assigned to the bureau's financial and business beat. That meant tramping through the Treasury, the IRS, Labor, Commerce, Justice, Agriculture, and Post Office departments on the lookout for stories. It was so easy then to drop by the offices of government officials for a word or two. That began to change after President Kennedy was killed. Security tightened, slowly at first, then more harshly. I spent little time at the Post Office Department, whose main mission was to deliver the mail on time. But, one sunny spring afternoon in 1959 I found myself standing around the desk of Postmaster General Arthur Summerfield with a half dozen other print reporters.

On the desk lay an unexpurgated copy of D.H. Lawrence's lustful novel, *Lady Chatterley's Lover.*

Not only would Lawrence's tale not be delivered on time, it wouldn't be delivered. Summerfield announced that the book was being banned from the mails and that all copies sent through the postal system would be confiscated. He told us in explanation of his action that "any literary merit the book may have is far outweighed by the pornographic and smutty passages and words, so the book taken as a whole is an obscene and filthy work."

With a back of the hand to the era's conventional taste, the unexpurgated *Lady Chatterley's Lover* was being published in the United States for the first time by Grove Press. The book's past was notorious, beginning with self-publication in Italy in 1928. Its use of taboo language far exceeded anything acceptable at the time in contemporary fiction.

"General, would you read us a passage or two to demonstrate your claim?" I asked him. "No, I won't," was his curt reply. I thought he even blushed.

Now, the general was a mild mannered man from Michigan. He seemed embarrassed by my question. I had no position on the book. I hadn't read it, but censorship, generally, is abhorrent to me. Back then the post office was a cabinet department, not the quasi-government institution it became later. Summerfield was an influential member of Eisenhower's inner circle. His business background in the automotive industry camouflaged a crafty political mind that played an important part in putting the war hero in the White House. I was awed by his office. It was the biggest I'd ever seen. It was enormous. Its first and most prominent occupant was James A. Farley, a legendary politician of the New Deal. A big, rugged Irishman, Farley oversaw completion of a monumental new post office headquarters in the nation's capital. Tucked inside was an office for the postmaster general that seemed to be half the size of a basketball court. The walk from the office entrance to the Postmaster General's desk was so long that Farley joked that by the time visitors reached him they were so intimidated and exhausted that they had forgotten why they came. Farley developed an uncanny ability to recall names and faces in a long political life that included campaign manager for Franklin Roosevelt in the presidential elections of 1932 and 1936 before he split with Roosevelt in 1940 over his bid for a third term. Sally and I met Farley only once at a dinner party in Trohan's home, so we never tested his prowess. But, he sure looked a person straight in the eye.

Obviously, Summerfield's edict was laden with legal danger. After Grove Press sued in Federal Court in the Southern District of New York to lift the ban, I followed the story through the courts even though the law suit did not name Summerfield as a defendant. Instead, it chose the New York City postmaster and charged that he had unlawfully confiscated copies of the book. In checking my memory of the court action, I found a quote of the venerable Associate Supreme Court Justice Oliver Wendell Holmes in which he said, "The use of the mails is almost as much a part of free speech as the use of our tongues." Of course, his use of the word *almost* is tantalizing. Justice Holmes didn't extend his remark, which was made before the unexpurgated *Lady Chatterley's Lover* reached American shores.

Summerfield's ban was overruled initially by a lower court. Summerfield appealed. But, Appellate Judge Frederick van Pelt Bryan quickly upheld the lower court. He called Summerfield's action "contrary to law and clearly erroneous." He said the post office violated the freedom of expression in the Bill of Rights. The judge revealed that he had read the book and found it inoffensive. He said it was not obscene based on its "redeeming social or literary value." Bryan ordered the post office to lift all restrictions on sending copies through the mail. Summerfield conceded defeat. He took no further action and the long held authority of the post office to impound books was over. The long tradition of banning books in Boston also came to an end.

Lady Chatterley's Lover went on to sell two million copies within a year, including one to me.

Summerfield, though he lost his legal battle, was not a lonely warrior. Decency in the arts has always been difficult to characterize. Many have tried, but there is still no uniform definition of obscenity. In 1964 Supreme Court Justice Potter Stewart tried to explain hard core pornography, or what was deemed to be obscene, when he said, "I shall not attempt further to define the kinds of material I understand to be embraced…but I know it when I see it." His statement is well known as summarizing the irony and difficulty in trying to define obscenity.* Social commentators said later that the emancipation of *Lady Chatterley's Lover* began a sexual revolution in America. But, pioneering studies that appeared soon after on human sexuality disclosed that men and women were blithely romping with each other all along. The revolution was the willingness to discuss sexuality publicly. Inevitably, the openness has led to contentious political issues that defy easy solutions.

---

*Judith Silver, Coollawyer.com

CHAPTER ELEVEN

THE UKRAINIAN-AMERICAN WHO CHALLENGED THE SOVIET UNION

'd spotted Lev Dobriansky quickly from the doorway of the men's grill on the second floor of the University Club. He was seated at a table midway back in the room, the first to arrive for our lunch together. There was no missing his tanned bald head and stocky shoulders. He smiled as I pulled back the chair across from him and sat down. "I don't suppose the Russians would be happy if they knew I was breaking bread with you here just a stone's throw away from them," he said. He gestured in the direction of the gray stone Soviet embassy across the alley from the club. His eyes twinkled. "No, I suppose not," I replied. "You're not their favorite American right now."

I'd called Lev that mid-July morning in 1959 to ask him to meet me. I knew him through the club's athletic facilities. I often saw him at the swimming pool or in the sauna when we both worked out. At the time, and for many years thereafter, he was professor of Russian economics at Georgetown University in the nation's capital. In the last few days, I'd also come to know him in a different light. Of Ukrainian descent, he was active in Ukrainian/White Russian émigré circles and he had conceived the idea of a Captive Nations Week. The Kremlin was not pleased. It was upset and mad, and had expressed its displeasure through diplomatic channels a few days earlier when the White House issued a proclamation designating the third week in July as Captive Nations Week. The proclamation asked Americans to pray for the deliverance of their citizens from communist controlled, totalitarian regimes. The White House action was based on a joint Congressional resolution which listed the eastern European countries in the Soviet sphere, along with those within the borders of the Union of Soviet Socialist Republics, as bonds of the Kremlin.

Everyone was surprised by the Soviet's angry reaction. President Eisenhower was stunned, although he didn't mind getting the Kremlin's goat. He'd signed the proclamation without a second thought, thinking it was for domestic political consumption.

Lev said he worked with Sen. Paul Douglas, a Democrat from Illinois and an economics professor himself at the University of Chicago, to guide the resolution through Congress. Both were strong anti-communists. Lev was by birth and Douglas by observation while touring Russia with an American trade commission. Douglas told me that after seeing Russia personally, he was convinced that Marxist economic theory was unworkable. I was interested in writing about Lev's role in the creation of Captive Nations Week as a sidebar to another story unfolding half way around the world. Several hours before I met with Lev, Nikita Khrushchev, the Russian premier, had denounced the American action in his famous "kitchen debate" with Vice President Nixon at a trade fair in Moscow's Sokolniki Park.

"This resolution stinks," Khrushchev had shouted at Nixon. Those present said that the Kremlin leader's face was red with anger. "It stinks like fresh horse manure and nothing smells worse than that." Nixon, aware that Khrushchev had once been a pig farmer, retorted that pig manure was worse.

The vice president and Khrushchev were touring the fair's American National Exhibition, in which an entire American middle income home had been built, including a model kitchen with the latest in appliances. The two sparred among glistening dishwashers, countertops, built-in washing machines and driers. Khrushchev refused to acknowledge that the United States products and living standard were superior to those in the Soviet Empire. He taunted Nixon saying the United States had 150 years to reach its high standard of living while the Soviet Union was only 42 years old and in another seven years it would be on a level with America.

"...after that we will go farther," Khrushchev exclaimed. "As we pass you by, we'll wave 'hi' to you and then if you want, we'll stop and say, 'please come along behind us.'...If you want to live under capitalism, go ahead, that's your question, an internal matter, it doesn't concern us. We can feel sorry for you, but really, you wouldn't understand."

Lev told me that he believed the Soviet Union was fragile and, eventually, would break apart. Time proved him correct and Khrushchev wrong. Lev was born of immigrant Ukrainian parents in New York City. It was said of him that he understood ethnic politics like no one else. During our lunch he said that he believed Khrushchev was so angry over the resolution and proclamation because they included not only Russian satellites in Eastern Europe, but also countries that were part of the Soviet Union. It's the first time that we've recognized by public law that there are enslaved populations within the Soviet Empire, he said. Lev was delighted that he'd touched a raw nerve in Moscow. He said that the idea for a Congressional resolution came to him when Imre Nagy, the prime minister, was executed in the aftermath of the unsuccessful Hungarian revolution against Kremlin dominion.

The Hungarian revolt against Soviet tyranny was the first big tear in the Iron Curtain. It came in the autumn of 1956 as I left the financial news department to become a general assignment reporter in the city room. It began in early October and it was crushed 12 days later by the Kremlin invasion of its troops and tanks in one of the darker moments of the Cold War. Some 200,000 refugees fled across the Hungarian border into Austria and Yugoslavia. Eventually, up to 40,000 were airlifted or brought by ship to the United States. Their destinations included Chicago and Milwaukee.

I was sent to Milwaukee to meet the first arrivals there. I did a series of stories on the refugees and the groups and government officials working to get them settled and off to a solid start. A year later I wrote a series, timed to their first anniversary, which took a look at refugees who had come to Chicago. The articles generated the most mail I ever received as a journalist. One day I arrived at work to find two large gray canvas post office mail bags atop my desk. They contained several thousand letters. Of those I read, some were sympathetic and acclaimed the way the refugees had settled in with hard work and schooling. Some thought the refugees were being pampered. Others were critical of me for putting a positive spin on their exploits.

Perhaps I overcompensated because of the fervent anti-communism in me. I never anticipated the criticism. I thought everyone would welcome their advancement. Not so.

One letter in particular has stuck with me for its angry tone. It opened my eyes to a different perception of the revolutionaries. It was written by a man from upstate New York who picked up a Tribune at Chicago's Midway airport while waiting for his flight home. He was upset by my compassion for the refugees. He wrote that he had worked hard to achieve what he had in life. He said he had done it on his own without anyone's help and that no one wrote about him. He asked why the Hungarians should be aided to take jobs away from Americans.

It wasn't my view that the refugees endangered anyone's livelihood. I believed America was a generous nation with a big heart and open mind. The refugees, relatively few in number, were Americans themselves now, in the long tradition of immigrants. They had little in material things. Their strength was spiritual and a desire to be free. These men and women risked their lives to flee from enslavement under communism. In some ways, the United States had betrayed them. Radio Free Europe, administered by the CIA, had encouraged the rebels to believe western support was imminent. The Eisenhower administration policy was to promote independence of the so-called captive nations of Eastern Europe but only in the long run. Eisenhower was upset when Khrushchev crushed the revolt but he had determined that there was little he could do to help the landlocked Hungarians short of risking a global war. Eisenhower was not prepared to go that far.

CHAPTER TWELVE

AN OLD BOLSHEVIK COMES TO TOWN AND DOES A FAVOR FOR A CHICAGO PRIEST

The Cold War never traveled in a straight line. There were alternate periods of calm and belligerence. Two months after his verbal explosion in the "kitchen debate" Khrushchev flew to Washington as a guest of President Eisenhower. Larry Burd and I were at Andrews Air Force Base to meet him. The Russian premier was in a calmer mood than in his confrontation with Nixon and proud of his big new airplane. But, his spring ultimatum for the western allies to leave Berlin was still in force. If Khrushchev turned the government of Berlin over to the East German Republic, a sovereign state which surrounded the city, as he threatened to do, the western allies would have had no alternative but to leave.

It was Larry's story to cover as the Tribune's chief White House correspondent. I was there to back him if there was too much happening for one person to handle. I always enjoyed being backup. I got to see everything without the responsibility of writing the story. I made my notes, and I was ready if Larry needed me, but mainly I had a free ride to a history-making event. Larry would go on to cover Khrushchev as he toured the United States. My special press pass for the Russian premier's trip was clearly labeled Washington only.

Khrushchev's new plane was the largest in the world at the time, and was so high off the ground that special stairs were required at the air base for him and his entourage to disembark. Eisenhower greeted the premier as he stepped on American soil. After opening ceremonies, I watched the two world leaders, along with Khrushchev's wife, Nina, climb into a black, open convertible for the ride to the White House.

Angry at the press for crowding around them on an Iowa farm, Khrushchev
(bottom right corner) and his host, Roswell Garst, throw ears of corn at
the reporters and photographers (AP Photo)

Ike was squeezed in the middle between the two heftier Russians, and
looked uncomfortable. Mrs. Khrushchev also was wrestling with a huge
bouquet of flowers. Eisenhower spoke no Russian, and the Russian
couple spoke limited English, which added an element of awkwardness.

Just how much English Khrushchev knew is problematic. When he
visited Eleanor Roosevelt at Hyde Park, New York, during his trip,
he was running late and had to skip a lunch she had prepared for him.
As Khrushchev hurried away, he grabbed a roll from the table and
shouted back to her in English: "One for the road." But, it was important for the two men to be seen together in a joyful setting as their visit
began. Riding in a convertible with its top down on a pleasant, sunny

afternoon along a parade route of well-wishers and military bands certainly alluded to a happy and carefree mood. It was the leisurely security of the times that was so amazing, however. In retrospect, here were the two most powerful men in the world riding side by side in an open convertible for miles through streets thronged with onlookers and no one gave it a second thought.

One Sunday night, Ike drove into Maryland to speak to a national meeting of Republicans in the University of Maryland's Cole Field House. There were three cars in the procession: Eisenhower's limousine, a secret service limousine and a press limousine with four or five of us reporters. Once we crossed the District of Columbia line into Maryland and onto a four lane highway, the three vehicles formed a triangle with Eisenhower in the front and the other two slightly behind on either side riding shotgun. That was it. No police, no ambulance, no multiple black SUVs trailing along behind like today. It was after the assassination of President Kennedy as he rode in an open touring car through the streets of Dallas that everything about presidential motorcades changed. Our innocence ended that day and the world began a downhill slide into a darker side. But, when Khrushchev visited Eisenhower an ease of movement and access still existed.

There is no better example of that relaxed atmosphere than Joseph Prunskis, a Roman Catholic priest from Chicago, who was an assistant pastor in St. George parish on the city's south side. He came into the bureau in the early afternoon of Khrushchev's last day in the United States. He told me that he wanted to deliver a petition to the Russian leader, and he asked me if I knew how it could be done.

"Your clerical collar should do the trick, Father," I said. "Let's walk over to Blair House."

It was now Sunday. Blair House, where Khrushchev was staying, was across the street from the White House. The previous Wednesday Father Prunskis had intercepted Khrushchev after the Soviet leader's speech at the National Press Club. Addressing him in Russian, saying "Good day, Mr. Khrushchev," the Kremlin leader halted and the priest, continuing in Russian, asked him if he would permit Prunskis's 72-year-old widowed mother in Lithuania to join him in Chicago. "I'll do that," he quoted Khrushchev as replying.

Prunskis fled Lithuania in 1940 when it was occupied by the Soviets as part of the Molotov-Ribbentrop non-aggression pact between the

Kremlin and Nazi Germany. His mother had remained in Kaunas, a center of resistance to Russian authority, before and after WWII. Now Prunskis wanted to see Khrushchev again.

The day was pleasant and sunny as we walked the few blocks from the bureau to the presidential guest house, where a dozen people casually occupied the sidewalk in front when we arrived. Automobile traffic moved by on Pennsylvania Avenue. The front door was open and through a screen door, Russian voices could be heard inside. Father Prunskis climbed the steps of a small porch and knocked. After an exchange in Russian with a man who appeared, he vanished inside.

Later, as we walked through Lafayette Park on our way back to the bureau, Father Prunskis, recapped for me what had taken place. He said that Mrs. Khrushchev was preparing to leave for a farewell call on Mrs. Eisenhower, but she delayed her visit to speak with him. He gave her a petition, signed by his brother, John, and two sisters, Dr. Anna Jarunas, a dentist, and Miss Anele Prunskis, which requested that their mother, Ona, be allowed to join them in Chicago.

"I'll take care of the matter personally," Father Prunskis quoted Mrs. Khrushchev as saying. "I'll call the petition to my husband's attention when he returns from Camp David."

"Although I had only a few minutes with her, she didn't hurry me," the priest told me. "I'm sure she would have granted me more time, if it had been necessary. She was friendly and didn't rush me a bit. I explained that I had not signed the petition because I thought the signature of a priest may prejudice officials against my mother."

"You should not have been afraid to sign it," he quoted Mrs. Khrushchev as replying.

Earlier that morning, Khrushchev had declined to attend church services in Gettysburg with the president. Instead he had hiked the paths of Camp David with aides. Later, he visited Eisenhower's Gettysburg farm. That evening, Khrushchev went to the Russian embassy, where he held a press conference and made a nationwide television/radio speech to the American public. After the press conference, Larry went back to the bureau to write his wrap-up story of Khrushchev's trip across the United States. I stayed to cover the Russian leader's talk. Khrushchev made his comments in Russian sitting at a small table with an interpreter at his right side, rephrasing Khrushchev's words in English as he spoke.

"People who have been to the Soviet Union have no doubt spoken of the very good feelings entertained for you by the Soviet people, and of their wish to live in peace and friendship with you," Khrushchev began. "I will now take back with me the conviction that you entertain similar feelings for the Soviet people of this."

Khrushchev was on his best behavior, but saying at the same time that a possible thaw in the Cold War would require great effort and patience. He told his audience that it is not easy to overcome all that has accumulated over the many years of the Cold War. He said it is impossible, therefore, to count on a sudden change in the situation. Khrushchev made a strong pitch for co-existence, saying that there can be no tranquility in the world unless the United States and Russia live side by side. He pressed for separate peace treaties for East and West Germany, the desire behind his threat to make East Germany a sovereign state that would strip control of West Berlin from the western allies.

The Soviet leader praised Marx, Engel, and Lenin, but did not mention Stalin, in naming the men who blazed the trail of communism. He pictured Russia as a social paradise wrapped in political purity. He said unemployment is not a worry in Russia and boasted again that his country would soon be the number one industrial power with homes, schooling, and sick care for everyone. In reality, Russia was a poor country. Behind the scenes, Khrushchev sought better trade relations with America. After his talk, Khrushchev flew out of Andrews Air Force base back to Moscow. I stood on the tarmac and watched him go.

Russian experts and scholars did not think Khrushchev-Eisenhower talks accomplished much beyond beginning a long period of east-west negotiations to mitigate the Cold War and lessen the risks of a shooting war. The two men issued a joint statement that all international disputes should be settled through negotiations, and not by force. The Russian leader did get to see a slice of America in a train ride to New York City, which he thought was noisy and choked with too many vehicle exhaust fumes. In Iowa he visited a farm. He witnessed the filming of the Can-Can for an upcoming movie in Hollywood. He thought it vulgar. In San Francisco he had a long and friendly talk with Harry Bridges, leader of the left-leaning Longshoremen's Union. He saw a steel mill at his request in Pittsburgh. He showed little interest in IBM's giant computers in a visit to a company plant in California but he was fascinated by its cafeteria with what he called its wide selection of food and easy going democratic atmosphere. He ordered cafeteria style eateries set up in Russian factories upon his return to the Kremlin.

Meanwhile, preparations began for Eisenhower to visit Russia in the summer of 1960. Before that, he and Khrushchev were to hold a summit in Paris in mid-May. But, the most careful of plans can go unfulfilled. On May 1, 1960, the Russians, after futile attempts on previous intrusions, shot down an American U-2 spy plane over-flight deep inside their country. The Cold War turned ugly once again. Khrushchev dominated the summit with anger over the U-2 flights. Eisenhower never visited the Soviet Union.

Ona Prunskis did come to America. In the lull between Khrushchev's American tour and the U-2 incident, Father Prunskis, on March 19, 1960 received diplomatic word that his mother had been granted a Soviet exit visa, per his wishes, and she flew to the United States via Moscow to join her family in the Midwest.

CHAPTER THIRTEEN

THE U-2 AFFAIR: SLOW WALKING THE TRUTH

The U-2 incident unraveled slowly for both the press and the public. I thought the truth was slow in coming, but intelligence gathering is difficult to cover. So much of it is, by necessity, secret, and, by nature, deceptive. Sources within the intelligence community are hard to cultivate. Until the plane disappeared on May 1, it was a top secret information gathering operation that involved a handful of people on a need-to-know basis. Once the plane went down, the affair became a cat and mouse game between the White House and the Kremlin. Espionage is always an inside game. Both governments knew that each spied on the other. Spying was one of the premier activities of the Cold War. Both sides had its defectors. Risks were taken. Novels and movies of espionage tales were some of the most entertaining and thrilling fiction of the 20th century, as American and Soviet agents on screen, and in books, tried to outdo their counterparts.

But, sometimes truth caught up with fiction, and like the U-2 incident, the outcome was nasty.

When Eisenhower gave the go ahead to build the U-2 in late 1954, he was well aware of the dangers in its use for clandestine espionage missions. Evan Thomas in his excellent book *Ike's Bluff* quotes an oral history which Secretary of State John Foster Dulles gave to his alma mater, Princeton University. Dulles said that Ike told those present that day in the White House, "Well boys, I believe the country needs this information, and I'm going to approve it (the U-2). But, I'll tell you one thing. Some day one of those machines is going to be caught and we are going to have a storm."[3]

I felt some of that storm was caused by the Eisenhower administration itself in the U-2 incident. I never fully understood the need for the U.S. to voluntarily put out a cover story that the U-2 was a weather plane. Why the convolution? Only a few people in either country really knew what was going on. This was clearly a situation of unknowns. Why wade into a swamp whose depth was unclear? Russian officials were mum. Why shouldn't American officials be the same? Why not wait for events to unfold?

But American officials didn't. Two days after the plane disappeared NASA said an aircraft on a Weather Service mission in Turkey had disappeared. The statement drew scant attention. The Tribune buried its coverage in a paragraph on an inside page. The Russians continued their silence. But a deception was underway that would be embarrassing, and which I thought was unworthy of an American government. The Russians had tried and failed to shoot down over-flights of their country but the U-2 flew so high at 70,000 feet that Soviet surface-to-air missiles couldn't reach it and their MIG fighters couldn't climb that high to intercept it. An SA-2 missile finally traveled high enough to checkmate the May 1 intrusion of Soviet airspace.

The Eisenhower administration wondered what had gone wrong. In 1902, two years into the 20th century, a song with the title *Bill Bailey Won't You Please Come Home* became an enduring hit sung through the decades by jazz singers and Dixieland bands. It was even popular at campus parties in my college days. So, on May 1, 1960 a message arrived in Washington saying Bill Bailey didn't come home. It meant that the U-2 flight that day hadn't reached its destination in Bodo, Norway after takeoff in Peshawar, Pakistan.

So, where was it? It was now day five since the U-2 had disappeared. Russia had the answer and in a moment of high drama, Nikita Khrushchev, in a speech before the Supreme Soviet, disclosed the details. He said that a foreign aircraft that crossed the Soviet Union border five days earlier had been shot down on orders of the Soviet government. Khrushchev said investigation showed it was a U.S. plane. American officials kept stiff upper lips as they faced the problem of how much the Soviets knew. They debated, in turn, how much information, if any, they should make public.

Ike kicked off the American response with a brief word that an inquiry would be made by the State Department and NASA, with the

State Department, not the White House, handling all public statements. Ike then slipped into the background. Much of the government reaction in the U-2 shoot down involved the State Department. The Tribune didn't have a full-time State Department correspondent, so when the story broke wide open we needed someone there. I was soon on my way to Foggy Bottom, as the former wetlands near the Potomac River where the state department stood was called, a description that long had carried a double meaning.

In its first response, the U.S. requested that the Soviet government provide it with full facts of the Soviet investigation and the fate of the pilot. It didn't fess up that the plane was flying a spy mission.

"We've been informed by NASA that, as announced, a U-2 weather research plane based at Adana, Turkey, piloted by a civilian, has been missing since May 1," we learned from the State Department statement handed out to reporters. "During the flight of this plane, the pilot reported difficulty with his oxygen equipment. Mr. Khrushchev has announced that a U.S. plane has been shot down over the USSR on that date. It may be that this is the missing plane. It is entirely possible that, having a failure of oxygen equipment, which could result in the pilot losing consciousness, the plane continued on automatic pilot for a considerable distance and accidentally violated Soviet air space. The United States is taking this matter up with the Soviet government, with particular reference to the fate of the pilot."

Just what the State Department thought was "a considerable distance" was not defined. The U-2 had taken off from Peshawar to photograph military installations in the Russian areas of Sverdlovsk, Kirov, and Archangel. It was shot down over Sverdlovsk, 1,200 miles inside the Soviet Union, by all measurements quite "a considerable distance." It would be the same as a Russian over-flight that took off from New York City being shot down somewhere around Omaha, Nebraska.

Nonetheless, during Q and A following his reading of the State Department statement, Lincoln White, the department spokesman, felt free to elaborate. "There was absolutely no, N-O, no deliberate attempt to violate Soviet air space," he said. "It is ridiculous to say we are trying to kid the world about this."

NASA, unaware of its now secondary role, added in a statement the additional details that U-2 research airplanes had been in use since 1956 in a continuing program to study gust-meteorological conditions found at high altitudes. It said that the pilot was employed by Lockheed Aircraft Corporation and that he had reported having oxygen difficulties in an area over Lake Van, Turkey.

A haze of uncertainty hung over the capital. Suspicion was growing that things may not be as they were reported. When I returned to the office, we discussed the possibility that, despite White's assurance, this was an intelligence operation gone wrong. We didn't think the weather story made sense. It seemed bogus, a cover story in the finest tradition of spy craft. Why study the weather in far off Turkey? The nonchalant posture of the U.S. to a plane shot down seemed telling. Why no anger? Why no protest? The war drums weren't banging. We concluded that the low-key response signaled a CIA mission caught (pardon the expression) *red* handed. We made calls to key senators and congressmen on Capitol Hill to no avail. The CIA was mum. The White House kept referring everyone to the State Department and Eisenhower took off for his farm in nearby Gettysburg for the weekend, as though nothing were amiss. But, we kept probing.

This was a story with a lot of dead time. The fountainhead of news was in far-away Moscow. All the U.S. could do was respond to Kremlin initiatives. Nothing happened stateside outside of controlled briefings. Dodging reporters, principals sneaked in and out of the White House. This isn't difficult. There are many entrances to the executive mansion. Sometimes reporters would divide up to watch the different gates, but group participation was rare. Competition usually overruled cooperation. Show me a reporter who relies only on briefings for information and I will show you a lousy journalist. Many times sources outside of the White House are more helpful than those inside.

The Russians weren't fooled. They'd attempted to shoot down U-2 high altitude reconnaissance over-flights since the first one in 1956, the year mentioned by NASA. Nevertheless, Khrushchev went out of his way to omit details of the shoot down in his speech. He seemed to open the possibility for Eisenhower to wash his hands of the matter by emphasizing that he did not know if the American president was aware of the flights. He suggested the U-2 was being operated by "cold warriors" in America. The "cold warriors" were, of course, Allen Dulles and the Central Intelligence Agency he headed.

Allen Dulles was once a Tribune guest at a White House Correspondents Association dinner, where I sat next to him and was taken on a world tour of U.S. trouble spots. I felt he was telling me more than I wanted to know. But, that wasn't happening now.

Ike had expected Khrushchev to bring up U-2 flights during his visit to America but he didn't. Now, in his own way, the communist leader attempted to protect the president and save the upcoming mid-May summit with him in Paris only days away. Although I learned later that some American officials suggested ditching the weather plane story and telling the world the truth about the U-2, the predominant thinking among them was that the Russians would find no evidence to prove the U.S. government was conducting espionage flights. The Americans did not think that the pilot had survived (he had poison to take if faced with capture) and they assumed that the light-skinned jet, which looked much like a glider, would disintegrate in a missile strike. If not, there was a dashboard button for the pilot to push to do the same thing.

Khrushchev finally had enough. In all, there had been 24 U-2 flights across the Soviet Union. The Soviet leader had signaled to the Americans how they could handle the situation to his satisfaction. They hadn't done so. So he showed the U-2 plane to the world largely intact, and produced the pilot, Francis Gary Powers, alive and well for the world to see.* In an embarrassing reversal of previous statements, the United States admitted the American plane shot down over Russia was on an information gathering mission as charged by Khrushchev. But, it still fudged on the truth, saying that there was no authorization for the latest flight from officials in Washington. The statement, again read by Lincoln White, said that unarmed U-2 aircraft had been flying along "the frontiers of the free world" for the last four years to avoid a surprise attack.

The admission came after a daylong conference attended by frustrated American diplomatic and military officials who had seen their alibi weakening daily and finally blow up. They knew in advance of Khrushchev's disclosure that Powers was alive. Yakov Malik, the Kremlin's deputy minister of foreign affairs, had blabbed about the coup at a diplomatic reception in Moscow, where his words were picked up by American

---

* Powers' trial for espionage began August 17, 1960 in Moscow.
Barbara, his wife, and his parents, Mr. and Mrs. Oliver Powers,
attended and talked to him. Powers was sentenced to 10 years in
a Russian prison but he was exchanged for the Soviet master spy,
Rudolf Abel, on February 10, 1962 in Berlin.

foreign service officers. Ambassador Llewellyn Thompson cabled Washington that Kremlin officials were questioning Powers, who had parachuted to safety. American officials in Washington had known within days of the first flight back in the summer of 1956, that the Russians were aware the U-2 was tracking its military installations and missile sites. The Kremlin filed a formal protest through diplomatic channels, but refrained from making the information public because they didn't want to admit that they couldn't shoot the U-2 down. As to the no authorization from Washington, it became known that Ike had given permission in late April for one last flight before his Paris summit with Khrushchev scheduled for May 1. It's true that Ike didn't okay a specific flight for May 1, but he did give a window for a flight to take place. The hairsplitting cut veracity close. But politics will do that. So interpret the U-2 incident as you will. It's just history now. The world, as always, has moved on.

CHAPTER FOURTEEN

THE U-2 MORPHS INTO THE SPACE AGE

've never thought I was naïve. I'm fully aware after years as a journalist that things aren't always on the level. I've seen some pretty good lying in my time. Still, when I arrived in Washington, I thought that the White House, with its vast resources, would always be up front about events; that it would always stick to the truth. The U-2 affair ended that innocence. That didn't mean I disapproved of intelligence operations. It only meant that I'd be more skeptical of things at first glance. A deep dent had been made in my trust to accept things as presented. There is no substitute for friends if you are a journalist. Stories don't fall from the sky. Government officials and bureaucrats are good sources of information if they know and trust you and you trust them. While I was awed by the U-2's amazing ability, I would never look at the White House in quite the same way again.

Even while the U-2 flew, The United States was moving on to the use of orbiting spy satellites. It had been 2½ years since Russia launched the first artificial earth satellite, a small sphere traveling high above us through space, the sun reflected on its polished metal sphere. Sputnik upset the American psyche, with massive handwringing by the public over Russia's triumph. Eisenhower couldn't understand America's reaction. Secure with the knowledge of Russia's military weakness garnered from U-2 flights and knowing the United States would soon launch its own satellite, he wondered what all the fuss was about.

More important, no nation came forward to protest intrusion of its air space by Sputnik. That meant American reconnaissance satellites under development would be able to roam in space at will at much higher altitudes than the U-2. Four months after Sputnik, the U.S. sent its own satellite, Explorer I, aloft from Cape Canaveral, Florida.

The race to dominate space had begun.

Corona was the first American spy satellite. Several satellites were launched between June 1959 and September 1960, also under the operational eyes of the CIA. The overlord of Corona, just as he had been for the U-2, was Richard Bissell, a special assistant to Allen Dulles and later director of plans. As with so many of the early CIA officials, he came out of the Eastern establishment. He had been schooled at Groton and Yale. Before Corona, Bissell guided clandestine programs for building the U-2 as well as its supersonic successor, the SR-71.

In late summer of 1960, I accompanied Eisenhower to the big missile center at Huntsville, Alabama, where the president took his first look at work underway on the powerful Saturn rocket that would fly Americans to the moon. The Eisenhower presidency was coming to an end. He would leave office in a little more than four months. Reassured of U.S. superiority, he fought attempts to increase military spending and warned against a growing military-industrial complex. He was proud that his administration had not fought a war.

"The United States never lost a soldier or a foot of ground in my administration," he said proudly. "We kept the peace. People ask how it happened. By God, it just didn't happen. I'll tell you that."

Huntsville was my first trip with the White House press corps. There were 25 of us aboard the turbo-prop plane chartered from Capital Airlines that climbed into the sky at 7:30 a.m. from National Airport. I was up early and at the terminal for private aircraft at seven o'clock. I wasn't going to miss this. Eisenhower was still having coffee at the White House when we took off. He wouldn't leave Washington for another hour and 10 minutes at 8:40 a.m. on his own propeller plane, Columbine III. The press plane was filled with veteran White House correspondents and photographers. I was the only newcomer. Frank Holeman of the *New York Daily News* motioned to me to sit with him. Across the aisle were Bob Pierpont of CBS and Ray Scherer of NBC. Also along was Felix Belair Jr. of the *New York Times*, by far the snappiest dresser among us with his cuff links, tie clasp and ivory cigarette holder. I spotted the shaved head of Jack Sutherland of *U.S. News & World Report* in a seat several rows ahead. Charlie Roberts of *Newsweek* plopped down beside him. All would become frequent traveling companions and good friends. Art Lodo and Bill Smythe represented Fox Movietone News. Yes, in 1960, there were still newsreels in movie theaters. Telegraph was still the predominant way for print reporters to move copy and Carroll Linkins was there for Western Union. That's all changed in the computer age. Filing by Western Union is a thing of the past. Even telephones seem passé.

Besides inspecting the Saturn that day, Eisenhower dedicated the missile center in Huntsville as the Marshall Space Flight Center in honor of the late Gen. George C. Marshall, chief of staff in WWII, and Ike's boss when the president was supreme allied commander in Europe. Later, as secretary of state, Marshall developed the Marshall plan to rebuild war torn Europe. A red granite bust of Marshall was unveiled by his widow, Katherine. With the dedication over, Eisenhower, my press colleagues and I, joined Wernher von Braun, the German-born rocket expert, who directed the space age facility and its 5,000 employees.

"I have long looked forward to visiting this spot," Ike told von Braun as other reporters and I encircled them, listening in. "For an old foot soldier like me, it is a revelation to see firsthand the efforts underway to probe into the mysteries of the universe."

Donning a white safety helmet stamped with a presidential seal on the front, the president rode an elevator up three stories to get a top side view of the 80-foot-high, eight-engine first stage of the rocket as it rested on a firing pad. Along with Ike, I was seeing the American space age in its infancy. I'd seen German rockets in the sky in WWII, both the V-1 and V-2. The V-1 was a primitive contraption. In reality, it was just a flying bomb. In fact, it was nicknamed "buzz bomb." In Belgium one night in WWII, a V-1 flew directly over me on its way to Antwerp, about 60 miles westward, an important allied port of entry to the European continent. It sounded like a thrashing machine. Fire belched from its engine exhaust as it lumbered slowly along about 800 feet high. When it was a few miles beyond me and my fellow soldiers, still in sight, its engines cut off. No one uttered a word. We just waited. In seconds a mighty explosion rocked the area as the V-1 hit ground in a farm field. A grist mill that was company headquarters shook violently, rifles and helmets hanging on its walls flew off their hooks, glass windows shattered. Those of us outside could feel the shock waves hit our bodies.

The Germans launched their first V-1 on London on June 13, 1944 from Normandy, a week after D-Day. I saw the launch pads there after the war. They looked like swimming pools slanted about 45 degrees skyward with one end open. Three months later, in September, 1944, the first V-2 was launched. The V-2, its automatic guidance system and lift-off power perfected, soared 50 miles above the earth, the first manmade object to reach suborbital space. It was a true rocket, the dawn of the space age. We saw only their vapor trails as they sped toward London.

In retirement in Florida, I had a neighbor, George Burgle, a German scientist who had worked with von Braun at Peenemünde, the Third Reich's rocket proving ground and research facility on Usedom Island in the Baltic Sea off of Germany's northern coast. At war's end, George and his family lived in what would soon become East Germany. He was coveted by both Russian and the Allies for his work on guidance systems. The Allies got him, but his escape was a heart stopper. George was contacted by the British in the village in which he lived, and plans were made for him to flee with his family into Allied territory. On departure day, George went to the railroad station ahead of his wife, Alma, and their two children, who, by plan, would come later. The family was onboard a waiting train when Russian soldiers arrived, prepared to take them captive. A contingent of British soldiers surrounded the Burgles, sang and pretended to be drunk. The Russians pushed and shoved to reach the Burgles and remove them from the train. The British pushed and shoved back until the train began to move. George said the Russians scrambled off the train as it began to gain speed.

The trip to Huntsville was a short one. We were back in nation's capital by late afternoon. I filed my story from the bureau and I was home in time for dinner.

CHAPTER FIFTEEN

FLYING WITH PRESIDENTS

I was on many more presidential trips through the years, some more hazardous than others. Eisenhower didn't fly much. He usually drove to and from his farm in Gettysburg. Helicopters were used sparingly for presidential missions during his administration. There would be no jets for White House use until President Kennedy was chief executive. It was only then that the presidential plane was designated as Air Force One.

In earlier years, presidents and would-be presidents on the campaign trail traveled by rail. The definitive transition to air came as the nation moved into the 1960s. As a boy in Galesburg, in the heyday of trains, I saw FDR, Alf Landon, and Herbert Hoover speak from the rear platforms of club cars as they made whistle-stops in my hometown. Wendell Willkie came through town in 1940, but he got off of the train and spoke in front of the Burlington Route station. I remember how raspy his voice was from making so many speeches every day. We'd get out of school to go. Educators thought the whistle-stops were real-life civic lessons.

Now, airport rallies are often the order of the day on presidential campaigns. The 1964 presidential campaign was the first in which candidates used jet airplanes. Jets made it possible to cover widely separated areas of the country in one day, topped off by a night rally and a clean hotel room. Hotel stays can have their bad moments, however. I remember our overnight in Grand Rapids with Nixon and the dilemma in which Dick Dudman, of the *St. Louis Post Dispatch*, found himself the next morning, as we boarded the bus around 7:30 a.m. The hotel laundry had not returned the dress shirts he had put out to be washed as he slept, and he was wearing nothing but an undershirt beneath his suit coat. He took a lot of teasing

As presidential trips by air became a way of life, press travel with the president developed its own routine. The White House handled travel arrangements and billings for the press, the cost of charter flights for those making a trip divided among newspaper correspondents, magazine writers and broadcast organizations. Departure times were announced. Luggage was brought to the White House and transported to the press aircraft by the travel office.

The pattern was solid except for LBJ, who could be obstinate about making up his mind whether to go to his Texas ranch for the weekend or stay in Washington. When Thursday nights rolled around, we could never get a definite word about flying to Texas. We were told that to be safe, bring a suitcase on Friday. There were times I lugged my suitcase and portable typewriter back home. Trips to and from the White House to the airport were by bus. If the press stayed in one location for several days, like Gettysburg, Hyannis Port, San Antonio, Texas when Johnson was president, or San Clemente, California with Nixon, rental cars would be waiting. We would sign up beforehand with Cleve Ryan, the TV lighting technician, who ran a little business on the side with rental agencies. Hotel arrangements were made by the travel office. In the beginning of air travel, Capital Airlines, with headquarters in Washington, was used exclusively, but romances developed among the press and flight attendants who were regulars on trips. Homes were broken up. Soon, to avoid such situations, press charters were shared among different airlines and rotating flight attendants.

I'll always have a soft spot in my heart for Kennedy because of those pleasant summer weekends he gave me on Cape Cod, especially in August, when he flew to the Cape every Friday and returned to the capital on Monday. It was then I concluded that White House correspondents should vote for a presidential candidate based on where he spent his vacations. Kennedy would retreat to his home in Hyannis Port as soon as we arrived. We seldom saw him again except at Mass on Sunday. There would be one press briefing a day in the Yachtsman Inn, where the traveling press stayed. The rest of the time was mine along with the other reporters.

On Friday, August 24, 1962 I was the newspaper pool reporter for the trip. I flew in the backup helicopter from the White House to Andrews

Air Force Base in Maryland. On the plane, Kennedy was up front in the presidential quarters. I was in the cabin in the back with his staff. On my seat was a preflight report with an imprint of the presidential seal and signed by Col. James B. Swindal, aircraft commander.

Details of the trip were in the report: The distance to Otis Air Force Base in Massachusetts was 405 miles (352 nautical miles). Our flying time would be 50 minutes, plus 10 minutes to land. With a five-mile-per-hour tail wind, our ground speed would be 550 miles per hour. Our flight altitude would be 23,000 feet with a cabin altitude of 300 feet. The time change was none. The weather forecast en route was clear. At our destination there were a few clouds with the temperature at 70 degrees.

This was the first presidential jet, a modified Boeing 707. Kennedy was the first president to use it a few months earlier. So, I was aboard Air Force One at the beginning of the jet age for presidential flight. I had a mystical feeling about the aircraft, that it personified the power and majesty of our nation itself.

I was a pool reporter several times with Presidents Johnson and Nixon on Air Force One. I traveled with Johnson from Suriname, just north of the equator in South America, to Randolph Air Force Base in Texas. LBJ was on his way to his ranch after attending a summit of Latin American nations in the South Atlantic seaside resort of Punta del Este, Uruguay. We had landed in Suriname to refuel. It was stifling hot and humid. A tent where a crowded reception was held for LBJ took on the smell of a menagerie.

I was a pool reporter on a Nixon flight from San Clemente to Honolulu, Hawaii. After two days in Hawaii we flew to Midway Island, home of the dodo bird, and the area of one of America's great victories at sea in WWII. Nixon met the president of South Vietnam there to discuss America's continued role in that war-torn country during the Nixon presidency.

Airports at the start of the jet age didn't always have runways long enough to easily accommodate jet aircraft. Once, flying with President Kennedy to the west coast, we stopped in Pierre, South Dakota, to mark the beginning of construction on a federal dam. The landings were okay, but the presidential plane tore up part of the asphalt runway on its takeoff. The press plane was held on the ground, unsure the remaining runway was long enough for takeoff. After discussion and some calculations, it was decided to give it a try. We made it into the air by a few yards.

A similar event took place in covering President Johnson, but this was

PREFLIGHT REPORT

FROM _ANDREWS_ TO _OTIS_

THE DISTANCE IS _352_ N.M. _405_ S.M.

THE FLYING TIME IS _50 MIN. PLUS 10 MIN. LANDING_

DUE TO A _5 MPH_ _TAIL_ WIND WE EXPECT TO

HAVE A GROUND SPEED OF _550_ MILES PER HOUR.

OUR FLIGHT PLAN ALTITUDE IS _23,000_ FEET.

OUR CABIN ALTITUDE WILL BE _300_ FEET.

TIME CHANGE _NONE_

WEATHER FORECAST

ENROUTE _CLEAR_

DESTINATION _A FEW CLOUDS_
TEMPERATURE 70°F

Colonel Swindal
AIRCRAFT COMMANDER

Air Force One preflight weather report when I was pool reporter from Washington to Hyannis Port on August 24, 1962 a bit more harrowing. We flew to Fort Campbell, Kentucky, where the president reviewed troops bound for Vietnam. The next stop was southern Indiana to campaign for Democrat candidates in the midterm elections of 1966. I always had the feeling that the White House considered the press corps expendable. This was doubled in spades when LBJ switched to a small, one engine plane at Fort Campbell for the next leg. We continued on in our big jet. The second we hit the ground at the next airport, the pilot hit the brakes. After a few more seconds, the plane turned sharply as it came to a halt. Out the window I could see a barbed wire fence a few feet away.

The takeoff was equally close. As we barreled down the runway, Jack Sutherland, of *U.S. News and World Report*, stared out the window. The instant we left the ground he began to count: "One, two, three." We soared into the air. We cleared a fence at the end of the runway by a foot, maybe two. "Three seconds," he said. "We cleared the fence by three seconds."

I'll always remember an incident while covering Barry Goldwater's campaign for the presidency. We had made a stop at Newport, Tennessee, tucked in the so-called tristate mountain area bordering both Kentucky and Virginia. After the rally, we took off and climbed steadily. Suddenly, the plane, an American Airlines charter, turned back toward the airport and descended into a steep dive.

In the seat behind me I heard Jack Steele of Scripps-Howard exclaim, "God! We're crashing!"

But, there was nary a word, never any explanation, from the pilot as to what was happening. I gripped the arms of my seat and glanced across the aisle at David Schoumacher of CBS. He shook his head a bit and held up the palm of his hand toward me as if to say "don't panic."

I saw Goldwater jump from his seat and head to the cockpit, then return and calmly sit down. We leveled off a few hundred feet above ground. Soon the plane began to climb again. I learned later that what happened is known as a low level, high speed pass. A few weeks earlier, a vintage Ford Tri-Motor (the "Tin Goose") had landed at the airport on a barnstorming tour. The tower had asked it to do a low level, high speed pass. That must have looked like slow motion compared to the Goldwater jet. Schoumacher had been an air force pilot and he knew the plane was never out of control. Others, like Steele and I, weren't so sure.

My initiation into the jet age came in WWII on a clear and chilly warrior morning in April, 1945. With no inkling of what I was about to see, our armored column of tanks and halftracks was off again cutting up the German army trapped in the Ruhr Pocket. Suddenly, the fastest aircraft I'd ever seen zoomed by low above us.

"Jesus!" I exclaimed.

"What the hell was that?" shouted Ralph Dreisbach, our halftrack driver.

I was in the machine gun turret and could easily see the plane. Ralph couldn't from his seat, lower down and buttoned up in armor but he heard the roar of its engine. The plane came, and went, in what seemed a split second, a fighter with the knights cross insignia on its fuselage. Everyone in our column strained his neck to catch a glimpse of this breakthrough German aircraft, even hoping that it would return for a second look. And it did. This time, the jet flew along the side of the column, so low that I could see the pilot from my perch in the turret. The German made no attempt to fire on the column; he looked us over and then hightailed it away.

I was so awestruck I made no attempt to fire on the plane, much less hit it, since it seemed to outstrip the wind. If I had been a reporter for the Chicago Tribune that day I would have filed a dispatch on witnessing this new phenomenon.

One of the mysteries of WWII has to be Hitler's delay in developing his jet fighter, considering the early test flights by the Luftwaffe prior to the war. The engines in German jets, like the one I saw, were developed as early as 1935. The kerosene fuel of the plane was readily manufactured from coal, which Germany had available right in the Ruhr Valley through which our column moved. That day I saw tipples jutting skyward above mines.

It was another 14 years before I finally flew in a jet on a United Air Lines flight from Chicago to New York City. The airliner was brand new, part of United's first fleet of commercial jets. As jets became common, they changed commercial and political worlds as much as the military world. They transformed Washington from a sleepy southern town to a high-pressure capital of lobbyists and special interests that could jet in from anywhere in the country in a few hours. Before jets, many trade associations were concentrated in Chicago, the nation's rail hub, centrally located in mid-America. But, who wants to ride trains to Chicago when you can easily jet to Washington, the greatest power center of all the cities on the earth.

CHAPTER SIXTEEN

OLD SOLDIERS REMINISCE

As I wrote earlier, Eisenhower drove to his farm in Gettysburg most of the time when he wanted to get away from the White House. So, it was an easy drive for me one day several years after he left the presidency, when he asked reporters to come there for comments he wished to make backing a return of the Panama Canal to Panama. We stood around a temporary desk on the floor of the Gettysburg College gymnasium as he discussed his reasons for his position, then he started to reminisce about WWII in Europe, where he'd been supreme commander of Allied forces.

"I was one of your boys, general," I remarked.

"In Europe?" he asked.

I nodded.

A smile broke across his face. "What outfit?" He asked

"Eighth Armored Division, 49th Armored Infantry Battalion, Company C, a staff sergeant," I replied.

"The Eighth Armored," he mused. "Your commander was Brigadier General Divine."

"Yes, he was," I said. "That is, he was in Europe. In the States, we had Major General Bill Grimes."

The Eighth Armored history records that Eisenhower personally selected John Divine, previously commander of Combat Command C of the Seventh Armored Division. Grimes was known affectionately as "Granny" by his troops. He was a weathered old soldier but too along in years for a battlefield. There were a number like him, who oversaw divisions as they trained in the States.

As I drove back to Washington, I was awash with personal memories of the war. I had enlisted in the army shortly after Pearl Harbor with the caveat that I'd stay in school until called to active duty. I preferred the navy, but I'd been rejected by a navy doctor because my dad had been ill with tuberculosis in his left lung when I was 11. His illness was a tough time for me. He and I had no contact for many months as he recovered in Hines Veterans Hospital outside of Chicago. He'd been in the Army Air Force in WWI, serving in Europe, as I did.

It was in the years of WWII that the Tribune's circulation climbed to more than one million copies sold daily. Readers were eager for war news. The Tribune provided it in depth. My parents regularly sent me articles about the war, especially the syndicated columns by Ernie Pyle, the most famous of WWII war correspondents. The Tribune had its own war correspondents, of course, scattered on battlefields around the globe. John H. (Jack) Thompson parachuted into Sicily with Maj. Gen. James Gavin, then a colonel leading the 505th Parachute Infantry Regiment of the 82nd Airborne Division. Jack went ashore at Omaha Beach on D-Day, June 6, 1944, with the First Infantry Division, Colonial McCormick's outfit in WWI. I walked Omaha Beach with Jack in 1988, when together we attended the dedication of the Battle of Normandy Museum outside of Caen.

"The landscape and vegetation has changed so much," he pondered as we tramped along in the sand. The air was calm, waves soft on the shoreline, the noise and smoke of battle gone. "It's difficult for me to recognize where I waded onto land." He pointed a few yards ahead. "Maybe, it was over there."

I learned a lot about human behavior as I moved along through WWII. The education was certainly a mixed bag. I interacted with men and women of great dignity in trying circumstances. I met cowards and scoundrels. Some who crossed my life were memorable. I saw life, at times, at its rawest. Death was certainly on a short leash, at least mentally, as I moved into combat. I think that's true of any soldier. My company went ashore at Le Havre, in Normandy, France on January 3, 1945 and quickly moved eastward to take up positions vacated by more seasoned troops in Patton's Third Army, as they pivoted north to Bastogne in the Battle of the Bulge. A week earlier, we had been in reserve on the Salisbury Plain in southern England.

A hellish winter blanket of cold and snow covered France as our

Jack Christian, my close wartime buddy, and I talk during a pause in the Eighth Armored Division's advance deep into Central Germany in WWII

convoy crawled along on icy, desolate roads towards the front. Hour after hour, I stood in the .50 caliber machine gun turret of my squad's halftrack, snow in my face. But, at least my feet were warm from the engine heat. A halftrack is all iron except for a cloth seat cushion for the driver. It's a rolling ice box of frigid metal. When the convoy halted from time to time, squad members in the back of the halftrack would scramble forward to warm themselves atop the hot, iron covered engine. Darkness had come when we moved close enough to the battle line to hear the rolling rumble of artillery, and witness white and red flashes from big guns dot the nighttime sky. Snow swirled in our head-light beams as the wind blew it across the highway. Icy pellets stung my face. I heard the plaintive high pitch of a European locomotive whistle and saw a train approach on a rail line parallel to the road. Large red crosses marked the sides and roofs of the passenger cars, their window shades drawn. It seemed lifeless as it moved slowly along, a hospital train on its way to the rear.

I stood silently in the turret to watch it pass. Its message was clear. I could be severely wounded or killed in the days ahead. It's difficult to express what I felt in mind and heart. Certainly, the scene racked me emotionally. I experienced a lonely feeling of resignation. I would soon be in harm's way.

I have no chronological memory of the war. Remembrances come and go, scattered about without orientation. They are etched into my episodic memory. Still vivid in my mind is crossing the Rhine River in midmorning on March 24, 1945, the last major waterway blocking our access deep into Germany. Hours before, the first infantry troops had crossed in boats. Then, armored divisions, including the Eighth Armored Division, lumbered over hastily-built pontoon bridges and drove eastward.

One dawn, a rain storm moved across our departure line. Soon, the morning became a gray mix of mist and fog. Across a field, in the first row of houses, it was quiet. We expected German fire, but none came. We walked into the town. I don't recall its name. Maybe it was Dorsten or Kirchhellen. Perhaps, it was Bruckhausen. They, like many others, were in our path as we encircled the Ruhr Valley. In military history, it became the Ruhr Pocket, where a pincher movement by American Ninth and First Armies trapped 300,000 Nazi troops defending this gem of Hitler's industrial might. The Eighth Armored Division was now part of the Ninth Army. Often I didn't know exactly where I was fighting. I had my own little place of combat each day. The big picture I left to others.

A few blocks into the town, artillery shells whistled overhead. There were shouts of "Incoming! Incoming!" I hustled into the closest house. It was empty of Germans, military and civilian alike. Most of the men scurried down into the basement. I stayed upstairs with a couple of others to signal a possible German counterattack. It was a solid stucco house. The first floor, after we stuffed mattresses into window frames, was safe enough from flying shrapnel. There was a second floor and attic above to help absorb a direct hit.

The shelling ceased eventually. As I waited for the signal to move forward again, I sat down at a desk and began to idly rummage through its items and papers. I was dumbfounded as I picked up a colored postcard with the imprinted words "Greetings from Camp Ellis Illinois." I flipped it over in my hand to read the other side. Using my college German, I haltingly determined that the writer was a prisoner of war in Ellis. He wrote that he was healthy, and he hoped all was well with everyone. The message was to a woman, maybe his wife, or perhaps to his mother. I wasn't sure.

There I was in his home and he was only 20 miles or so from mine in Galesburg.

It was a strange feeling, this wartime juxtaposition of uncertain odds. I had fleeting thoughts about where and how he was captured. Normandy? Had he been in Rommel's Afrika Korps? There in that room, his room really, I felt an intimacy with a foe I would never meet or know. I never saw Camp Ellis. Officially dedicated in July, 1943, and closed in 1945, it came and went while I was away. The 18,000 acres of farmland it covered are mostly corn fields again three-fourths of a century later. The golden corn stalks rustle once more in the autumn winds, and the Spoon River the camp bordered winds its way slowly through the countryside.

CHAPTER SEVENTEEN

SALLY TAKES A CAPITALISTIC APPROACH TO THE RUSSIANS

A spooky atmosphere pervaded the Soviet Embassy in Washington during the Cold War, an aura of curiosity and mystery that sent both chills and excitement through one's body. Here was the philosophical enemy nesting in the nation's bosom. When we had out-of-town guests, the first thing they wanted to see was the White House. The second was always the Soviet Embassy. In those days, before the Russians built a new one at the far end of Embassy Row in northwest Washington, their embassy was just several blocks from the White House through Lafayette Park and up 16th Street, where it was neighbors with the University Club and the National Geographic Society.

The Soviet Embassy was closer to the White House than any other embassy in the capital, although politically it was farthest removed. Very few people were ever seen going inside the building, which sat on a small plot of ground surrounded by a see-through black wrought iron fence. It was a handsome four-story edifice in a French architectural style with its gray stone exterior and slate mansard roof. But its windows were always shuttered, a fact that lent flavor to a grim feeling of intrigue and sinister doings as people skipped past. It had been purchased in 1913 by the old Czarist government from the family of George Pullman, maker of railroad sleeping cars.

Sally certainly had those feelings of mystery and cunning. So did Sassy Boswell, her closet friend and our neighbor. Both felt they could work those emotions to their advantage as co-chairs of the 1960 embassy tour of the Alexandria Junior Woman's Club. They knew having the Russians on board would be a game changer in attendance and lead to increased proceeds for the Alexandria School for Handicapped Children, the club's charity.

They wrote a letter to the Soviet ambassador to the United States, Mikhail Menshikov, inviting the embassy to be on the tour, knowing that it would be the first chance for the general public to see inside. A couple of weeks went by. Then, one day, a letter typed on coarse brown paper arrived in Sassy's mailbox. It invited the two women to come to the embassy to discuss arrangements and suggested a date. It was no secret in Washington that the FBI had an apartment in a building across 16th Street from the embassy, and that it filmed everyone who came and went from the building. I got in touch with Harold "Bud" Leinbaugh, my friend from college days and an assistant to J. Edgar Hoover, the storied head of the organization. I informed Bud that Sally and Sassy would visit the embassy at 10:00 a.m. on the appointed day and why.

I thought of informing Bud after the fact to make their visit a bit enigmatic to the door watchers. Maybe the FBI had the ability to listen in on the conversation. Bud told me once that the bureau had a listening device that could pick up conversations a block away. But maybe that was outside and a few years later. Agents whose sons were in my son, Jon's, scout troop insisted that they even knew the color of the socks Russian officials in the capital wore. I thought that might be a stretch beyond reality.

To say that Sally and Sassy were excited and also somewhat apprehensive as they entered the Soviet compound, walked to the heavy wooden front door and rang the bell, is an understatement. But I was sure they would sweet-talk the Russians into joining the tour. People would want to see the Soviet Embassy even if they skipped others already signed up along Embassy Row on Massachusetts Avenue—Iran, India, Malaya, Thailand, Japan, Turkey, and Argentina. The tour ticket price was $3. The Soviets agreed to join them. It would be interesting to know how far up the ladder of the Soviet hierarchy Menshikov had to go for approval. One thing of which I'm certain, Menshikov alone didn't make the decision to let the public roam the embassy.

All was now in readiness for Saturday October 22, 1960. The weather cooperated. It was a beautiful, warm fall afternoon. Everything pointed to a successful turnout. Even Sally and Sassy did not anticipate what happened. An hour before the tour began, a line four abreast assembled on the sidewalk outside the Embassy and snaked down the block and

Sally (on left) and Assistant Secretary of Labor Esther Peterson serve tea to embassy tour patrons

round a couple of corners, past the entrance to the *Washington Post* building, like a crowd waiting to see a hit movie. Aroused to action, the *Post* had a panoramic photo of the line across the entire top of its front page on Sunday morning.

When the afternoon was over, more than 2,000 curious people had streamed through this little patch of the Soviet Union.

The *Post* sent over a fellow journalist, Myra MacPherson, to write a story. I was manning our bureau as usual on weekends and couldn't be there. The first two floors of the embassy were open for the tour. A gold-trimmed banister greeted those climbing to second floor. Myra said people on the stairs commented about the "lovely" chandeliers. "I think it is very clever the way they have the chandeliers reflect in the mirrors," she quoted one viewer as saying. "Looks like twice as many."

The Russians showed a movie: *Happy Journey to Moscow.* Taken the year before when some U.S. governors toured the Soviet Union, it had a background of rippling streams and stirring music. In a second film, ballerinas leaped and spun. But, as one boy told Myra: "no cartoons." There was no vodka or caviar either, only large portraits of Lenin and Khrushchev looking down from the walls on the moviegoers.

Comments to Myra about the film of the tour of governors ranged from "I thought it was a wonderful picture" to "everyone is singing and happy; seems as if they are avoiding a lot." A bulletin board propped in the corner of one room had more photos of happy people, and phrases in English like "Disarmament — The Way to Peace."

Comments by the touring spectators were not mundane. They were telling other Washingtonians, for the first time, what the inside of the foreboding building was like. In second floor drawing rooms were ornate gold statues and furniture. The hammer and sickle emblem of communism stood out on the banister leading to the third floor. Draperies in communist red brightened the windows. Ambassador Menshikov's office was on the second floor. Once upon a time, before the Cold War, it had two large windows looking across the lawn to the street. But by 1960, the windows had been tightly bricked up on the inside, although from the outside they continued to look like ordinary windows with glass panes. A new room had been built inside the old one. Between the outer and inner walls there was a magnetic field as a defense against electronic eavesdropping.*

Menshikov's office was closed for the tour and the third and fourth floors were also off limits. The top floors were working rooms for embassy personnel explained Valentin A. Shorin, third secretary of the embassy. On the third floor there was an apartment, which consisted of three rooms and a kitchen for the ambassador and his family, Shorin told the touring sightseers.

With the U.S. presidential election just days away, one of the Russians asked Sally who she was working for: "Jack or Dick?" He said he'd seen a headline he liked very much — "Ike Tells Rocky, Stay Away from Jack and Dick." So many n-e-e-k-names, he said.

Plenty of Soviet literature abounded. A marble-top table held a 158-page booklet titled *The Trial of the U-2-Exclusive Authorized Account.* There were pamphlets on *Causes of the Summit Failure* and *Soviet Policy in the Current International Situation.* Late in the afternoon, when all the pamphlets and booklets laid out were gone, embassy staffers hurried to the basement to haul up hardcover books about life in the Soviet Union.

When I got home that evening, Sally was still flushed with excitement.

"Oh. Russ, it was all so wonderful," she exclaimed. I was proud of

---

Harold "Bud" Leinbaugh and Anatoly Dobrynin's autobiography In Confidence her as I listened. "So many people came. We raised so much money for the school. The Russians said they would be happy to do it again."

She and Sassy were thrilled by the large attendance, and the money garnered. They'd seen the Embassy as a chance to make money in true capitalist fashion and the Soviets weren't going to let a chance to convert someone to communism go unused. Maybe, in microcosm, the disparate aims were what the Cold War was all about.

CHAPTER EIGHTEEN

TO *TASS* WITH MY CONDOLENCES

Several years later, during the Johnson presidency and somewhat by happenstance, I also engaged a Russian in the capital on a personal level. He was Vitaly Gan, a reporter for the Soviet news agency, *Tass*. I looked upon the occurrence as it unfolded as somewhat whimsical, but I'm sure Gan was deadly serious. Tip O'Neill, when he was Speaker of the House, used to say that "all politics is local." I'm sure Gan was not familiar with that bit of political philosophy.

In the late 1960s, the Soviets wanted to open consulates in several American cities, including Chicago. There were already a number of foreign consulates in Chicago, listening posts certainly, but mostly to promote trade. The Soviet effort did not go smoothly with Chicago's reigning politicians, including their incomparable mayor, Richard J. Daley.

In fact, Chicago's political leaders responded with a hard and firm, "*Neyt.*"

I often went to State Department briefings, usually held in the late morning. On occasion, I would fall into conversation with Gan, who spoke remarkably good English. Our talks were nothing serious, just idle chit chat.

One afternoon I parked my car, as I often did, in the Ellipse between the White House and the Washington Monument. As I stepped out and locked the door, Gan appeared, seemingly out of nowhere. He was wearing the Russian equivalent of a foreign correspondents trench coat. His tousled hair bounced on his head. Some thought *Tass* reporters were KGB agents. Maybe so!

"I have a question for you," he said after saying hello. I nodded and told him to shoot away. He got right to his subject. "Why is there opposition in Chicago to a Soviet consulate there?"

I chuckled. "Well, Vitaly, the answer is easy," I replied, as we leaned against my car talking like two buddies who'd accidentally run into each other. "There's a large Polish population in the northwest part of the city. It's a large voting bloc. Polish leaders in Chicago are against the consulate. It's the same with Lithuanians on the city's southwest side. There are probably enough votes in the two groups to swing an election."

A sly smile crossed Gan's face. Poland! Lithuania! Both were under the Kremlin yoke. After a moment of thought, he replied, "I see." I wasn't sure, however, that Gan understood the hard fought and gritty ward politics of Chicago. Though the word commissar was no doubt clear to him, it is doubtful he was familiar with terms like precinct captain or ward healer.

"Vitaly," I continued, "There are many immigrants from Slavic and Eastern European countries in Chicago. They resent Kremlin domination of their native lands. They don't like your Iron Curtain. In Chicago, they can speak with their votes."

I asked him if he was familiar with the name Richard J. Daley. He nodded.

I explained to him that Irish politicians like Daley controlled the city, but to stay in power they had to woo other ethnic groups with favors. I said they had to be particularly mindful of pleasing the Poles because of their big numbers and a streak of independence. I added that in one election the Poles even put up their own candidate, Benjamin Adamowski, to run again Daley and he almost won. Daley understands his need to keep political peace with the city's Poles I told Gan, saying that in 1960, as part of President Eisenhower's People to People program, the mayor had chosen Warsaw, of all cities on earth with which to partner, never giving a second thought to a town in his beloved Ireland.

I suggested to Gan that the Kremlin might be up against an unbeatable foe.

Anatoly Dobrynin, the popular and longtime Soviet ambassador to Washington, tells in his autobiography *In Confidence* about the high-ranking Kremlin diplomat, Vyacheslav Molotov, passing through Chicago by train in 1955. The Soviet envoy was on a cross-country trip from New York City to San Francisco to celebrate the tenth anniversary of the founding of United Nations in the California city. Dobrynin wrote that while the train paused in Chicago, Molotov was booed by a large and agitated crowd that gathered outside of his private car. He asked the then Soviet Ambassador to the United States, Georgi Zarubin, what the crowd meant. Dobrynin wrote that Zarubin replied without batting an eyelash "That is the American way of greeting."[4] Molotov looked puzzled, according to Dobrynin, and noted it was a strange way to greet visitors. Dobrynin added that Zarubin knew full well, of course, the anti-communist and ethnic make-up of those outside of Molotov's window.

Like me, Gan is long gone from Washington, and there's still no Russian consulate in Chicago.

CHAPTER NINETEEN

THE FBI TIP ABOUT JFK I KEPT TO MYSELF

I met John Kennedy in May of 1957 as a city room reporter when I covered a speech he made to the annual dinner of the Democratic Party of Cook County in the Conrad Hilton Hotel in Chicago. He was a senator then, the presidency just a gleam in his eye. There was no hint of family tragedies to come. We did not know that four years later I would cover him in the White House.

I found Kennedy in a tower suite on the top floor of the Conrad Hilton, my fingers crossed that he had a copy of his speech. Thankfully, he did. We engaged in shop talk. That is really what our connection that night was for both of us. I sought assurances that he would stick to his text, explaining that if the dinner ran late I might have to leave to make a deadline. He assured me that he would, adding that in any event he would stand by the text. I wished him well and went down to the ballroom. Other people were arriving in the suite, among them his sister, Eunice, and her husband, Sargent Shriver. The Shrivers lived in Chicago, where he managed the Merchandise Mart, which was owned by the Kennedy family.

To my pleasure, and I hoped his, Tribune editors put his speech on the front page of next morning's paper. Considering the large Polish population in Chicago, the placement should hardly have been a surprise since his speech centered on Poland's plight as a captive nation of the Soviets.

There is little I can write about Kennedy that is not known. I'm not writing about him; I'm writing about my experiences in connection with him. I never shared inside tidbits with him. My relationship with him was that of a journalist in the nation's capital. I didn't cover his 1960 presidential campaign. That was assigned to Joe Hearst of the Tribune's Washington bureau, one Roman Catholic covering another. I mention this because it played a part in Hearst getting the assignment. Tribune editors thought Hearst would have a sympathetic feel for the controversy Kennedy's religion ignited in the campaign.

That didn't mean I was uninterested in the campaign. The day after the first Kennedy-Nixon debate the nation's capital churned with talk over who had won. It so happened that I had lunch on that early fall day with Harold "Bud" Leinbaugh, my college buddy, who was with the FBI. I had also grown up with his wife, Rosemary Swanson. We were in a small Italian restaurant around the corner from the Justice Department. Bud and I met two or three times a month for lunch. He was an excellent source of information. Most of it stayed between us, but sometimes there was the germ of a story.

That day, as we left the restaurant, he mentioned that Kennedy had had a WWII liaison with a suspected Nazi spy. He said audio tapes of them together, pillow talk included, were stored in the Justice Department basement. There was a surge of excitement in me. Leinbaugh was telling me something off-beat, different, something with the hint of scandal. I wanted to hear the tapes. Bud said that was impossible, but that he could give me some facts about the episode. The key to the story to me was whether Kennedy had revealed any government secrets. I wanted to listen to the tapes to determine whether he did. That would have been a big story. The affair itself seemed insignificant to me.

Of course, the tale had the best espionage elements of seduction and conspiracy. The woman involved, Inga Arvad, was a gorgeous, blue-eyed, Danish blonde who spoke several languages. Kennedy, handsome and virile, was from a wealthy American family with high political connections, and he was doing intelligence work for the United States Navy. A fiction writer couldn't have asked for two better-matched characters — James Bond before James Bond.

Here is what happened. A letter to the FBI from a tattler at the Columbia University Journalism School in New York City touched off the FBI's interest in Arvad, who had come to the United States and was a student at the school. The letter expressed concern about Inga's admiration of Hitler. Arvad did have a connection to Hitler. She had interviewed him twice, and she had lunched with him. She was his companion at the 1936

Olympics in Berlin. Hitler described her as the perfect Nordic beauty. Her marriage to Paul Fejos was coming to an end. He was a Hungarian movie director and Amazon River explorer for Axel Wenner-Gren, a Swedish entrepreneur and gun maker. Wenner-Gren was close to Nazi officials and banned from the United States. Fejos was her second marriage; her first had been to an Egyptian diplomat at age 17.

Arthur Krock, the noted *New York Times* columnist, met Arvad during her second year at Columbia after a session of the Pulitzer Prize Board at the university's Journalism School. The Danish beauty asked Krock if he could help her find a newspaper job. Krock, dazzled by her looks, recommended her to Frank Waldrop, editor of the *Washington Times Herald*. Waldrop hired her to write the *Times Herald's* "Did You Happen to See" column of short interviews with capital personalities.

Arvad was 28 and Kennedy was 24 when they met. When she interviewed him for her column, their affair began.

Kennedy had joined the United States Naval Reserve on June 24, 1941, as a seaman second class. But with the influence of Navy Captain Alan G. Kirk, he was appointed an ensign that October and assigned to the Office of the Chief of Naval Operations in Washington. He worked on a daily digest that summarized local and foreign affairs. He had a security clearance and access to classified secret information. When the FBI learned from the Office of Naval Intelligence about Jack and Inga, it stepped up its surveillance. In the taped conversations with Arvad, he never discussed his work, in pillow talk or otherwise. Meanwhile, Arvad told Cissy Patterson, owner of the *Times Herald*, about her past, and insisted that the FBI clear her name.

Leinbaugh told me that once the couple was bugged, Hoover contacted Joe Kennedy, suggesting that Jack's father break up the romance. Jack did as he was told. He broke off with Inga. According to Leinbaugh, Joe Kennedy then had high navy officials transfer his son out of the Office of the Chief of Naval Operations, a move that eventually led Jack to the South Pacific and his dramatic wartime experiences there as commander of PT Boat 109, told first in a book by my friend, Robert Donovan of the *New York Herald Tribune* and *Los Angeles Times*, and later in a movie based on the book.

The FBI continued a 24-hour watch on Inga without the eavesdropping, because by then she knew about the latter. President Roosevelt wanted the surveillance kept because of her connection to Wenner-Gren.

The FBI redoubled its efforts but found nothing suspicious. It closed the case in August, 1942. A month earlier, Arvad had resigned from the *Times Herald* and drifted westward, where she went to work as a publicity writer for MGM in Hollywood. In 1947, she married cowboy film star, Tim McCoy. I had watched him on the silver screen as a young boy at Saturday matinees at the Colonial Theater in my hometown.

My insistence that I listen to the tapes turned out to be a wise decision. It is said that in journalism competition, it is better to be first with a little on a big story than last with a lot. But, I don't believe that half a loaf would have been good here. It became obvious in later years that many persons in Washington knew of the affair and all of its details at the time.

With no access to the tapes, I never pursued information on Kennedy and Arvad. The tapes became public years later, when Charles Colson, counsel to President Nixon, played them in his White House office one afternoon for a select group of reporters. I was not there. So, in the end, the air went out of the spy case. The pivotal role the episode played in Kennedy's life cannot be denied, however. It forced a decision that eventually made him a heroic castaway on a remote South Pacific island.

I liked covering Kennedy. Only six years my senior, he was the first of our generation to become president, the first to be born in the 20th century. That in itself was thrilling. The old order that had seen the country through the Great Depression and WWII was fading away. Eternally, people rule, become old or die, their places taken by others, younger and more vigorous. It was my generation's time to take center stage. As Kennedy said in his inaugural speech, the torch was being passed.

I've often wondered if I would have felt the same if Richard Nixon had been elected in 1960. I covered him as a journalist. He was also of my generation. Nixon was a different personality in 1960 than he was as president eight years later. In 1960 he did not bear the scars of ensuing political battles and media attacks that left him bitter and defensive.

I relished covering presidents of my time, that chance to see them up close on a regular basis. It wasn't for me to like or dislike them. It was my job to report on their administrations, both the good and the bad. My aim was to be the pure reporter. On the title page of his memoir, in the copy he gave to me, George Christian, LBJ's press secretary, wrote "to Russ—one of the best of the breed—with admiration." I hope there was truth to that.

Kennedy took television coverage of the White House a step further than Eisenhower. His press conferences from the beginning of his term were live. The Eisenhower White House didn't allow the release of the TV footage of Ike's press conferences until the transcripts were reviewed. Kennedy also moved the conferences out of the Indian Treaty Room to the larger State Department auditorium. Usually, JFK held his conferences in late afternoon so he could dominate the evening TV newscasts — another blow to newspapers.

Kennedy had a wonderful presence. He was a good listener, relaxed and calm. Nixon, on the other hand, would sometimes look over your shoulder while talking to you, plotting who he wanted to see next. Kennedy had a great sense of humor. It was charming and spontaneous. He was confident in spoofing himself. No other president could do that until Ronald Reagan came along. I liked Kennedy's supply side tax cuts. He was pragmatic in his approach to governance, cool under pressure, and I thought he resisted statist trends.

Of course, there was Kennedy's sexual recklessness. I was told that during his presidency friends challenged him about potential political problems caused by his promiscuity. He was said to reply that as long as he was alive, no one could touch him, and once dead, it no longer mattered. He was wrong about the latter. His philandering has clouded his legacy.

It was important to me that I thought he was fair. The Chicago Tribune did not endorse Kennedy's presidency and it often took pot shots at him in its editorials. Typical of Washington, some of his aides held that against me, especially Pierre Salinger, his press secretary, but I never thought that Kennedy himself did. Kennedy was too much a man of the arena and he had been a journalist himself for a short while.

Harold Linder, a Wall Street investment banker, was appointed by Kennedy to be president of the government's Export-Import Bank. When I wrote that Linder had made a secret bank loan to an Argentine subsidiary of an American company in which he held an interest, an angry Salinger told me that no one took my story seriously. Maybe I was whistling in the dark, but I felt that Kennedy would be curious enough to probe into the inside aspects of the story. I doubt Linder ever believed that a loan in far-away Argentina would become public. At times, exposure comes from the long way around. No politician likes to be bested, and least of all to be blindsided by his own appointee.

I'm sure Kennedy found out after a time that my tip came down from the Rockefellers who had large business interests in South America. Fascination with intrigue was common to the presidents I covered. They all loved the inside game. You could see it in their eyes, always eager and keen to get one last morsel.

I've pondered at times through the years, mostly late at night as I drifted off to sleep, what might have happened if the Kennedy-Arvad affair had become public during the 1960 campaign. Fair or unfair to reveal, I'm sure it would have been explosive and controversial. The election was one of the closest in history; just 112,827 votes separated Nixon from Kennedy in the popular balloting. The question that besets me has always been: would 112,827 voters have changed their minds because of the revelation and thrown the Electoral College vote to Nixon? Kennedy's margin of the popular vote was a tiny 0.1% among the total cast. Nixon needed 269 electoral votes to be victorious. He got 219. Nixon lost Illinois by 0.19%, Missouri by 0.52% and New Jersey by 0.8%. These states had a total of 56 electoral votes. A reversal of a few votes in the three states and Nixon would have won.

But it is dangerous to play God.

CHAPTER TWENTY

JFK'S INAUGURATION

The air was cold from a chilling Arctic wind. And snow? It was deep enough to cause lots of trouble. I didn't think the foreboding weather was the best combination for the inauguration of a new president. But so it was on January 20, 1961, for the swearing-in of John F. Kennedy. The untimely bad weather had pronounced its coming the afternoon before. By inauguration eve, it had closed airports and left motorists stalled on choked roadways.

Snow in Washington, as rare as it is, can be gentle or it can be monstrous. It can fall quietly to create a winter wonderland, or it can bluster down from a cloudy sky with a driving force that blots out the landscape. It chooses its own way. The snowfall of Kennedy's inauguration wasn't my decision. Otherwise, I would have done it differently. The capital is beautiful when the snowfall is soft and fluffy. But, it wasn't pretty this time.

At nightfall, I'd decided to stay late in the office in hopes streets would be clear of traffic eventually for my homeward journey. Sally was disappointed, since her plans to attend the ceremonies were suddenly uncertain, but she wasn't totally defeated. Looking out of my office window around dinnertime, I saw that the swirling snow had eased from a few hours earlier. She decided that was a good omen.

Around 9:30 p.m. I struck out for home. I was a solitary figure as I walked to my car in the Ellipse south of the White House. Anyone going to a pre-inaugural dinner party was already there, high-stepping through the drifts in fashionable attire. Out-of-town revelers who made it to Washington were mostly snowbound in their hotels. Thousands were stranded along the east coast and in the Midwest. Nothing was moving east of Chicago. Some heads of state were late, or didn't make it at all. I brushed some eight inches of snow from my car, let my engine warm up for a few minutes, and pulled away. I was the only one on the road as I rounded the Lincoln Memorial, and crossed the Potomac River Bridge into Virginia.

Driving south along Mount Vernon Memorial Highway, I encountered abandoned cars. Slowly, slipping and sliding, I wove around them snug in my little Renault with its front wheel drive. From the snow blown up against them, it was obvious the empty vehicles had been there for hours. Their numbers increased as I passed National Airport, strewn along like forgotten toys. By the time I reached Alexandria, I must have encountered 500 unoccupied and neglected autos. I wondered where all their owners had gone. Once home, Sally put off a decision about attending the inaugural. For me, I had to be in town the next day. I was assigned to cover the inaugural parade. The question as we climbed into bed was would there be one.

We were up early the next morning. Radio weather reports said that main roads were open, and traffic was moving. But it remained cold. The high temperature predicted for the day was 22 degrees. The wind was clocked at 19½ miles per hour. The wind chill measurement had yet to be developed. That would come in the 1970s. But if there had been a wind chill measurement to report, it would have been 15 degrees. Nothing was expected to change before swearing-in ceremonies at noon outside the east front of the Capitol.

An inauguration is really about just one person—the president-elect. Everyone else who is there is a bit player. On movie sets they are called extras.

Kennedy performed beautifully.

Liberty themes were harkened to several times in his speech, which took 13 minutes and 59 seconds, one of the shortest inaugural addresses, but judged one of the most powerful ever. Controversy remains about how much of it Kennedy actually wrote. In some ways, Kennedy was a man made by others. But his gift of oratory, the wonderful cadence, was important to the speech's success. I'm sure different parts of the speech were liked more than others by those who listened. Sally and I concurred that our hearts beat faster when he said, *"Let the word go forth to friend and foe alike, that the torch has passed to a new generation of Americans born of this century."* Sally said she felt warmer for a few minutes after those words. Our generation was in this together now. It was our country to advance and defend. Sally and I didn't know if we'd like Kennedy up close as a friend. But we did know we liked him from a distance. It wasn't my duty to decipher his inner thoughts, anyway. My work was to report his presidential actions to readers of the Tribune. I liked covering him. He was easeful to be around. A feeling of grace and well-being enveloped the capital during his time. It was the feeling that Sally and I liked. Our attitude had nothing to do with politics. During his time in the White House, all too short, our lives were in balance—comfortable and interesting.

I dressed in the warmest clothes I had when I left home that morning. I wore thermal underwear, lined boots, wool socks, a flannel shirt and corduroy trousers, a heavy cable knit sweater, storm coat, a wool stocking cap and gloves. When I reached the office, I reported the situation in the capital to Sally. The first encouraging sign I saw was that all the abandoned cars on the Mount Vernon Parkway north of Alexandria were gone. So was the snow on the pavement. The 2.2-mile parade route up Pennsylvania Avenue from the Capitol to the White House was dry and clear after an all-night effort by city workers and military to remove the snow with heavy plows and salt.

Buses were running. Events would go on as scheduled. It was decision time for Sally. She had a ticket to a seat below the inaugural platform. President-elect Kennedy and President Eisenhower, only hours away from leaving office, were getting ready to meet at the White House to ride together to the Capitol, a symbol of the peaceful transfer of power. In her heart, Sally wanted to be among those present when that transfer took place. There would be more inaugurations before we left Washington but this one, being our first, was special. Sally decided that she would go; it was being part of history. Like me, she bundled up in thermal underwear, left over from our Chicago days, slacks tucked into fur lined boots, a sweater or two, a storm coat, wool socks, and a knit cap over her ears.

It would be a day of walking, first over the snow covered countryside to the bus stop at the fire house a mile away from our house, then from the bus terminal in Washington to the Capitol, another mile or more. She'd decided the night before not to drive the station wagon to the ceremony. Except for bus rides, she would be outside most of the day. There were no cell phones or iPads in 1961. It's hard to imagine now, but people were out of contact from each other for many hours at a time. At the same time,

Kennedy and Eisenhower leave the White House to ride together
to the Capitol for JFK's inauguration (AP Photo)

there was less worry about a person's movements, less concern about a mishap. As it turned out, I did not talk to Sally again until I arrived home for dinner that night. She was still aglow with excitement.

"It was very moving," she said.

Kennedy and Ike arrived at the Capitol dressed, at Kennedy's request, in daytime formal wear—silk top hats, morning coats and grey striped pants. But when Kennedy spoke he was bareheaded. He had put his top hat on his chair. The action on his part is said to have triggered a decline in the sale of men's hats.

Always judged his best line is: *"And so, my fellow Americans, ask not what your country can do for you, ask what you can do for your country."* The sentence is preceded by, *"Let every nation know, whether it wishes us well or ill, that we should pay any price, bear any burden, meet any hardship, support any friend, oppose any foe, to assure the survival and success of liberty."*

As Sally's adventure on Inauguration Day ended, mine began. She started for home; I headed out of the office for the parade. I noticed, as I walked along Pennsylvania Avenue to the press area in Lafayette Park across from the White House, that viewer bleacher seats along the way, for which they had paid $3 to $25, were clear of snow if they wanted to get to them, or cared to. Thousands did. Hours before, boy scouts and soldiers had brushed off the snow from all 58,000 seats, but many were empty as the parade began.

Some marchers were also missing. They were hundreds of miles from the capital, stranded by the snow. As I arrived in the press area, a lone black limousine approached on the parade route with CBS pennants attached to its front fenders. It stopped in front of broadcast booths built across from the reviewing stand for the occasion, and out stepped Ed Murrow. Boy, I thought, that's classy. The CBS booth would have heaters to boot. As for me, have you ever tried to jot down notes with pen and notebook clutched in heavy wool mittens?

Marchers had problems with cold feet and chapped hands. The weather was equally hard on the bands. It was difficult to slide the trombones, and lips tended to stick to cold mouthpieces. But everyone loves a parade; those in it, and those watching it pass by. The new president and first lady led the parade as it wound its way from the Capitol to the White House. They alighted at the White House and stepped into the glass front, heated reviewing stand. Forty-four governors were scattered through the procession, among the floats and displays, leading their state delegations. Clopping along with them were 275 horses—the most ever—and 22 mules and a burro. Two "horse ambulances" were placed strategically off of the parade route. They were large vans, with space for a horse to lie down, and a cradle to help a horse stand in. Each was manned with a veterinarian and an assistant. There were ambulances for the governors too, if they needed them.

It took 2½ hours for the parade to pass by the reviewing stand. Dusk had arrived as I trudged back to the office to write my story. My drive home was much easier than the night before. Sally had arrived home hours earlier in mid-afternoon. Of course, snow and cold, like everything, has its time and place. It just shouldn't threaten to gum up the inauguration of a president. Fortunately, in this case, man and machines and a few electric space heaters outfoxed nature. Sally also conquered the day. She forever could say, "I was there." Sometimes, however, she remarked that she had never been so cold for so long.

CHAPTER TWENTY-ONE

THE LYNCHING OF
MACK CHARLES PARKER

The challenge to segregation in the United States was gaining momentum as President Kennedy took office. A year earlier, black college students had conducted sit-ins at an all-white lunch counter in a Woolworth five-and-dime store in Greensboro, North Carolina, and the action spread. When asked about it, President Eisenhower replied that he was deeply sympathetic with efforts of any group to enjoy the right of equality that they are entitled to under the constitution. The fight continues, in one form or another, to this day. I saw a lot of it.

A wish to be a contender is as American as apple pie. Respect for one's ability is a reasonable demand. To put up a fight needs no apology. Blacks traveled a rough road from slavery to their life in the middle of the 20th century. But a sign of racial betterment began in February, 1948, when President Truman ordered the United States Armed Forces to desegregate as quickly as possible. I was in my last semester at Washington University in St. Louis. In July, Truman issued Executive Order 9981 calling on the military to end racial discrimination. In 1951, the chief of staff of the armed forces ordered all military commands to desegregate.

When I fought in Europe with the Eighth Armored Division in WWII, black soldiers were mainly in supply units. On the western front, they were assigned to the Red Ball Express, hauling supplies to fighting units twenty-four hours a day, a remarkable feat of endurance. Several thousand volunteered to join troops on the front line when the Germans broke through thinly-manned American positions in the Battle of the Bulge. But, throughout the war, segregation was the order of the day.

When the Korean War broke out in 1950, blacks became part of the manpower needed for fighting units. That need for combat soldiers hastened the 1951 order to desegregate immediately. I've often reflected why I was not recalled to active duty during the Korean War. After an oral examination before an army review board in St. Louis, I had become a second lieutenant in the army reserve while at Washington University. As a line officer, with combat experience in an armored infantry unit, I seemed ready made for Korea. But my orders never came.

I don't recall desegregation of the military creating great controversy, but it didn't affect civilians. It seemed to happen more or less offstage. In contrast, anxiety and pushback followed the ruling of the Supreme Court of the United States in 1954, that separate educational facilities for black and white students were inherently unequal. The court ordered that integration take place at "all deliberate speed." But, in a culture inbred with centuries of racial discrimination, change is slow and difficult. Foot dragging was strong in the South, where lynchings still took place. In the summer of 1955, the same year Rosa Parks refused to give up her seat to a white man on a city bus in Montgomery, Alabama, a 14-year- old black Chicago boy, Emmett Till, was murdered in Mississippi while visiting relatives. He was accused of whistling at a young white woman, Carolyn Bryant. On August 27, Till was kidnapped, brutally beaten, shot, and dumped into the Tallahatchie River, near Money, Mississippi. Bryant's husband, Roy, and his half-brother, J.W. Milam, were tried for Till's killing and acquitted. The Tribune followed the story closely, both in Chicago and in Mississippi, and editorially condemned what had taken place.

Four years later, the lynching of Mack Charles Parker happened. His murder is in the FBI's file of cold cases now, but like the Till murder, it scorched the nation's soul. Parker was a 23-year-old black man charged with rape of a white woman. His white killers dragged him from the Pearl River County jail in Poplarville, Mississippi, beat and shot him. Like others before it, the lynching was a classic example of lawless killing by violent action.

My connection to Parker's murder was the revelation in a copyright story in late May, 1959 that the FBI had tracked down those responsible. I disclosed that the names of the alleged murderers had been turned over that day to Gov. James P. Coleman of Mississippi at his farm house outside the state capital of Jackson. A reporter rarely knows firsthand the impact his story has as it ricochets around the country, whether it changes attitudes or hardens attitudes, if it stirs a nation's conscience, or merely sharpens cultural battle lines.

Federal agents pulled out of the case the same day of my story. Attorney General William Rogers told me that the FBI withdrawal was based upon a ruling that its investigation established that the lynching party had not violated the federal kidnapping statute, and that no other successful federal prosecution could be maintained. In order for the Justice Department to prosecute a kidnapping case under the Lindbergh Law, a state line has to be crossed. However, Rogers said the FBI can investigate a kidnapping on the assumption that a state line might have been crossed. The Pearl River flows between Mississippi and Louisiana.

Lynching has a long history in America, but by 1959 it was condemned as part of an archaic social order. The first known lynching goes back to an angry mob of Pilgrims who hanged one of their own, John Billington, for bad behavior. The term became common from its association with militia officers, Captain William Lynch of Pittsylvania County, Virginia, and Colonel Charles Lynch of Bedford County, Virginia. Both men harassed and bullied Tories and their sympathizers during the Revolutionary War, often tarring and feathering them, and even hanging them.

The Parker affair had familiar post-Civil War earmarks: a segregated society; angry hooded and masked white men utterly void of remorse, who appointed themselves judge, jury and executioner; a midnight raid on a conveniently unguarded jailhouse; a common knowledge in both white and black local communities as to who had participated, and denial of the black man's right to stand trial in a court of law with a presumption of innocence.

As a lasting backdrop to the era, Harper Lee's iconic novel *To Kill a Mockingbird* was published in 1960. The book went to the heart of racial injustice and prejudice.

My story reported that up to 10 men were involved in the Parker lynching. Eventually, the names of eight men became public. They were from communities and the rural area surrounding Poplarville. All are dead now. I disclosed that the motive for the killing was twofold: to make an example of Parker, and to avoid courtroom questioning of the white woman by Parker's black attorney, R. Jess Brown, a civil rights activist from Vicksburg.

But no arrests were ever made. No indictments were ever returned by a grand jury.

The lynching took place on April 24, 1959, three days before Parker's trial was to begin in the Pearl River County courthouse. The FBI probe uncovered the following. There was an outdoor meeting of the conspirators in a rural area the night before the abduction, at which plans were made to raid the jail in the courthouse in Poplarville and remove the prisoner. Lots were drawn to choose members of the lynch mob. Entrance to Parker's cell was obtained through threats to the jailer, who left a key readily available and went home. Other prisoners said Parker was beaten and dragged screaming from his cell in the unguarded jail. Parker was shot twice by his abductors as they drove on Highway 26 toward Louisiana. They dumped his body into the water from the middle of the Bogalusa Bridge over the Pearl River flowing between the two states. His body was found several days later floating in the river. Collusion among the gang members continued after the abduction with a conspiracy of silence, but with 60 FBI agents on the scene, details emerged and a scenario took shape. Federal agents found slips of paper used in the drawing.

The rape occurred on the rainy night of February 23, 1959. Parker and four of his friends were going north on Mississippi Highway 11 to their homes in Lumberton from Poplarville, where they had spent the evening drinking and playing poker in a local bar. The rape victim, her husband and a four year old daughter were returning to their home in Poplarville from Gulfport on the same highway when their car ran out of gas. The husband left for help. Parker's companions told the FBI that when Parker spotted the car, he first thought it was abandoned. He stopped, hoping to strip it of something of value. When he directed a flashlight inside, however, he saw the woman and her daughter huddled in the front seat. He returned to his car and took off, but he suggested to his friends that he might return and attack the woman after dropping them off in Lumberton.

Sometime later, a lone black man in old clothes forced the woman and daughter from their car into his. She told authorities that he drove to a lonely logging road and raped her. A few days later, Parker was arrested. He denied involvement. Nothing was found at the scene of the crime to directly involve him. Lie tests were inconclusive. The victim picked him out from a lineup, but she said she couldn't be absolutely sure. Authorities claimed to have supporting evidence from other blacks.

Two days after my original revelations, I covered Gov. Coleman's testimony before a Senate subcommittee on constitutional rights. Coleman assured the senators, some of them segregationists, that he would have the evidence in the Parker case submitted to the next regular session of the grand jury in Pearl River County in November. Asked by subcommittee members about information that might be in the federal report, Coleman replied that this is "touchy ground." He explained that Mississippi law requires that all evidence presented to a grand jury must be kept secret for six months.

"If I were to discuss it here, it would be trying the case in the papers in advance of the grand jury," he said. "I think it is best not to go into detail, and I ask to be excused."

The governor, a segregationist himself, appeared before the subcommittee to voice opposition to several pending bills on civil rights legislation, but much of his two hours of testimony was devoted to discussion of the Parker case. He explained the legal difficulty of presenting the FBI evidence to any special grand jury called before November. He said he was quite sure any indictments returned by a special grand jury would not be sustained by the Mississippi Supreme Court. He said further that if a trial were held on the basis of the indictments, its findings almost certainly would be overturned. Coleman, himself a former circuit judge and prosecuting attorney, explained that the state's high court repeatedly has ruled invalid the findings of any grand jury that is called to hear a special case.

"I don't see why we should wash the linen two or three times just to make a show," the governor said.

Coleman referred to the lynching as regrettable. He expressed the opinion that the evidence compiled against Parker in the rape case showed him guilty. He said he was sure Parker would have been convicted. Parker was indicted by a regular session of the Pearl River County grand jury. A move made by his attorney to quash the indictment because there were no blacks in the panel from which the grand jury was drawn was overruled by the court. Under Mississippi law at the time, a person had to be a qualified voter to be eligible for grand jury duty. Coleman told the subcommittee that none of the 4,000 blacks in Pearl River County voted. He said he had been told on "good authority" that some were registered, but they had not paid the necessary poll tax.

A poll tax of $1.50 had to be paid to vote in Virginia when we moved there and it disenfranchised a lot of people, especially poor minorities. Even though political change was underway in the old Confederacy, it was another decade before payment of a poll tax as a prerequisite to voting was eliminated in Virginia.

Segregationist governors like Coleman were also slow to react to the Supreme Court decision desegregating schools. When eight black students enrolled in Little Rock Central High School in Arkansas in the fall of 1957, Gov. Orval Faubus sent the Arkansas National Guard to the school to prevent the blacks from entering the building. White mobs threatened to lynch the students. President Eisenhower sent the 101st Airborne Division to the school to protect the students. He federalized the National Guard, so instead of preventing the students from entering the school, the guard protected them. The Tribune sent Clay Gowran to cover the story. His wife went with him and they took up residence for almost two months.

I always attended integrated schools. I thought nothing of it; it was a way of life. Among the blacks in my graduating class was Curtis Hamblin, who worked with me on the *Budget,* the school newspaper. His family had lived in Galesburg for many years. As an adult, he lived in Los Angeles and returned for our 25th class reunion. A relative, "Ziggy" Hamblin, had starred as a football player at Knox College, the town's liberal arts institution. There is now a Hamblin residential hall on the Knox campus.

In high school, black boys took part in football and track, but it wasn't until my junior year that the color line was crossed in basketball, when Don Wallace was added to the varsity team. Throughout our childhoods, Don had played backyard football and basketball with me and other boys who grew up with him on the north side of town. His dad was on the police force as the ambulance driver and liaison with the black community. When Elizabeth Smallwood, another black schoolmate, sat behind me in our junior high school home room, she teased me unmercifully by tickling my neck and ears with the eraser on a pencil she used for schoolwork. It was all in fun, to me.

During my sophomore year in high school, a wintery blizzard blocked highways across Illinois on a Friday night when we were scheduled to play Rock Island, whose team included a black player. Because of the storm, the Rock Island team came to Galesburg from the Quad Cities, 50 miles away by train, instead of a team bus, and had to stay in Galesburg following the game. The question arose as what to do with the black player overnight, since the town's hotels catered only to whites. Quietly, arrangements were made with Bernie Schimmel for him to stay at Galesburg's premier hotel, The Custer, with his teammates. The Schimmel family operated a string of top-notch hotels in the Midwest, including the Custer. It was a touchy situation that few people knew about.

I don't know how much my black schoolmates knew about segregation beyond our school days of benign neglect, but they learned quickly if they left town for an outside world, where segregation was obvious to all. That also applied to Jews, whose families moved freely among Galesburg townspeople socially, and in business. Sharon Ross, a beautiful young Jewess, who was a year ahead of me in school, told a group of us on her first holiday vacation that she had never understood what discrimination was until she entered Northwestern University, where Jewish co-eds were segregated in their own Greek sororities.

My hometown was settled by abolitionists in 1837. That same year, it became the headquarters of the first anti-slavery society in Illinois. In time, it became a stop on the Underground Railroad, a network of routes with safe houses that used to hide slaves as they escaped to non-slave states or Canada. As a boy, old buildings were pointed out as onetime safe houses. Aging, uniformed veterans of Union forces in the Civil War always led parades on Memorial Day and the Fourth of July when I was young. The Civil War was very real to me. Actually, more time has passed from the end of WWII to now (73 years) than the 58 years from the end of the Civil War to my birth.

Still, unwritten rules existed. Despite its abolitionist history, a dividing line between the races remained in the Galesburg of my youth. Blacks attended school dances, but there were never mixed couples on the floor. Blacks used the public library and other facilities. But movie theaters were another matter. Blacks had to sit in the last rows of the balcony in the Orpheum, the town's number one picture palace, and they had to use separate stairs off of the lobby to get there. In the West Theater, which had no balcony, a couple of rows off to one side in the back were designated for them. I ushered at the West for two summers in my mid-teens, but I don't recall many black patrons.

One hot summer day in the mid-1930s, some black teenage boys showed up at Lake Storey's public beach north of town to swim. Police were called to chase them away. The town then built another beach and bathhouse across the lake for blacks only. It was after WWII that the Lake Storey beaches were integrated. By then, the civil rights movement was in full bloom. There were neighborhood grocery stores when I grew up so it didn't seem out of place that a black grocery store existed.

Blacks had their own nightclubs. The social life of black families was mainly among themselves. There were two black churches in town—one, Allen Chapel, was African Methodist, the other was the Second Baptist. Other churches were white. That is quite different from the Episcopal churches I attended in Florida, where I've lived in retirement for more than a quarter of a century. The Florida congregations were a mixture of white, black and Hispanic.

The slowness of integration following the Civil War was unfortunate and society still suffers immeasurably from it. Whites were asked to change comfortable life patterns, and their new reality did not come easily for them. When I worked at the Chicago City News Bureau, I was deeply troubled by the suppression of reporting of racial disturbances among whites and blacks. One location was the newly integrated Park Manor public housing site on the city's south side. Although I understood a desire not to spread racial unrest, it didn't seem right to let the disturbances go unreported because of an unwritten agreement between Chicago officials and newspaper executives. I thought their action was a violation of the public trust. For me, a canon of a free press is telling things like they are. But when unrest erupted, as it did sporadically, and police responded, it was mentioned only in a "memo to editors" sent by the City News Bureau. Troubled times are not new to the world, and once underway evasion only prolongs them.

Unplanned, but significant, was the way sports helped integrate universities in the South, when southern coaches realized they could no longer compete nationwide without the skills of black athletes. The University of Alabama was the first to cross the color line. Its all-white team took a drubbing in Tuscaloosa in 1970 by a University of Southern California team that boasted several star black players. Paul "Bear" Bryant, Alabama's now legendary coach, was quick to react. By 1973, one-third of the starters on his Alabama squad were black. While blacks were unwelcome in classrooms for a century, they were quickly welcomed on the gridiron, where victory was priceless.

Jackie Robinson broke the color line in professional baseball after WWII. Sally and I went to see him play the first time he came to St.

Louis with the Brooklyn Dodgers in 1947. We sat way up in the upper deck in left field in Sportsman Park, home that year to the world champion St. Louis Cardinals, the only seats we could get for a sold-out ball game. Robinson couldn't stay at the Chase Hotel with his white teammates. He had to lodge elsewhere in the black community. St. Louis had all the remnants of a segregated southern town in the early post-WWII years. Cardinal players threatened to strike as the season began if Robinson played, but they didn't after the league announced that striking players would be suspended. They played rough with him, however. In one game, Enos Slaughter, a star Cardinal outfielder, cut a seven-inch gash in one of Robinson's legs sliding into him. Slaughter was married to a Galesburg woman for a few years. He wasn't the most polished of men.

Though segregation ended in the major leagues, the Negro National League of professional black players continued for several years as a segregated operation, including the Chicago Giants. The Giants would play to sellout crowds of 55,000 in Comiskey Park, home of the American League White Sox, but the Negro League and its games were never covered by the Tribune, or other Chicago newspapers, except the *Chicago Defender*, a black-owned paper published on the city's south side, with its expanding black population. The Negro League played an east-west all-star game every summer in Comiskey Park, but it also drew no coverage from the Tribune, or other Chicago dailies, except the *Defender*.

Like so much of the time in the civil-rights era, I covered federal policy makers, especially those in the Justice Department, but not actual events that took place elsewhere beyond the nation's capital as a result of their decisions. These situations were always tense and dangerous, with U.S. marshals and armed troops present. Unrest accompanied the 1962 enrollment of James Meredith, the first black student at the University of Mississippi. It was the same at the University of Alabama a year later, with the enrollment of Vivian Malone and James Hood.

I was present for the historic March on Washington on August 28, 1963. It was a joyful crowd, with a sense of accomplishment, although much sorrow was yet to come. I remember the day as sunny, warm, and clear. President Kennedy remained in the White House. By late morning, the 200,000 marchers were packed around the reflecting pool on the Mall. In the shadow of the Lincoln Memorial, I heard The Rev. Dr. Martin Luther King, Jr. give his famous "I Have a Dream" speech that expressed his hope that someday all would be brothers.

But complex relationships existed between leaders of that era, including the Kennedy brothers and Dr. King, as well as J. Edgar Hoover, director of the FBI, and King. In early December, 1964, King and Hoover met at the Justice Department. I was among the crowd of reporters outside of Hoover's office. Neither spoke to the press after they met, but we were told their discussion was about derogatory comments the two had made about each other, as well as information compiled on King by the FBI. There were rumors, later revealed to be true, of federal wiretaps on King. I asked Deke DeLoach, a top Hoover aide, who sat in on the meeting, to fill me in on details. He said he would on the stipulation that there would be no FBI attribution. I knew Deke well and I trusted him, but I declined his offer. I believed the relationship between the FBI director and the civil rights leader was too explosive to write about on my own and without attribution to either the FBI or King. Perhaps I was too careful, but I didn't want egg on my face if either or both men questioned publicly the truthfulness of my account of their meeting.

John Kennedy was dead by the time Hoover and King met face to face. But during the 1960 presidential campaign, Kennedy made a telephone call to Coretta Scott King that transformed the black vote. Martin Luther King Jr. had been arrested in Georgia on a traffic technicality: he had lived in Georgia for three months, but still had an Alabama driver's license. He was sentenced to four months of hard labor in a Georgia chain gang, and spirited away to maximum security prison. His wife was frantic. Harris Wofford, a Kennedy aide, suggested the Democratic candidate call Mrs. King to express his concern. Kennedy agreed it was a decent thing to do. Bobby Kennedy, meanwhile, called the judge who had sentenced King to tell him he thought King's sentence was harsh treatment for a minor traffic ticket. Soon thereafter, political pressure forced the release of King.

Even in politics, niceties matter. King's father, Martin Luther King Sr., was a Nixon supporter. But Nixon had not called King's daughter-in-law. On a Sunday morning at the Ebenezer Baptist Church in Atlanta, where the Kings were co-pastors, the senior King told the congregation that he had expected to vote against Kennedy because of his Roman Catholic religion. But he said he would now vote for Kennedy because he had the moral courage to stand up for what he knew was right. The election was two weeks away, enough time for black voters to follow the lead of the elder King.

CHAPTER TWENTY-TWO

A FURNISHED APARTMENT FOR $95 A MONTH

When I first moved to Washington, I found a furnished apartment for $95 a month in the Chastleton at 1701 16th Street NW, an easy walk to the bureau. All I really needed was a bed to climb into every night. The rent was a sign of the times. The Chastleton had been called the Hotel Chastleton when it opened in 1920 as a luxury apartment building. Eight floors high, its architectural style is described as Beaux Arts. To me, its high, arching lobby was reminiscent of a Norman castle. But its grandeur and upper-crust clientele were in the past. Many of its residents were middle-level foreign embassy staff. The halls in early evening often reeked of curry.

When I told people where I was living, they knew of the Chastleton's past glory. The tales gave me my first intimate feeling of the human side of the nation's capital. Numerous well-known senators had lived there. I was told that in the early 1930s, General Douglas MacArthur had a suite there for his Eurasian mistress, Isabel Rosario Cooper, a former chorus girl from Shanghai. When the divorced MacArthur returned to Washington from the Philippines to become army chief-of-staff, he brought Isabel along. Eventually, the affair cooled and Isabel prowled the nightspots of Washington and Baltimore. After their affair ended, Isabel sold MacArthur's love letters to her to Drew Pearson and Robert S. Allen, writers of a column, "Washington Merry-go-Round," and dropped out of sight. Major Dwight D. Eisenhower, then MacArthur's assistant, was dispatched to find her without success.[5]

A fully renovated Chastleton in 2018 enjoys a third life as a luxury condominium building. Asking prices for apartments are advertised from $140,000 to $600,000. With monthly condo fees thrown in, the prestige of living there runs much higher than my earlier rent. My guess is that the living conditions are also better.

I crossed MacArthur's path twice. The first time was in April, 1951, when he came to Chicago as part of his triumphant return home from the Far East after he was sacked by President Truman over disagreements on strategy in the Korean War. Television was in its infancy. There were, as yet, no TV sets in Tribune newsrooms. Somewhere, second hand, I had picked up a six-inch oval screen Zenith that was shaped like an elongated box. It had a handle so it could be carried like a suitcase. It even looked like a suitcase with its brown, alligator-like leather cover. The screen was just large enough to be seen from six feet away. In our apartment, we placed it on a small table at one end of our davenport. Sally and I would watch it lying down with our heads resting on the davenport arm at the other end. Stations weren't on overnight. They signed off at midnight with the playing of "The Star Spangled Banner." Then, the ever present test pattern came on.

For MacArthur's arrival and parade, I lugged the Zenith set down to Tribune Tower and set it up with a rabbit ears antenna so the Metropolitan staff could watch his arrival at Midway Airport and the parade that followed. Television coverage was primitive by later standards. There were no roving cameramen with shoulder cameras moving among the millions of Chicagoans who lined the streets. Cameras were in set locations at the airport, and along the parade route. Early the next morning, as the sun rose, Sally and I walked a half block to Sheridan Road from our apartment building on Fargo Avenue to see MacArthur's motorcade en route to Milwaukee. Like everywhere he passed, people lined the curb three and four deep to wave and to catch a glimpse of the war hero.

The other time was at the White House, when he came down from New York to confer with President Kennedy. Retired, a bit frail, he wore civilian clothes as he chatted in the West Wing Lobby with reporters in that strong MacArthur voice. Only a handful of reporters were gathered around MacArthur. Among them was Bob Gruenberg of the *Chicago Daily News*. Bob served in the Pacific theater in WWII. One day as he sat in a foxhole writing a letter, MacArthur happened by. He asked Bob if he was writing to his girlfriend. Bob replied no, the letter was to his mother. The night before MacArthur's White House visit, Bob retold the story to a MacArthur aide.

In the West Wing Lobby, the aide walked the general over to Bob. MacArthur shook his hand, and asked him about his mother. The cameras flashed. It was a nice gesture by MacArthur. The general was mum about details of his meeting with Kennedy, but Theodore Sorensen, the president's confidante and speech writer, said in later years that MacArthur and Kennedy discussed Vietnam. MacArthur's advice was not to use American ground forces on the Asia mainland. Kennedy discussed Vietnam with MacArthur on several occasions and I've always believed Kennedy would have heeded MacArthur's advice. Of course, I will never know. The unanswered question will always be whether the martyred president would have undertaken a buildup of American troops in Indo-China if he had lived. MacArthur gave the same advice to President Johnson when he succeeded Kennedy. The country, to its sorrow, knows how that turned out.

I moved from the Chastleton to our new home in Virginia when my family joined me from Chicago. I don't know if I ever became a true Virginian even though we lived there for 29 years. I loved the state's natural beauty and its geological makeup of the Blue Ridge Mountains, the Piedmont, its estuaries flowing into Chesapeake Bay, certainly one of the most fascinating bodies of water in the world. But I was always more attuned to the national scene. The children think of themselves as Virginians. Sally's father was from Kentucky and she had a feel for the South. There is a certain charm about the South that has its winning ways. There always will be a dark side to harass its history, however, and that is pre-Civil War slavery. Our house was 16 miles south of Washington, but I had one of the most beautiful commutes in the world as I drove into the city on the tree-lined Mount Vernon Memorial Highway along the west bank of the Potomac as it slowly rolled southward toward the sea. Our house was near the Potomac River, a half-mile from the Mount Vernon estate of George Washington. It was in a cluster of new houses dubbed Stratford Landing that ran along Little Hunting Creek on land that once was part of the first president's estate. Originally, the estate was called Little Hunting Creek Plantation. The first house was along the creek. Lawrence Washington, George's half-brother, renamed the estate Mount Vernon in honor of a vice admiral in the British Royal Navy, Edward Vernon, under whom he served.

All that took place before the Revolutionary War. The Washingtons became owners by a 1674 land grant during the reign of King Charles

II. When George became the sole owner through inheritance, he kept the Mount Vernon name. The tract covered roughly 5,000 acres. George divided this into five farms—Dogue Run, Muddy Hole, Union, Mansion House, and River. Stratford Landing was on the old River farm.

CHAPTER TWENTY-THREE

THE CUBAN MISSILE CRISIS

Lee Forrester, our bureau's copy editor, and I walked along Pennsylvania Avenue past the White House at dusk when an array of TV klieg lights went on under the North Portico of the Executive Mansion. "It must be Gromyko," I remarked. "Let's go in." We flashed our press passes to security guards at the avenue's west gate and hurried up the drive. We knew Russia's foreign minister and President Kennedy were meeting. Lee and I were only onlookers, as usual curious about things. Lee was going home and I was headed for a quick bite of food before returning to the office. Larry Burd, our regular White House correspondent, was covering the Kennedy-Gromyko meeting for the Tribune. By the time I returned to the bureau, he'd filed his story and left.

None of us knew of an unfolding backstage drama. Everything seemed more or less even tenor. The capital was magnificent, as always, with the colorful leaves of fall. Its citizens scurried about in the warm twilight, doing what mattered to them, unaware anything was amiss. But, these were the beginning October days of the 1962 Cuban Missile Crisis, the most dangerous episode of the Cold War. Gromyko was jovial with us reporters. He said his talk with Kennedy was "useful, very useful." There has always been speculation as to just how much Andrei Gromyko knew, if anything, about his country's clandestine deployment of offensive nuclear missiles on the Caribbean island. It came out later that Khrushchev had kept knowledge of the operation from his diplomats. Anatoly Dobrynin, the Kremlin's ambassador to the United States, said in his memoir *In Confidence* that he learned what his boss had done the same night the American people did.

Larry's story dwelt mainly with Berlin, where the Russians threatened to sign a separate peace treaty with East Germany and force Western allies out of the city. The Russians were pushing hard for a settlement on Berlin. On Cuba, Larry wrote that those in the meeting said Gromyko assured the president once again that Moscow's military assistance to Cuba was for defensive purposes only. Kennedy once again informed Gromyko any changes in that situation would have grave consequences. The Gromyko-Kennedy meeting took place October 18. As he spoke, the president had photographs in his desk drawer of a missile site taken by an American U-2 reconnaissance plane four days earlier. Meetings were already underway among American officials on how to respond.

I went to the State Department that evening. Members of the Tribune's Washington bureau took turns staying late to answer queries from Chicago, update stories filed by colleagues, and cover any breaking news. October 18 was a duty night for me. With nothing better to do, I joined reporters standing watch on a working dinner Secretary of State Dean Rusk and subordinates were having with Gromyko. I might as well be there, as in the office, returning in time to check things over before a bureau teletype operator closed down the wire to Chicago at ten o'clock. Shortly after I arrived, John McCone, CIA director, and Secretary of Defense Robert McNamara entered the lobby. Asked if they were going to the dinner, they said they were and walked on to an elevator. I thought it strange that McCone would dine with Gromyko, or for that matter, McNamara, too. But, I let the moment pass. With no clue of their real intent, I had no waters to fish in.

Looking back, it was a most surreal setting that night. What a story if I'd known enough to piece things together. Gromyko and Rusk, who was aware of the missiles, were in a diplomatic reception room on the eighth floor, other American officials were deep in discussions on Cuba one floor below in a conference room off of Undersecretary George Ball's office, and we reporters were hanging around the lobby—so close, yet so far—from what was happening. It amazes me still how knowledge of the missiles, once discovered by the U-2, was held so tightly within a small circle of men charged with a response. I can't recall a hint of what was happening. Maybe, it was an avatar-like instinct, inborn and emotional, that made them so cautious, a necessity to protect a feeling of betrayal until the situation could be remedied.

But it was vital that there be no leaks while they debated what to do.

Rumors about the missiles had been around for some time within the Cuban exile community in Florida, where talk had begun in late July that a buildup of Russian military equipment and men was underway in their native land that included missiles that could strike the United States. Sen. Kenneth Keating of New York claimed on the Senate floor that he had proof missile bases were under construction. The reports were so persistent, along with growing concerns of American intelligence officials, that President Kennedy in early September quietly approved a CIA request that the entire island be photographed by U-2s. Early reconnaissance photos showed unmarred landscapes. Then, refugees reported suspicious activity by Russians was going on around San Cristobal, 100 miles west of Havana. On October 3 it was decided to send a U-2 back over San Cristobal for more high-altitude photos. But the return was delayed a week by a hurricane, then by cloud cover for a few more days. Finally, the sun returned on October 14 and a U-2 took the photos President Kennedy had in his desk drawer. The landscape had definitely changed.

The president was reportedly in pajamas and a robe in his bedroom when first shown the photos around 8:45 a.m., Tuesday, October 16 by McGeorge Bundy, the president's special advisor for national affairs. All the wherewithal of the crisis is declassified now. The records are an intimate, inside peek of events. Kennedy had been reading the morning papers. A CIA officer had arrived at the White House a short time earlier with the photos and interpretations of them. Preparation of the material had taken 24 hours after the U-2 returned from its flight. So, it was Monday afternoon, October 15, before the task was complete and reported to Deputy CIA Director Lt. Gen. Marshall Carter in lieu of CIA Director McCone, who was away from the capital due to a death in his family. Analysis of the photos continued into the early evening at the CIA as Bundy, Defense and State Department officials were briefed down the chain of command. In all, at least 10 high administration officials were informed of the missile sites that night. They, in turn, discussed the situation among themselves.

Life outside of their group was normal enough. The New York Yankees won still another world series and the Metropolitan Opera opened its 78th season. College football games were played across the land. The Kremlin, too, was active. It causes one to wonder if Russian actions were contrived to divert attention from Khrushchev's madcap adventure. The Kremlin chief in mid-October expressed a desire to visit the United States again to see Kennedy and to appear before the United Nations. He pressed hard for a Berlin treaty. Gromyko visited the White House three times within 12 days during the crisis, always to discuss what he called "the Berlin situation."

With mid-term Congressional elections approaching, Kennedy was frequently away from the White House campaigning for Democratic candidates. In Boston, former president Eisenhower told a Republican rally that JKF was weak on foreign policy. Meanwhile, Castro had become unduly quiet, saying nothing on U.S. surveillance of his island by air and sea patrols looking for evidence of illicit arms exports to other Latin American countries. The Pentagon was asked to comment on a navy squadron of 12 jet fighters that took up residence in Key West, Florida, 90 miles from Cuba. A spokesman said there was "no reason to get excited about it." He said it was "the ordinary thing to do" in view of reports that Cuba had acquired at least two dozen MIG fighters from Russia.

A group, later known as the Executive Committee of the National Security Council, held its first meeting with the president in the White House cabinet room within hours after Bundy briefed him. Among those present were Rusk, McNamara and Ball; Attorney General Robert Kennedy, the president's brother; Chairman of the Joint Chiefs of Staff General Maxwell Taylor; Bundy and Theodore Sorensen, the president's special counsel as well as principal speech writer. McCone joined in when he returned to the capital. The group had a tough role to play. Documents show that they met constantly in the days that followed. In addition to the threat to U.S. citizens, America's prestige and credibility were at stake, both with allies and Latin American countries. Khrushchev had to be uncloaked.

Meanwhile, the President continued with events scheduled in advance for him. He became his own decoy as he flew off to Connecticut, to fulfill a promise made weeks before, to campaign in Stratford, New Haven and Waterbury for Democratic candidates. In his absence, the group hashed, and rehashed, the situation. It almost goes without saying that Bobby Kennedy's presence in the Excomm group was important, not only because he was the leading law officer of the land, but because of the closeness of the two brothers.

I was responsible for covering the Justice Department. Looking back, I lived a two-tiered existence during the crisis, walking about on a surface of calm while underneath all hell was ready to break loose.

Excomm members slowly settled in on the action to take. Air sorties were considered and rejected. An invasion of Cuba was debated. Morality entered the discussions. Ball drew a parallel between a U.S. first strike and the surprise Japanese attack on Pearl Harbor in WWII. "This coming in there, a Pearl Harbor, just frightens the hell out of me as to what goes beyond," Ball argued. "You go in there with a surprise attack. You put out all the missiles. This isn't the end. This is the beginning, I think." McNamara had suggested a naval blockade of the island, and this idea came increasingly to the forefront. In a morning meeting on October 18, according to transcripts, Bobby told his brother that George Ball had a hell of a good point. "It's the whole question you know of, you know—what kind of a country we are."

Llewellyn Thompson, recent ambassador to Moscow, who had joined the meetings, suggested that a blockade, with only intermittent activity, could lead to a period of negotiation that would defuse matters. By the fourth day after the U-2 discovery, the Excomm group coagulated, like blood on a wound, around a blockade, an action that would allow Khrushchev some room to maneuver, to give him a chance to pull back. A first strike would close off a diplomatic solution. Late that night Bobby Kennedy called Deputy Attorney General Nicholas Katzenbach, a former professor of international law at Princeton, at his home. He told him to begin work on a legal basis for a blockade. Ambassador Thompson had convinced the group that there had to be a solid legal basis for American action. He said Russians were big on "legality." Another consideration: a strong legal case could also influence world reaction favorable to the United States.

Now a decision had to be made about the president's campaign activities. On Friday, October 19, as planned, he went on the trail again, this time to the Midwest, including the Tribune's home town of Chicago. It was in Chicago that suspicions of a crisis took hold. The president reached the city late in the afternoon, after rallies in Cleveland and the Illinois capital of Springfield. But the next morning in the Sheraton Blackstone Hotel, where Kennedy was staying, Pierre Salinger, his press secretary, announced that the president was dropping the rest of his trip. He said the president had a cold and was returning to Washington to spend the rest of the day in bed. He said that the president was being treated with aspirin and antihistamines for what Rear Admiral George Buckley, assistant White House physician, described as "a slight infection of the upper respiratory tract with a one degree temperature."

The alleged illness was a cover story. It was a ruse to get the president back to the capital. Kennedy was fine even though he, too, took part in the charade when he told Gov. Gaylord Nelson of Wisconsin as he boarded Air Force One at O'Hare field, "I don't feel too badly. This is mainly precautionary. I'll call you Monday about coming back to Wisconsin." The president had planned to speak at an airport rally in Milwaukee on the first leg of a five state campaign swing that day, with Nelson accompanying him to Milwaukee on the presidential plane.

The abrupt change in presidential plans raised eyebrows at the Tribune. Its telegraph desk in Chicago queried the Washington bureau while Kennedy was en route back to the capital, asking if there was an emergency there that required the president's return. Larry Burd, who'd been on the campaign swing, said when he came into the bureau that Kennedy did not seem ill to him. He thought the president had returned to Washington for some other reason. Media, in general, sensed something was up and began asking questions. Adding to the speculation was an AP story that Vice President Johnson had stopped campaigning in Hawaii because of a cold and was returning to Washington. Secretary of State Dean Rusk canceled a speech in Virginia because of "the press of business." Was it too much to challenge all this as more than a coincidence?

As for me, I'm not a great believer in coincidence.

The need for a lockdown on information, too, was diminishing. The president and the Excomm group were moving from planning to action. Their work was still unknown, something still concealed, but everyone suspected now that something was up. Bundy briefed Kennedy when he reached the White House. The president read the first of five drafts of a proposed speech prepared overnight by Sorensen. The Pentagon finished preparations for a naval and air blockade. Army units were on the move over southern highways for everyone to see.

So, what was going on in those last hours before the president told the world about the missile sites? Katzenbach and a team of lawyers put their finishing touches on a blockade proclamation. State Department officials prepared for a session of the Organization of American

States. Former Secretary of State Dean Acheson readied himself for a flight to Europe to brief the North Atlantic Treaty Organization Council and Gen. Charles de Gaulle, who had pulled France out of NATO. Dispatches were prepared for American embassies worldwide. Allied diplomats in Washington were briefed. Preparations were made to notify ships on the high seas. A letter was readied for Khrushchev. Larry O'Brien, the president's congressional liaison, telephoned Democratic and Republican congressional leaders spread across the country campaigning to inform them that the president wanted all of them in Washington as soon as possible. A few who couldn't arrange commercial flights got the rides of their lives in jet fighters. At noon, Salinger announced that the president would speak to the nation on a matter of great urgency at 7:00 p.m. Kennedy took an early afternoon swim in the White House pool. Ambassador Dobrynin, who was in New York City, to see Gromyko off to Moscow, was asked to come to Rusk's office at 6:00 p.m.

Dobrynin was his affable self with us reporters when he arrived to see Rusk at the State Department. I saw no signs of tension in his manner. But when the ambassador departed a half hour later, he was grim and shaken. In his hand was a text of Kennedy's speech and the president's letter to Khrushchev. Queried if there was a crisis, he responded, "Ask the secretary." Asked to appraise the situation as he hurried off, he snapped, "You can judge for yourself." It was a moment that focused the mind on what was at hand. The Tribune was between two early editions. I called in developments at the State Department.

As I'd written earlier, Dobrynin had been in the dark about the missiles. The ambassador wrote in his memoir that he asked for instructions from Moscow in mid-September on how to answer questions about the reports from Cuban exiles that Russian offensive weapons were arriving on the island. The curt reply was that in talking to the Americans, he should say that there are only defensive Soviet weapons in Cuba. U.S. officials, in the aftermath of the crisis, discussed whether to demand Dobrynin's recall from Washington, but concluded he didn't know of Khrushchev's plotting. Dobrynin wrote in his memoir that he thought he had been an involuntary tool of deceit. But, Khrushchev would need him in the coming days.

I thought Kennedy's speech laid everything on the line for Khrushchev — get your missiles and soldiers out of Cuba, or the United States will do it for you. It's long ago now, but I still feel a rush of excitement at the thought of having watched it all from so close at hand. The president said Russian ships sailing the high seas near Cuba would be stopped and searched for offensive weapons. In his talk, JFK rebranded the blockade, referring to it instead as "a quarantine," a softer word with no precedent as an act of war, and a less belligerent tone in diplomatic terms. Khrushchev's goal had been surprise: he would present the U.S. with the accomplished fact of missiles deployed, ready for use, and guarded by 40,000 Russian troops. That's a lot of soldiers. It was Khrushchev who was surprised, instead. He was the one in a pickle now. Fortunately, the quarantine gave both leaders time to negotiate as Ambassador Thompson had predicted. It would be a day or two before a Russian ship heading to Cuba would reach the quarantine line of U.S. Navy ships stretched across the Caribbean ready to interdict them.

With the gauntlet down, the Washington bureau had to determine how to cover the crisis. It decided to concentrate on the White House and the Pentagon with reporters at those two locations almost around the clock. We thought these would be the command centers if war came, unless they were blown to smithereens right off by ICBMs. I was assigned to the Pentagon from 3:30 p.m. to 1:00 a.m. I figured I would be among the dead if there was a nuclear Armageddon. But, deep down in mind and heart, I didn't think Khrushchev was dumb enough to engage in a nuclear exchange. I've often wondered why Sally and the kids didn't pile in our station wagon and take off. But, there was only so far to run. Quickly, the crisis became a waiting game. Letters went back and forth between Kennedy and Khrushchev. Our home life went on. As I waited to go to the Pentagon each night, I did yard work and washed the cars. I listened on my shortwave radio, an old army field piece, to English language broadcasts of Radio Moscow, which often aired Kremlin statements about the crisis. Jon and Holly went to school as usual. Sally went grocery shopping. One noon, the two of us slipped out to lunch and talked about what a great adventure Washington had been for us. Another morning we took little Allison with us on a drive around the countryside. I called my dad in Illinois every night around ten o'clock from the Pentagon to tell him it appeared we'd survived another day. Intermediate range missiles from Cuba could hit Chicago and the Midwest since their strike distance ranged from Lima, Peru to Hudson Bay in Canada. But, as each day passed, tensions lessened. Negotiations, not warfare, became the mantra. Khrushchev, through Bertrand Russell, the British philosopher and pacifist, suggested, somewhat vaguely, a summit meeting and he said he would make no reckless decisions. Former president Dwight Eisenhower was so confident that there would be no war that he flew to Illinois the last weekend of the crisis to campaign for the re-election of the Republican senator from the state, Everett Dirksen.

I wrote two stories in 10 days at the Pentagon. Not much output, to be sure. But, I was there in case something happened at night. The days were covered by Phil Dodd, our regular Pentagon correspondent, beginning at 6:00 a.m. My first article was datelined October 24, the day the quarantine went into effect, and it reported the release of four air reconnaissance photos of missile bases that defense department officials said were "more recent and more revealing" than ones taken earlier. The photos, which showed greater ground detail, were of two bases: one for medium range ballistic missiles, and the other for those of intermediate range. One photo of the medium range base showed oxidizer and fuel trucks. At least two dozen vehicles were seen clearly. Missile ready buildings were clearly visible, as were two launch pad erectors. The other story, datelined October 27, carried the report that a U-2 was shot down over Cuba and its pilot, Maj. Rudolf Anderson Jr. was killed. Anderson was the same pilot who first filmed the missile sites. Dodd always encountered much more information during the day. The first interception was of an oil tanker, which had been allowed to proceed without a search; a Panamanian freighter under Soviet charter had been boarded and searched, but no contraband cargo was found and it was allowed to continue on its way. I, and the whole world, breathed a deep, and I mean deep, sigh of relief when a Soviet ship carrying military hardware throttled its engines rather than run the quarantine line. It was drama on the high seas signaling that Khrushchev had backed down.

Second-guessing is easy. But, we might have had a blockbuster of a story if I had tailed Bobby Kennedy instead of hanging around the Pentagon. Dobrynin wrote in his memoir that he and Bobby met late at night during the crisis as go-betweens for the White House and the Kremlin, usually between 11:00 p.m. and 3:00 a.m. either at Kennedy's office in the Justice Department, or at the Russian embassy. He said that at the embassy they conferred in the sitting room of the Dobrynin's apartment with no one else present. Dobrynin's wife, Irina, would make them coffee and then go to bed.[6] It hardly seemed a world sweating out a possible nuclear holocaust. But, the outside world knew nothing of this. The two had become a back channel in Washington-Moscow relations after Dobrynin's arrival in the American capital in March 1962, seven months before the missile crisis. The President introduced them at a diplomatic reception in the White House in May, telling the ambassador that Bobby was "an expert in confidential contacts with the Soviet Union whom Dobrynin should get to know better." A week later, Bobby invited the ambassador and his wife to lunch at his home across the Potomac in Virginia. From then on, they met frequently on the Q.T.

Moscow's first reaction to President Kennedy's speech was a dispatch 13 hours later in *Tass*, the Russian news agency. This was followed by a letter to JKF from Khrushchev the following day that called the quarantine illegal, but threatened no counteraction. Rather, it said President Kennedy was no longer appealing to reason, but wished only to intimidate the Russians. The crisis reached its tipping point the night of October 27 after the U-2 was shot down. Bobby asked Dobrynin to come to his office in the Justice Department. He had a letter from President Kennedy to the Russian leader accepting his terms that Russia would withdraw its missiles and military units and in turn the U.S. would never invade Cuba. The president's letter ignored Khrushchev's demand that American missiles in Turkey be withdrawn, a proposal Kennedy had publicly rejected a few hours earlier. The missiles in Turkey were the crux of the Bobby-Dobrynin discussions. Bobby told Dobrynin that his brother intended to withdraw the missiles (which were obsolete), but not for four or five months because they were part of a NATO arrangement. He asked the ambassador to quietly pass this information on to Khrushchev.

One result of the Cuban crisis was direct teletype communications between the White House and the Kremlin which became known worldwide as the hotline. This private wire was available 24 hours a day for the two governments to correspond with each other if another emergency arose. There is no doubt that the tense diplomatic exchanges during the crisis were plagued by delays due to tedious communications systems. The Russians especially used Western Union to send messages back and forth between their embassy and the Kremlin, certainly an archaic practice by modern methods. It was no different than you or I sending a telegram. Nowadays, world leaders just pick up the telephone to talk to each other. But, in 1962 they used what was available. Kennedy and

Khrushchev exchanged letters five times in the crisis. Dobrynin relates in his memoir that the procedure was not without anxiety, especially the handling of Kennedy's last reply to Khrushchev. The ambassador wrote that after receiving the text of JFK's message at the embassy, it was encrypted in code. Once ready, Western Union was called to pick it up. In due time, a uniformed Western Union boy on a bicycle arrived at the embassy. As he rode off to return to the Western Union office, the Russian translation in hand, the ambassador wrote that he could only hope the boy would not dally along the way to talk to a girlfriend.[7]

Khrushchev was so anxious to let Kennedy know that he'd accepted his terms that he broadcast his reply over Radio Moscow while the written text was en route to Washington via Western Union. He also delivered a copy of his answer to the American embassy in Moscow. It seemed in the end that the Russian wanted to leave no margin for error. He wanted the crisis which he created over and done. Two years later, in October 1964, Khrushchev was ousted from power. His misplaced Cuban adventure did not sit well with his colleagues. He had overplayed his hand. The old Bolshevik didn't fight his removal, saying he was along in years and tired. He was given a pension, an apartment in Moscow and a countryside dacha. Back in Cuba, Castro thought placement of the missiles was mishandled. He claimed that Cuba, as a sovereign nation had a right to the missiles on its own behalf and that they could have been legitimately purchased from the Soviets. That would have created an entirely different and more complicated set of circumstances for the United States and other Western hemisphere nations.

CHAPTER TWENTY-FOUR

I STILL CRY

I t is 55 years since the assassination of President Kennedy but sadness still lingers within me. I can't throw off the feeling of a life unfinished. He never got a chance to grow old, as I have. Certainly, I was used to uninvited death. I'd been in WWII combat. As a police reporter, in my early years as a journalist in Chicago, I'd seen the mayhem and ugliness of organized crime. It struck me one night, as I stood on a sidewalk over the bloody body of a gangland shooting victim, that I'd become hardened to violence. I'd become emotionally immune to tragedy. I had no more feeling about the murder, than if I had been sitting on the curb eating a ham on rye sandwich.

It was different with Kennedy. I felt deep sorrow about his death. And it wasn't only the death of one man; it violated the nation he led. I always knew I enjoyed covering President Kennedy more than the rest—Eisenhower, Johnson or Nixon. I never saw Kennedy angry; I did the others. With Kennedy, there seemed to be a grace under pressure, equanimity to take life as it comes. Still, there was an infectious vibrancy about him that rubbed off on others. That's what hurt so much—to know that he was gone forever. I never looked at the world quite the same again after his death. Life, as a whole, became more jaded and shopworn.

Everyone remembers where they were when the first news flash came that Kennedy had been shot. I was crossing the Mall in the shadow of the Washington Monument when I heard a voice call out my name. Bill Eaton, of the United Press, ran up behind me. "Kennedy's been shot," he yelled. We ran together to the pressroom of the

Department of Labor a block away, where we read the stories on the wire service tickers coming in from Dallas. No one said much. We were too stunned. I was clearly aware of Secret Service details that guarded presidents. I knew many of the agents as friends, but I never thought that they would be confronted with an assassination. I tried to call the bureau but telephone lines were jammed across the city by too many users. It would continue that way for hours.

The story at that moment was in Dallas, not the capital. Everything was concentrated there. The principals were there—Vice President Johnson and Mrs. Kennedy. Some cabinet members were en route to Hawaii. The only person of consequence in Washington who I covered was the president's brother, Bobby. I left the Labor Department and walked the few blocks east to the Department of Justice. The building was largely abandoned. I finally found Nick Katzenbach, the Deputy Attorney General, alone in his office sitting before a TV set. He waved me in. I asked him if he knew the whereabouts of the Attorney General. He told me that Bobby had gone to his home in Virginia for lunch and he had been there when the shooting in Dallas happened. Katzenbach said Ed Guthman, Kennedy's press secretary, was with him. I watched the TV coverage for a while with Katzenbach. We knew by then, in midafternoon, that the president was dead. I left and went on to the bureau.

Bob Young was with the press corps in Dallas for the Tribune. He was in direct contact with Chicago in mapping his coverage. I sent a couple of paragraphs about Bobby Kennedy from Washington that could be inserted into his story. Things began to move quickly. Louise Hutchinson was flown in from the city room in Chicago to cover Mrs. Kennedy. Wayne Thomis flew to Dallas from Chicago to replace Bob Young, who returned to Washington with the new president, Mrs. Kennedy and the body of the martyred president. Lyndon Johnson had been sworn in on Air Force One, as it prepared to take off from Dallas' Love Field, perhaps misnamed for the moment considering the circumstances. I went to the White House in the early evening for a press briefing at which detailed arrangements for the next few days were announced. Names, places and times were included as though a contingency plan had been pulled from a drawer upon the president's death. The new leadership reacted swiftly. A political vacuum could not be allowed to form. No signs of confusion or weakness could be shown to a world engaged in a Cold War. It was announced that LBJ had already met with legislative leaders, to seek their united support, and that he would meet with world leaders coming to Washington for Kennedy's funeral. When I returned to the office, Trohan asked me to write a story on the reshaped political picture for the coming 1964 presidential race now that Kennedy wouldn't be running for re-election. In newspaper jargon, these are called thumb suckers. But, as I reread the analysis after a half century, it held up well. It's hard for me to imagine in my old age how fast I could gather and write a story back then. I didn't quote anyone, the piece was largely off the top of my head but all the names, both Democratic and Republican, were there, although some of the possibilities I mentioned didn't come to fruition until the race of 1968. This may have been my first purely political article.

I worked a half day on Saturday writing a story about Arlington National Cemetery and the grave site where Kennedy would be laid to rest. Trohan told me to take Sunday off.

My family and I stood silently on a knoll on the south lawn of the Treasury Building on Sunday as the horse drawn caisson with Kennedy's flag-draped coffin slowly turned the curve on Pennsylvania Avenue, and moved on towards the sun-covered Capitol dome glistening in the distance. A lone horse, its saddle empty, trailed behind. The muted ruffle of drums clocked the cadence. It was a brisk afternoon, clear and cool. The president's body had lain in repose through the night and morning in the White House. It would now lie in state in the Capitol rotunda for public view. The crowd around us was somber. I noticed that some held rosaries. Many wept. Others placed a hand over their hearts. As the cortege grew smaller in the distance, word spread through the crowd that Lee Harvey Oswald, held in Dallas as Kennedy's assassin, had been shot and killed. A man next to me turned on his transistor radio to seek verification. Though the volume was low, we heard a newscaster's account of the chaotic scene in the Dallas police building, where Jack Ruby fired a revolver point blank into the accused assassin's body, a picture we saw run again and again on television.

Ruby, a 52-year-old former Chicagoan, owned and operated two Dallas nightclubs. Oswald, months earlier in March, had bought the Italian military rifle he used from a Chicago mail order outlet. Ruby said he killed Oswald to spare Mrs. Kennedy the agony of a trial. He shot the assassin as he was moved through a crowded hallway outside an inner security section of the police building, preparatory to his transfer to the county jail. The irony is that Ruby never should have been there. But, as a hanger on around the police headquarters, he was a familiar face to officials, supposedly harmless. Oswald's death ended any attempt to learn his motive to kill JFK and conspiracy theories remain. But evidence points to the 24-year-old Oswald as a lone and emotionally detached gunman. He was said to be a better than average shot who learned marksmanship in the United States Marine Corps. He was described as a hazy thinker, full of muddled grievances, a restless man self-proclaimed as a Marxist, who lacked a grip on life. I accept Oswald as the lone sniper, but I have what-ifs.

What if Oswald had been questioned and watched in Dallas by the FBI, who knew him as a troublemaker? In the course of preparing for Kennedy's visit to the Dallas-Fort Worth area, the FBI investigated 16 individuals in the two-city area but Oswald was not among them. What if the book depository building had been secured and its windows sealed? What if Oswald had obtained visas a few weeks earlier from the Cuban and Russian consulates in Mexico City instead of being rejected, and had returned to Russia via Havana in the weeks before the assassination?

If any of those events had happened, perhaps Kennedy's death would have been avoided. For some, like conspiracy theorists Edward Jay Epstein and John Newman, the president's death will always be shrouded in mystery. They question CIA operations in Mexico City during Oswald's visit, a move on their part that is puzzling to me. They have produced nothing of significance, and since he didn't get his visas what difference does it make?

Back at work on Monday, I became a roving leg man calling in information to others writing stories. I walked along with world dignitaries, behind the president's coffin and his widow, as they slowly made their way over the many blocks from the White House to St. Matthew's Cathedral for a pontifical requiem mass. I will always remember the contrast between the diminutive Emperor Haile Selassie of Ethiopia, beribboned and silent, marching beside the towering figure of President Charles de Gaulle of France. Stretched out behind them were Prince Philip of Britain, Belgian King Baudouin, Queen Fredericka of Greece, Prime Minister Lester Pearson of Canada, German Chancellor Ludwig Erhard, and many, many other world leaders. After the mass, I peeled off from the entourage to Arlington Cemetery and went to the State

Department, where President Johnson held a reception and met with some of his world counterparts, especially close allies. Phil Dodd of the Tribune bureau was at Arlington for Kennedy's burial. From 1840 to Kennedy, every president, at 20 year intervals, had been the victim of either an assassination or died in office. Kennedy was our 35th president. Since his death, a half century has passed without the term of a president cut short by death. During that time nine presidents have occupied the White House. I covered some, and knew others before they assumed office. Five were Republicans and four were Democrats. Some were more interesting than others to be around.

With the death of President Kennedy, an abrupt change took place in the power structure of the Democratic Party. Suddenly, Johnson was its leader. The powerful blood relationship Bobby Kennedy had with his brother was gone. LBJ now held the forceful hand. But LBJ's situation was delicate where Bobby was concerned. Those of us with access to both men behind the scenes didn't have to see them publicly at odds with each other. We knew that an arctic coldness existed between them, that they had deep distrust of each other. They tried to keep a serene surface, but when things eat away at you privately eventually an outing takes place.

I made my first printed reference to their feud in a story in early March, 1964. The cold of winter had come and gone in the capital. In the warmth of spring, cherry blossoms had displayed their famed annual beauty. The transition to Johnson running the government had gone well. It was the unhealthy relationship between LBJ and Bobby that couldn't be conquered. Whispering about it was everywhere. Their suspicions and skepticisms of each other had been years in the making, back to the race for the Democratic presidential nomination in 1960. The Kennedys had outmaneuvered LBJ, and it was impossible for him to forgive them even after JFK choose him has his vice presidential running mate. Bobby had fought the selection and LBJ knew it.

Reference to the feud came during a White House briefing by Pierre Salinger, who had stayed on as press secretary after Kennedy's assassination. It was backhanded and awkward, but telling. Asked to comment on rumors that Johnson and Bobby were communicating through third parties, Salinger soft pedaled this, saying that the "two men see each other from time to time on various matters." Asked if the two men have sat down to discuss whatever differences exist between them, Salinger replied, "I'm not going to get into that matter."

There you have it. That "matter" was the feud.

The discussion with Salinger came about as the result of a large write-in vote Kennedy received for vice president in the just completed 1964 New Hampshire presidential primary, the first in the country. The write-ins were a sore point with LBJ, who wasn't going to be stampeded into naming Bobby as his running mate in the fall presidential election. Bobby pulled 25,861 write-in votes for veep in New Hampshire, slightly under Johnson's 29,630 for president. He had done so despite putting out a statement before the primary that LBJ should be free to choose his own running mate. Johnson was in a tough situation. He had to take the reins of his party without alienating Kennedy backers, who felt that power had been snatched from them although Johnson continued to move along JFK programs.

Bobby decided he would stay on as attorney general as long as LBJ wanted him. Johnson made no effort to discuss Bobby's political future with him. There was curiosity over what Johnson would do if Bobby demanded the spot in the name of his brother, who chose LBJ as his running mate. But, as time passed, Bobby told friends he wouldn't make that demand.

I think their dilemma weighed on Johnson more than Bobby. It was an emotional situation for both, but in different ways. Bobby's emotions revolved around his brother's death and the loss of the White House. Bobby no longer controlled the vision the Kennedys had for the future of the country. His influence was gone. For Johnson, the time was dangerous politically. He had to tamper Bobby down without seeming harsh and vindictive to both fellow Democrats and a mourning public. It was a brooding, cautious atmosphere for him. He had to avoid any action that would cause a public wave of sympathy for Bobby and jeopardize his own drive to win the presidency in the fall.

Eventually, LBJ decided he could win election without Bobby. He announced that none of his cabinet would be considered for the vice presidential slot, a move that eliminated Bobby, the sitting attorney general, and ended any thought that Johnson would share the 1964 Democratic ticket with Bobby as his running mate. And, as time passed, LBJ began to remake the White House staff in his own image. The Texas hill country of Johnson's birth is a vastly different culture than Boston and Cape Cod. He brought in Texans to replace Kennedy men and women. Instead of

New England Irish Catholics, you had Texas Baptists. Presidents always bring in White House staffers with whom they feel comfortable, and that leads to people from their home state. Scotty Reston wrote that when Kennedy was through with his appointments there would be nothing left of Harvard but Radcliffe, its women's counterpoint in those long ago days. Having people from different regions come and go as White House insiders maintains vitality in managing national affairs. I always felt euphoria in the White House as a new administration took charge of the national government. There was an esprit de corps, a feeling it could do better. Some did, others didn't. None stayed forever, and that is the majesty of the American Republic.

Bill Moyers arrived from Texas as a top aide, and soon became the White House press secretary. Bill and I lived a block apart in Virginia, but I hardly ever saw him outside of the Executive Mansion. Sometimes at night, I'd see his chauffeur-driven car pass my house with a reading lamp shining in the back seat with Bill finishing up correspondence carried home. Long hours were certainly an earmark of White House staffers. But, in time, LBJ thought Moyers had begun to make policy during his daily press briefings and George Christian was brought up from Austin to replace him. Moyers and Christian were favorites of mine, along with Jim Haggerty, Eisenhower's press secretary.

Despite the feeling of newness, there was continuity to governance. There were routine activities that carried over from one administration to the next. Sometimes, there was unfinished legislation, or a program, that had to move on. Johnson took it upon himself to move President Kennedy's civil rights proposals forward. President Kennedy had suggested an end to discrimination in public places and facilities. LBJ's actions resulted in the historic Civil Rights Act signed on July 2, 1964, a year after JFK initially undertook the task. Johnson was ambivalent about civil rights until he became president. Once in the White House he put his famous cajolery to work on Congress. No man understood Congress better than Johnson. He knew he needed Republican support to offset recalcitrant, anti-civil rights southern Democrats. He asked for help from Everett Dirksen, the Senate minority leader from Illinois, a pro-civil rights state. Dirksen gave him enough GOP votes for victory. In appreciation of Dirksen's efforts, Johnson went to Capitol Hill to sign the legislation into law with Dirksen at his side.

At times, LBJ could be gracious and considerate. Other times he could be a rogue and uncaring. One Sunday, Johnson attended the little white wooden framed church near his ranch. I arrived early and took a seat about half way down the center aisle. Shortly, the president and Lady Bird came in and slipped into the pew directly in front me instead of continuing to the front of the nave as they usually did. I felt uneasy being so close to him and I considered vacating my seat. Mostly, the press stayed in the back of the church or outside. But the president seemed oblivious to my close presence. Little did I know that I was about to witness the well-known cantankerous side of him. As soon as the sermon began, he and Lady Bird began to talk between themselves. I couldn't hear what they said, but I couldn't hear the preacher unimpeded either. When they weren't talking, the president was restless. He pulled a comb from a coat pocket and ran it through his hair. A short time later, he took out a nail file from the same pocket and worked on his fingers. He certainly had no interest in the sermon. Still, he went to church regularly and he was friendly with the clergy of the Texas hill country where his ranch was located. He sometimes entertained them in the ranch house. Johnson and I got along. Before his decision not to run in 1968, he kidded me that he would get the Tribune editorial board, often critical of him, to endorse him. I knew that would never happen, but I'm not sure he did. He had great confidence in his power of persuasion.

CHAPTER TWENTY-FIVE

GOLDWATER UP CLOSE

A lthough I continued to be responsible for coverage of the Justice Department and Bobby Kennedy, I was increasingly given political assignments that took me away from them. The Republican Party in Washington became my beat. That meant keeping pace with Sen. Barry Goldwater of Arizona, considered the front runner for the 1964 GOP presidential nomination. In late December 1963, I received a short note in the mail from Goldwater saying that he would announce his intentions in his home state on January 3, 1964.

I wanted to be there. It was one more way to become closer to the senator as a candidate since I was sure he would run. He had been quietly establishing field offices for more than six months. But the Tribune decided to send Sy Korman, the paper's west correspondent over from Los Angeles. I would pick Goldwater up again when he returned to Washington. He announced, as expected, that he would run. Goldwater was for me a somewhat difficult read. I had the feeling he was unsure of actually being president, that he had reservations about ably fulfilling the job. But, he had boxed himself in at the 1960 Republican convention in Chicago, when he inspired the party's conservatives with a speech declaring that someday they would take the party over. At that moment, he was anointed their leader.

As I watched his campaign unfold through the spring and summer, I sometimes sensed a desire in him to be elsewhere. If someone aspires to the presidency, he has to want it badly. He has to get up every morning in a fighting mood, ready to do battle against his foes, and there will always be many. The presidency is not an easy job. Young men grow grey as White House occupants.

I've always felt that, at any one time, there are perhaps a half dozen people in the United States with the ability, temperament, and judgment to successfully occupy the Oval Office. I never considered Goldwater as one of them. That didn't mean I was reluctant to cover him. There was plenty happening. The Republican Party became deeply divided, a philosophical split that would last for decades and it's not over yet. Goldwater was not alone in seeking the nomination in 1964. Republican Nelson Rockefeller, governor of New York, more liberal than Goldwater, soon challenged him, and the battle between them became acrimonious and bitter.

Also, in a somewhat quixotic venture, Sen. Margaret Chase Smith of Maine, a sharp, attractive woman of 67 years, announced her candidacy three weeks after Goldwater.

"I have few illusions and no money," she said at her announcement at a luncheon I attended at the Women's National Press Club. Her trademark, a single rose, adorned her dress. The women rattled the room with cheers for her as she went on to say: "I'm staying for the finish. When people keep telling you can't do a thing, you kind of like to try."

At the Republican convention in San Francisco, her name was placed in nomination by the Maine delegation and she kept it there until the finish, never conceding to Goldwater. Sen. Smith wasn't new to the national spotlight. She'd been mentioned as a possible vice presidential nominee on a ticket with Eisenhower in 1952. Truman was still president then, and when asked by a reporter what she would do if she woke up in the White House, she responded with a smile: "I would immediately apologize to Mrs. Truman. Then I would go home."

Goldwater was somewhat of a lone wolf among fellow Republican office holders. No Republican presidential candidate had ever run so far to the right as he did. He and his followers relished the idea but their movement ran counter to the party's long history of moderation. Nothing stood out more in this regard than Goldwater's vote in the senate against the civil rights bill 10 days before his party's presidential nominating convention. For many, he seemed to misunderstand the purpose of his country — its long struggle to move toward equality for all of its citizens, its hope to give everyone a shot at the pursuit of happiness. I thought his vote was political suicide and I wondered once again if he had a death wish about running. Goldwater also advocated the use of tactical nuclear weapons in Europe if the Cold War became a hot one. He thought Social Security should become voluntary. Both were unpopular political positions.

The Republican convention took place in July in Daly City's Cow Palace just outside San Francisco. I'd never been in San Francisco, so I looked forward to seeing the city's Chinatown, the Golden Gate Bridge, the old Bowery and Nob Hill, and to ride the cable cars, which I did every day traveling between my room in the Sir Francis Drake Hotel and the Mark Hopkins, Goldwater's headquarters. I spent most of my waking hours at Goldwater's command post on the upper floors of the Mark Hopkins, whose Top of Mark cocktail lounge became a fabled WWII meeting place for Pacific Theater servicemen and their women.

Late one afternoon, Cliff White and I sneaked away for a drink in the Top of Mark, and a feel of its atmosphere. I had easy access to Cliff and other Goldwater aides. But I saw little of Goldwater himself, outside of his visits to state delegations, and a 15-minute visit with former president Eisenhower in the St. Francis Hotel. Small talk with reporters was not a strong point with him. He considered constant media scrutiny as something to endure.

William Scranton's headquarters was also in the Mark Hopkins, but he received little attention from me, or the press in general. Scranton had announced his candidacy for the nomination just four weeks earlier in a late attempt to stop Goldwater. I drove over to Baltimore from Washington for his debut. But Scranton, a gentlemanly, old-line east coast patrician and Republican governor of Pennsylvania, was not a colorful candidate. His main concern was the fate of the GOP, as expressed in Baltimore, when he said that "the nation, indeed the world, waits to see if another proud political banner will falter, grow limp, and collapse in the dust."

It is 54 years later now, and I'm still waiting.

Although Goldwater appeared to have the GOP nomination sewn up, attempts to derail him were in motion up to the night of his nomination. Rockefeller kept fighting, as did Scranton. In a midnight letter to Goldwater on the first night of the convention, Scranton charged Goldwater with irresponsibility in racial matters and a man in the clutches of radical extremists. Goldwater called the letter intemperate, and returned it.

Scranton's name, along with Rockefeller's, was placed in nomination on the convention floor. But Rocky was dogged by his divorce and remarriage. Three days before the California primary, his second wife gave birth to a baby boy. No blessed event could have been more ill-timed. It put Rockefeller on the defensive once again. Goldwater openly questioned his opponent's morality, and pointed to his own long, divorce-free marriage. Victory in California gave Goldwater enough delegates for his nomination. When the roll call came at the convention, the tally was Goldwater, 883, Rockefeller, 114. Even Scranton received more delegate votes than Rockefeller with 214.

Political conventions were colorful and often raw with emotion before television slowly crushed all spontaneity. Today conventions have become so dull that the big four television networks—CBS, NBC, Fox and ABC—don't cover them from opening to closing gavel anymore. But that wasn't true in 1964 and all the acrimony and ill will within the Republican Party boiled to a high heat in the Cow Palace. The ugliest scene I saw in my years attending political conventions was during Rockefeller's pre-roll call speech. The booing, hissing, and cat calls from hostile Goldwater troops on the floor was so out of control that the noise drowned out the New York governor's voice. I had a floor pass and I was there among them. Looking down on the unruly delegates from the podium, Rockefeller called them extremist, and he accused them of being out of touch on the rising social issues of the day.

"These extremists feed on fear, hate and terror," he shouted, his face hot with anger. "They have no program for America and the Republican Party. They operate from dark shadows of secrecy. It is essential to repudiate, here and now, any doctrinaire, militant minority whether communist, Ku Klux Klan or John Birchers."

The next night in his acceptance speech for the nomination, Goldwater answered Rockefeller's accusation by saying "I would remind you that extremism in the defense of liberty is no vice, and let me remind you also, that moderation in pursuit of justice is no virtue." The line was widely criticized. Over time, it is the one utterance of Goldwater that I remember.

Upon Goldwater's recommendation, the convention nominated William E. Miller, a congressman from Upstate New York, as the party's vice presidential nominee. Goldwater said he choose Miller because "he drives Johnson nuts." To me, this was hardly a serious reason to be selected. I never uncovered a hint in the White House that LBJ was agitated by Miller, who was more moderate than Goldwater and was known mainly to his colleagues in Congress and constituents in his own blue collar district in upstate New York. Miller's selection showed what a closed affair, and inside game, Goldwater played.

Miller had a very solid career. An argument can be made that he was more qualified to be president than Goldwater. He was graduated from Notre Dame University, where he was elected head of the student government, and Albany Law School. In WWII, he was a first lieutenant assigned to the army's war criminals branch in Washington. After the war, he was one of the assistant prosecutors under Supreme Court Justice Robert Jackson that tried Nazi leaders as war criminals in Nuremberg. He served as chairman of the Republican National Committee. But, of his attributes, none was played up for political advantage. The campaign concentrated on Goldwater, and left Miller to himself. This led to the refrain:

"Here's a riddle. It's a killer. Who in the hell is William E. Miller?"

Miller, in a number of ways, made sense as a running mate to Goldwater. He gave the ticket a geographical and denominational balance. He was from the East and he was Roman Catholic, the first of his religion to appear on a national GOP ticket. It was 50 years until another Catholic appeared on a national Republican ticket when Paul Ryan was Mitt Romney's running mate.

Attempts were made to bring some unity to the party after the disruptive convention. In mid-August, I was up early to drive to Hershey, Pennsylvania to attend a GOP summit called by Goldwater. The daylong meeting was held in the ornate Hershey Hotel. Everything in the town seemed connected in some way to the Hershey name. An intoxicating smell of chocolate hung over the area. Not far away was the factory turning out the famous Hershey's chocolate bars and candy kisses. But all that sweetness couldn't penetrate the divisiveness of the Republican leaders. The rift among them was too deep. Former President Eisenhower served as moderator, but he, himself, was not happy with the Goldwater nomination. I saw forced smiles on the faces of other participants: former vice president Nixon, Rockefeller and Scranton and Gov. George Romney of Michigan. When the day was done and they all parted, they once again went their separate political ways. It was a tough time for these men. They had a nominee they did not want, and with whom they disagreed philosophically.

Some might feel that I'm too negative about Goldwater. But his campaign was truly an anatomy of a blowout political defeat. One morning, sometime before the New Hampshire primary, Denis Kitchel, Goldwater's campaign manager, had a small group of us over to his headquarters in the nation's capital. He spent some time laying out plans between then and Election Day. It was a small office. I remember Ben Bradlee, then with *Newsweek* before his legendary run as editor of the *Washington Post*, sat on the floor with his back to a wall and his legs stretched out in front of him. I remember Kitchel's view of voters in New England as old time Republican WASPs, taciturn and witty, sitting around the stove in a general store discussing world events. I thought: where's he been since the end of WWII? He seemed oblivious to the changing dynamics of politics in the New England states, the influx of Irish and Italians and their tendency to vote Democratic. It was as though John Kennedy had never been elected. As Ben and I walked through Farragut Square to our offices, we thought it would be tough for Goldwater to win in modern New England. In the end, Goldwater captured only five states across the south—Georgia, Alabama, Mississippi, Louisiana, and South Carolina—plus his own state of Arizona.

On the last Saturday of the campaign, we flew across country from Goldwater's home in Phoenix to a rally in Columbia, the capital of South Carolina. It was the wildest rally I ever saw. It all went out over an 87 station TV hookup across 14 southern states. The site itself was an auditorium on the University of South Carolina campus dating back to the Civil War. The building, not overly large, seemed to shake from the noise and foot stomping as Goldwater entered. The enthusiasm was unrestrained. Confederate battle flags draped the walls. A band played "Dixie" repeatedly. Goldwater banners were everywhere. The press contingent was greeted with boos and fist-shaking anger. We were not among friends and admirers.

A few days earlier, an event took place which can only be judged through the lens of history. It was a nationwide television address by Ronald Reagan on behalf of Goldwater. Reagan was co-chairman of the Goldwater campaign in California, but he was known best as a movie actor with a fading career who barnstormed the country making anti-big government talks for General Electric Company. In the days preceding the speech, I followed heated debates among Goldwater and his top aides as to whether or not it was a good idea to be associated with the Reagan speech. Some advisers were adamantly against endorsing it but finally Goldwater gave his approval.

Reagan's talk catapulted him onto the national political scene. It raised eight million dollars for Goldwater and gave his campaign a boost. It changed Reagan's life, and set him on a course to become president. I remember Lyn Nofziger, then a political correspondent for Copley newspapers, plopping down on the empty seat next to me when we boarded Goldwater's campaign plane the next day. He was excited and starry-eyed.

"If Reagan ever enters politics, he'll win every office he runs for," Lyn remarked.

Two years later, Reagan became governor of California. Lyn was his press secretary.

Many today refer to Reagan's address as "The Speech." It is known more widely by the title "A Time for Choosing," which is epitomized in the following lines: "You and I are told that we must choose between right and left. Well, I suggest there is no such thing as right and left. There is only up and down—up is man's age old dream, the ultimate in individual freedom consistent with law and order—or down to the ant heap of totalitarianism."

Reagan states in an autobiography that the speech changed his life. He said that after a fundraising talk days earlier at the Coconut Grove restaurant in Los Angeles, he was approached by a group of prominent California Republicans who asked him if he would give the speech on national TV if they raised the money for it. He agreed and suggested it be made before a studio audience. The speech brought hope for Republicans looking beyond Goldwater, and for a few days overshadowed the candidate himself.

On the Monday before Tuesday's Election Day, Goldwater flew to San Francisco for a rally and parade. As his motorcade wove slowly through the city's financial district, Goldwater atop the back seat of a convertible, confetti and balloons by the bushel tumbled out from the windows of skyscrapers along the route. I was in the press pool car behind him with the wire services. I would stay as the pool reporter until Goldwater's return to Phoenix that night.

From San Francisco we flew to Las Vegas. At the airport, the candidate, Paul Wagner, his press secretary, and I climbed into a small, single engine aircraft for a flight to a windswept mesa in Northern Arizona. We landed at a barren community called Fredonia. Goldwater had always ended his campaigns there. It was an intimate crowd, perhaps 50 people, mostly Native Americans, friends he considered good luck. It was dusk as our little plane set down. A cold, sharp wind blew so strong it seemed to carry Goldwater's words away as he uttered them. A telephone line had been set up with press headquarters in Phoenix for me to describe the event to my colleagues, who had flown onto Phoenix from Las Vegas. I assumed the role of a broadcaster on the spot describing events. But, it was to no avail, though I didn't know it then. The connection broke down and my words were heard only by the wind.

I typed up a pool report when we reached Phoenix but it was near 9:00 p.m. Pacific time and deadlines had passed for most media outlets in the East and Midwest. A farewell party for the press covering Goldwater was well underway in the Camelback Inn, where we were staying. Its hosts were the candidate and his wife, Peggy. No one was in the mood to file any more copy. Goldwater thanked us for our work. He said he had gotten to know many of us personally and enjoyed our company, if not our stories. That was the last we saw of him until we returned to Washington a few days later.

His staff in Phoenix expanded as the election neared, many coming from Washington. They were defiant despite the polls and were certain Goldwater would win. I knew that was wishful thinking and the returns came in as predicted—a landslide for LBJ. My colleagues and I waited for a concession speech or statement from Goldwater, but neither was forthcoming. I was told he was at his home in Scottsdale, and not in the best of condition. He did send LBJ a congratulatory telegram a day later. Goldwater's loss was by the second biggest margin in history at the time. He received only 38.5% of the votes cast. Only Alf Landon, the GOP candidate in 1936, suffered a worse shellacking with 36.5% in his defeat by FDR. George McGovern took over dubious second place honors from Goldwater when he received only 37.5% of the popular vote in his 1972 drubbing by Nixon. Goldwater's defeat was so overwhelming that he lost all influence in Republican affairs. Republicans returned to their more traditional positions, a little to the right of center and often their path to victory.

A day or two after the election, Earl Eisenhower, Ike's nephew and a Goldwater aide, took some campaign documents to Goldwater's home and he asked me to come along. I was in hopes of interviewing the defeated candidate. I waited by the swimming pool adjoining the

**I stand under an American flag at half mast at Goldwater's home
after LBJ defeated him in the 1964 presidential election**

house for a half hour before Earl returned and told me that there would
be no interview. I saw no one else the entire time. There was silence
all around. I noticed the American flag flying at half-mast on a pole
near the pool. I had Earl snap a photo of me standing under the flag.
The flag's position, a signal of mourning, is my lasting memory of the
Goldwater campaign.

CHAPTER TWENTY-SIX

ON THE BOARDWALK
BY THE SEA

Meanwhile, the Democrats were sure they had a winning ticket in 1964. Their national nominating convention took place in late August in Atlantic City. To my amazement, Goldwater took a three week vacation after becoming his party's presidential nominee. So, at the Democrat's gathering, I covered Hubert Humphrey, who was LBJ's choice to be his vice presidential running mate. Humphrey and Goldwater were as different as night and day. Humphrey was outgoing and gregarious and more approachable than Goldwater.

Humphrey had a long history in politics. He had sought his party's presidential nomination in 1960 when he ran in primaries against Kennedy. After his defeat, he returned to the Senate, representing Minnesota. He'd begun his political career as mayor of Minneapolis.

When Trohan sent me to Atlantic City earlier in the summer to arrange our facilities to cover the convention, I found a dilapidated, run-down seaside resort long past its heyday as a playground for the Eastern rich. The city was ill-equipped for a political convention. I found hotels with no telephones in the rooms, making communications difficult since there were no iPhones in those now ancient days. Dry cleaning and laundry facilities were limited and there were only a couple of first class restaurants, although I found plenty of salt water taffy for sale along the old boardwalk.

I wrote a story about the unfavorable conditions that brought the wrath of Atlantic City's mayor in a letter the Tribune ran in its "Letters to the Editor" column. This was all mothers' milk to a renowned convention city like Chicago. Still four years away was the 1968

Democratic convention in Chicago which sullied the city forever with the anti-Vietnam war riots and police brutality that took place along with the hateful atmosphere of the convention itself.

An attempt to revitalize itself with gambling casinos came years later in Atlantic City with mixed results.

Hotel rooms became my big problem. We were given a suite in the headquarters hotel for the top editor who came (Maxwell never went to Democratic conventions) and a room there for Trohan, but the rest of us were housed in a fourth-rate hotel that had all the earmarks of a tenement. I took one look at the rooms and went to Sam Brightman, who handled press arrangements for the Democratic National Committee.

"Sam, for God's sake, you've got us in flop house," I stormed. "Have you been over to look at that place?"

"You're the least of my worries, Russ," he responded. "Air conditioning! Air conditioning! That's my problem. So many rooms along the beach have no air conditioning. Who am I going to put in those?"

"Well, our rooms aren't air conditioned either," I told him. "Sam, the only light in our rooms is a bulb hanging from the ceiling. The building's a fire trap." I paused. We both were silent. He doodled on a note pad. "The old school tie, Sam, how about it?"

He laughed then. We relaxed. Both Sam and I had gone to Washington University in St. Louis. I knew the Tribune got poor pickings at Democratic conventions and good rooms at Republican conventions, since the Tribune traditionally supported Republican candidates. I didn't expect the bridal suite. But I had hoped for something better than the rooms I'd just seen.

"There are some motels in Ocean City," Brightman said. "It's 20 minutes away. Maybe, you should look over there. But, I give you warning. The road over there has a drawbridge about half way. It holds up traffic sometimes."

"We get up early. We go to bed late. It'll be two trips a day. There'll be no back and forth," I told him. "I'll risk the draw bridge."

When I called Trohan to discuss the matter, he agreed that I should concentrate on Ocean City. It was a picturesque little seaside town and it would be easy to travel back and forth to Atlantic City even with the drawbridge. But, first I had to deal with the proprietor of the motel I chose. He didn't come easy. Initially, he was perplexed that I wanted only one staffer per room.

"I can get up to six people in one room," he told me as we stood in his office. "Why should I rent them as singles to you."

I knew multiple occupancy was standard practice in Atlantic Ocean resort areas along the crowded east coast. I had seen it on Cape Cod when I traveled to Hyannis Port covering Kennedy. People out from Boston for a weekend would pile into rooms, four or five at time, and split the cost. So, I bargained with him.

"Look, I'll make up the difference if you're going to lose money with only one person in a room," I told him. "If you want to charge me your take for six people, I'll pay it. A couple of us will be here for a week. The others will be here Sunday night through Thursday, seven of us in all. The rooms will be empty again for the next weekend. How can you lose?"

"How do I know you'll pay me?" he shot back.

I was stunned. I didn't think I looked or talked like a con man. A bit exasperated I explained to him that the Chicago Tribune was one of the largest and most profitable newspaper corporations in the world. I said the Tribune always paid its bills. But, it was clear that corporations and journalists were not part of the world in which he dwelled. He dealt with groups in for a tan and splashing in a salt water ocean. The Jersey shore was his world and he couldn't think beyond that.

"I'll write you a check right now for half of the cost of the rooms," I said. "Cash the check to make sure it's good. I'll pay the rest when we get here."

He accepted my offer and I handed him a signed check on the Washington bureau's bank. He blocked out seven rooms for the dates we wanted and he gave me a confirmation receipt. At last, he was satisfied and so was I. The arrangement worked out well for us. The drawbridge was never a problem on our twice daily trips. We had air conditioned rooms to sleep in and a nearby café for uncrowded breakfasts.

President Kennedy before his assassination had picked Atlantic City to give delegates and their families a seaside vacation since he would be renominated in a cut-and-dried, uncontested event. That still held true for President Johnson in a way but LBJ had a problem. Bobby Kennedy lurked in the shadows. Bobby had made no effort to take the nomination away from LBJ but great emotion swirled around him. Everyone looked forward to his speech at the convention. The issue for Johnson was how to protect himself from this sentimental fallout;

how to prevent an emotional stampede on the convention floor to give another Kennedy the nomination.

LBJ's solution was to have the vote for his nomination before Kennedy spoke. Doing it that way made it impossible for a contest with Bobby to swell up on the meeting floor. Johnson was nominated. When Kennedy reached the podium on the last night, however, there was no doubt to whom the hearts of the delegates belonged. Bobby received long and loving ovations before and during his speech introducing a memorial film in tribute to his fallen brother. He brought many delegates to tears. Especially when he quoted lines from Shakespeare's *Romeo and Juliet:*

"When he shall die, take him and cut him out in little stars, and he shall make the face of heaven so fond, that the world will fall in love with night and pay no worship to the garish sun."

It was thrilling to watch. With his last words, Bobby endorsed Johnson and Humphrey and he asked the delegates to go forth in unison for the ticket.

During the convention, the Tribune's Washington offices were moved to 1750 Pennsylvania Avenue, a brand new high-rise, set back from the street with a plaza dominated by a fountain. It was stylish. We were a block west of the White House. We had familiar fellow tenants. Columnists Art Buchwald and Robert Novak were on the floor above us along with *Newsweek,* and Newhouse papers was on the floor below. A few weeks later the old Albee building, the bureau's home for decades, was demolished.

CHAPTER TWENTY-SEVEN

WINDS OF CHANGE

Our bedside telephone rang a little after seven o'clock on a Sunday morning in the late spring of 1967. Sally, half awake, muttered in wonderment over who the early caller could be. When I answered, a man asked if this was the home of Russell Freeburg of the Chicago Tribune. I said it was.

"Russ, this is Kirk."

I was somewhat surprised. The voice belonged to Clayton Kirkpatrick, the Tribune's managing editor. Continuing to talk, he explained that he and his wife, Thelma, were at Washington's National Airport to return to Chicago.

"I'm sure you saw me in the bureau this past week meeting with Trohan," he said. "I want you to call Willard later this morning and meet him for lunch. He's expecting to hear from you. He knows what's been going on, and he'll explain things to you."

Our conversation was brief. I told him that I would do as he said. He replied fine and hung up. The fellow he told me to see was Willard Edwards, the assistant bureau chief, who covered the Senate and headed up our reporters on Capitol Hill. Just what was he going explain?

I had some inkling about the reason for Kirk's visit. Late Friday, Trohan had called me into his office. Standing behind his desk, indicating the conversation would be short, he said he and Kirk had discussed the future of the bureau and that he'd recommended that Bob Young, who'd joined the bureau from Chicago in WWII, become bureau chief when he retired.

I asked Trohan if Kirk had said anything about my future. He must have realized at that moment that Kirk hadn't discussed his visit with me.

"Absolutely nothing," he replied, "he never mentioned your name."

My heart sank. His words became embedded in my brain. I had no quarrel with Young becoming bureau chief. He was senior to me. I'd never given thought to becoming bureau chief. But, I felt left out by Trohan's words. Sally and I discussed the matter over dinner that night and we wondered if it might be time for me to move on. I had an offer from *Time* magazine to join its Washington bureau. For us, it had been a long soul searching weekend when it was interrupted by Kirk's call.

Sally was wide awake now, sitting upright in bed. "Who was that?" I repeated the content of the call. "Do you think Walter lied to you?" she asked. There was a thoughtful pause. "Bob Young's not far away from retirement himself. Why make him bureau chief?" She snuggled up to me. "You'd be better."

We decided at breakfast to let events unfold further. Once again, we mulled over Trohan's comment that Kirk had said absolutely nothing about me in their talks. Shortly after I arrived in Washington, I'd received a warm letter from Kirk. He was an assistant city editor at the time.

Jan. 7, 1959

Dear Russ,

I was sorry that I did not say good-by and wish you well when you left. It was a pleasure to have you on the staff, and I hated to see you leave, although it's always good to see better opportunities come to the deserving. I saw a copy of a letter sent back on your progress so far. It clearly indicated you are making a good impression in your new Job. If there is anything we can do for your family while you are separated, don't hesitate to yell.

Good luck,
Kirk

Kirk had also commended me on the arrangements I made for the Tribune's coverage of the 1964 Democratic Party convention in Atlantic

City. I enjoyed working with him, and I thought he enjoyed working with me. Considering my interactions with Kirk in the past, Trohan's action and words were perplexing.

I contacted Edwards in midmorning to arrange our meeting. Shortly after noon, we walked from his home to a nearby restaurant. Willard and his wife, Leila, lived in a neighborhood of beautifully restored homes a few blocks from Capitol Hill. Like the Georgetown section of Washington a quarter of a century earlier, the area had been run-down and decaying. Now, once again, it was quiet and affluent. Willard could easily walk to work but he drove instead since the Tribune furnished him with a car just like they did for Trohan. Willard and the other fellows who worked on the hill would sometimes pile into his car and come down to the bureau late in the day. Trohan would be gone by then and a good time was had by all.

Trohan's usual working hours were nine to one, including Saturday and Sunday. He begged off longer hours saying he often entertained with dinner parties in his home. His office routine was to take the early wire copy of a developing story, type a lead paragraph or two of his own, then paste on the United Press version since the Tribune in Chicago did not subscribe to United Press and the bureau did. After he left for the day, it was up to the rest of us to update his story as needed. That's not to say he wasn't an outstanding reporter, especially in his younger days. But eventually, everyone loses his edge.

Once seated for lunch, Willard looked at me with a smile. "Well," he said, "you're going to be the next bureau chief." I was both surprised and relieved. But, Trohan's deceit befuddled me. I asked Edwards when this was going to happen and I filled him in on Trohan's comment on Friday night. He snorted and said Trohan was putting up a fight. He said the timing hadn't been decided.

"What about Trohan?" I asked.

"He's going to continue as a columnist," Edwards replied.

I had qualms about the uncertainty of the changeover. Little did I know then how justified they were. I was mystified that Kirk had not talked to me but one constant I'd noticed in Kirk over the years was his frequent use of middle men in his management style. I was puzzled over Trohan's about-face concerning me. He had mentored me from the beginning. He had introduced me to important people. He had asked his old friends among Western Union telegraphers to take good care of my copy on White House trips. He had asked White House Secret Service agents to look after me if need be. Still, there was an indirectness swirling about now that seemed to bode ill. I knew Trohan's reputation as a curmudgeon. I was appalled when he tried to keep my friend Carl Rowan, a renowned African-American journalist, from becoming a fellow member with him in the prestigious Gridiron Club because of his race.

I asked Willard if he knew why Kirk was taking such a roundabout way to let me know what was going on. He said Trohan's back had gone up like a cornered cat when Kirk defined his mission. From then on it had been a struggle, not over me, but Trohan's future. Trohan thought he had a right to determine when he would retire and how the bureau should be run until then. He didn't want to be only a columnist.

As we ate, Edwards began to reminisce. He said Trohan held a marker against Don Maxwell, the Tribune editor, going back to the 1948 Republican convention in Philadelphia. Colonel McCormick had assigned Maxwell, city editor then, to stay close to Illinois Gov. Dwight Green, fearing Green, a convention delegate like the colonel, would bolt from supporting Robert Taft to backing Thomas Dewey, who wasn't a McCormick favorite. Maxwell lost contact with Green, who met with Dewey and switched from Taft. In his anger, McCormick fired Maxwell, who pleaded with Trohan for an intervention. Willard said Trohan talked the colonel into rehiring Maxwell, and that Trohan reminds Maxwell, when he needs to, of the debt he feels Maxwell forever owes him.

What was now underway, however, was a monumental shift in the generational leadership of the paper. Maxwell, J. Howard Wood, the publisher, Trohan, Edwards, and several lesser editors in Chicago, as well as some members of the Washington bureau, were nearing retirement. The paper was putting younger people in place to succeed them in preparation for a smooth transition. Within a year, Kirk would become executive editor with Maxwell giving him ever more responsibilities.

There'd been only two Tribune bureau chiefs in Washington in more than half a century. Arthur Sears Henning held the position for 35 years beginning in 1914. Trohan had followed him beginning in 1949 at the age of 46 and held the title for 20 years. Willard said Trohan was not the first choice to succeed Henning, however. That role fell to Chesley Manley. Trohan was moved to New York City from Washington to cover the United Nations, replacing Manley there.

Luck was not Manley's ally, however. Before the official announcement was made he ran afoul of Colonel McCormick's wife, Maryland. In the excitement of meeting a train carrying the McCormicks into Washington's Union Station, he neglected to pick up and carry Mrs. McCormick's overnight case. She told the colonel that Manley simply wouldn't do, that he lacked the social grace necessary to be bureau chief. Manley and Trohan once again switched places.

After my Sunday meeting with Edwards, I went into the bureau Monday morning as usual. Trohan didn't say a word to me about Kirk's visit nor I to him. It was as though nothing had happened. On Wednesday, however, Trohan came to my desk.

"I've learned you know the details of my talks with Kirk," He said brusquely.

"You lied to me, Walter," I responded, as I rose from my desk chair.

Trohan turned and walked away. There was no apology. Living one's life is easier than writing about it later. As you write you essentially live it again but still without the ability to correct mistakes. As Trohan moved away, I thought belatedly that I should have let the lie alone. He, after all, remained my boss.

Several weeks later, other bureau members and I received invitations from Maxwell to a reception and dinner at the swanky Georgetown Inn. When we assembled, both Maxwell and Wood were there from Chicago. Kirk was not. After a round of drinks at a private bar, we retired to a banquet room. After dessert, as coffee was served, Maxwell made remarks praising Trohan's Tribune career, then, turning to Trohan he said Trohan would say a few words about the bureau's future. I was in the dark but I thought that maybe the changeover had been worked out.

Trohan rose to stand in silence for a few moments before saying, "Let's all have an after dinner drink." He then walked out of the room. Maxwell jumped up and went after him. When they didn't return, Wood suggested we all return to the private bar. Well, that's that, I thought, and after a quick drink I went to Maxwell and Wood, who were huddled at the bar talking, to say good night.

"Don't leave," Maxwell told me. He took me aside. "It's been decided that Trohan will keep the title of bureau chief and keep writing his column, while you'll take over managing the bureau as its executive director."

He glanced across the room at Trohan, saying that the dinner had been arranged solely for Trohan to make the announcement himself.

He looked at me again. "What do you want me to do?"

"If we're going ahead with the change, I'd like a date certain when the turnover will take place," I replied. "That's the only way to end this."

Maxwell called Trohan over. "I've explained the new arrangements to Russ. He would like a date set for the transfer." Trohan said nothing. Maxwell turned to me. "Pick a date."

"June 15th," I said.

Turning back to Trohan, Maxwell said, "This is the way I want it to be."

There was no acknowledgement from Trohan. He stood mute staring into the room. So, we marched ahead with me wondering if possibly sometime soon we could all be enveloped in some saving grace.

CHAPTER TWENTY-EIGHT

STILL MORE COMPLICATIONS

A s June 15 approached, a letter from Maxwell to Trohan appeared on the bureau bulletin board. Its first instruction was that it be posted. It detailed the changeover, but added that no public announcement would be made. I called Kirk to complain that it might be difficult to run the bureau if no one in Washington knew that I was in charge. He said Chicago would make sure that word got around.

"Do you want to go ahead?" he asked.

"Will I have a future at the Tribune if I don't?" I replied.

"Probably not," he said.

I asked why Trohan was so pampered. I told him I thought Trohan's actions were bizarre, perhaps neurotic, but I was never told why Trohan's unsavory behavior was accepted. I remarked that everyone is expendable. Kirk said that the present Tribune management had been together for many years and it was an emotional time for them as they turned the paper over to a new generation. I pointed out that the others seemed to be taking it in stride.

"I want you to do this," Kirk said.

It's true about the longevity. Maxwell had joined the Tribune in 1920, three years before I was born and a couple of months short of completing his senior year at the University of Chicago. Indiana born and bred, he was a Hoosier at heart. He had attended DePauw University in Greencastle, Indiana, for three years before transferring to the University of Chicago. Maxwell was so against government subsidies that he resigned as a trustee of DePauw when the school accepted a federal grant.

At the Tribune, Maxwell was mainly an inside man. As sports editor he was among the first to seriously cover a fledgling professional National Football League. He'd had street experience as a fuzzy-cheeked cub reporter with the Cleveland Press, however, where the city editor one day sent him to the home of a murder victim. He told the story of stepping up to the police chief on the front porch.

"Chief, man-to-man, what's the inside story here?"

"Man to boy," replied the chief. "I ain't going to tell you."

Both J. Howard Wood, like me a product of the Illinois prairie, and Willard Edwards joined the Tribune in 1925, the same year the paper's iconic Tribune Tower was completed on Michigan Avenue at the Chicago River. Here it anchored, with the uniquely white tiled Wrigley Building across from it, the south end of the "magnificent mile" of exclusive shops and hotels. Both are landmarks that epitomize Chicago to the world.

Trohan came aboard in 1929. All four cut their journalistic teeth during Chicago's gangster plagued Prohibition era. Now December 31, 1968 had been set as the date for them to retire together.

Wood, as a young reporter, became involved in a case about a policeman with a broken leg. Through his own investigation he stopped murder charges being brought against the officer. Although his leg was in a cast from a motorcycle accident, prosecutors were convinced the cop had murdered a school teacher, whose body was found burned as crisp as bacon in the furnace of her house. Wood wasn't convinced that a man with a broken leg had the physical strength to carry out the murder. He read the teacher's letters, personal papers, and books in her residence. He found she had underlined a portion of a book which mentioned purification by fire. She had made marginal notes hailing fire as the only way to cleanse the soul. Prosecutors concluded she'd immolated herself and the police officer with the broken leg went free. Later, Wood worked in the financial news department, where he became financial editor. He wrote a booklet *Inflation and Your Money*. He went over to the corporate side in 1942 to become auditor and controller of the Tribune. He became publisher in 1960. He was a graduate of Lake Forest College, and he attended Harvard for graduate studies.

Before Willard Edwards was transferred to Washington in 1933 he, too, covered the police beat. That meant coming into contact with gangsters of the Prohibition era. Edwards recounted in an interview for the

Truman Presidential Library that it was necessary in those days to have a bootlegger friend to gain inside information on gangland activities. He said he had befriended Dingbat Oberta. He described Dingbat as a jolly companion from whom he got information on occasion. "Then I awakened to the fact that he was not such a good companion after all," Edwards said. The epiphany came on a double date as couples danced in the backroom of an illegal saloon on the south side of Chicago. Dingbat was dancing with a girl in a dress with a bare shoulder. As Edwards watched, Dingbat pressed a lighted cigarette into her exposed skin. The girl screamed, Dingbat put back his head and laughed. He thought it was all very funny. Edwards concluded: "These are a different breed of men." Dingbat was found dead about a year later in a ditch, his body full of gunshot holes.

Even I, years after the end of Prohibition, had a gangster moment of sorts. One Saturday, when I worked in the city room, we received a report that the Capone gang was in negotiations to buy the Fox Head 400 brewery in Waukesha, Wisconsin. I called the home of Ralph "Bottles" Capone, Al's surviving older brother. During Prohibition, "Bottles" ran the legitimate soft drink operations of the gang, hence his nickname. Ralph's wife, Madeline, answered. She told me Ralph was out. She said she didn't know where, she never did, and she was stuck scrubbing the kitchen floor on a pleasant weekend afternoon. We discussed the downside of domesticity for a while. Ralph never called back, but rumors persisted that the mob held controlling interest for a time in the now defunct brewing company.

Edwards started at the Tribune after he was graduated from St. Ignatius Academy, a Jesuit institution in Chicago. He turned down a scholarship to Loyola University in the city to take the job. He covered both Truman and Lyndon Johnson on Capitol Hill and he traveled some with both men after they became president. An accomplished feature writer, he was sent to Flemington, New Jersey in late 1934 to cover the trial of Richard Bruno Hauptmann for the kidnapping and death of Charles A. Lindbergh Jr., the baby son of the famed aviator. The trial was held January 2 to February 15, 1935. Hauptmann was found guilty and sentenced to death. After the trial, Edwards returned to the Washington bureau. He told me that celebrities in search of publicity often came down from New York City to visit the trial for a day. One day his favorite movie actress showed up. To his disappointment, she was unkempt with several rings of dirt around her neck. He wouldn't tell me her name.

Trohan, a University of Notre Dame graduate, arrived in Washington in 1934. He told me he'd been brought to Washington at the request of John Boettiger, the bureau's assistant chief. Boettiger left the paper in December, 1934 to marry FDR's daughter, Anna. The couple had fallen in love when Boettiger covered Roosevelt's first presidential campaign in 1932. Boettiger and Trohan had covered politics together in Chicago, where Trohan had grown up on the city's south side. Trohan joined the Tribune shortly after the St. Valentine's Day Massacre. He was in the newsroom of the City News Bureau of Chicago at Clark and Randolph Streets in the loop when a police call came in of a shooting in the garage of the SMC Cartage Company at 2122 North Clark Street. He hopped on a street car to the scene and was the first reporter to arrive although every old-time police reporter in Chicago eventually made the same claim. Seven men in the George "Bugs" Moran gang had been lined up against a wall in the garage and shot by henchmen of Al Capone in a territorial war. It was the most notorious gangland slaying of the Prohibition era. But, by the time he reached Washington he was a seasoned political reporter.

Of the four men, only Trohan seemed unwilling to acknowledge the passage of time. The four had worked directly with McCormick in his fight against FDR's New Deal. But the colonel had been dead now for more than a decade. There had been little change in the paper. And, there's the rub. The paper remained highly profitable; Christmas bonuses to the staff were as big as ever. Wood had bought additional papers and TV stations. Purchases included the *Orlando Sentinel*, *Ft. Lauderdale News* and *Pompano Sun* in fast-growing Florida. Maxwell led the drive to build McCormick Place. Still, there was a specter of stagnation in the flagship Tribune. Although it remained one of the largest and influential of the nation's papers, its inner working seemed stuck in times past. Since the transition was going smoothly in Chicago, Trohan's behavior was disquieting. He'd told me, after I'd been in Washington nine months, that I had learned the ways of the capital quickly. He said that he first thought it would take me two years to come up to speed. There is no question that he pushed me along.

I assumed control of bureau operations on June 15, 1967 as executive director. I took over Trohan's desk in the newsroom, and his private office became his working place as a columnist. Helen Young continued as office manager and Trohan's private secretary. I went right on with the long tradition of a bureau head covering stories of his choosing. Lee Forrester, two years from retirement, remained as the bureau copy editor, assignment scheduler and daily coordinator with the telegraph desk in Chicago.

CHAPTER TWENTY-NINE

BREAKFAST AT EIGHT: *MEET THE PRESS* ON SUNDAYS

I t meant that I had to get up early. But it was worth it. I'm referring to the breakfast club of newspaper bureau chiefs and political reporters formed by Godfrey "Budge" Sperling, Washington bureau chief of the *Christian Science Monitor*. Budge asked me to be an original member of the group. There were a dozen of us in the beginning. We met in a conference room of the National Press Club at eight o'clock in the morning. Over orange juice, coffee, toast, scrambled eggs and sausage, we interviewed political leaders of the era.

For them, the sessions turned into more talking than eating. The only guest I can remember finishing his breakfast was Vice President Humphrey, who had little trouble eating and talking at the same time. The others, more or less, just poked at their food in competition with the Q and A. Bobby Kennedy agonized over whether to seek the 1968 Democratic presidential nomination at one breakfast. George Wallace brought along two bodyguards who sat behind him during the interview. Spiro Agnew caused a rumpus when he told the group that Humphrey was soft on communism.

We lunched with Ronald Reagan when he came to Washington on state business while governor of California. Budge sat me next to Reagan in the private dining room of the Madison Hotel we had rented for the occasion. Reagan and I had both grown up in the Midwest. I told the governor that we were probably the only two in the room who had gone to Silas Willard grammar school in Galesburg, where the Reagan family resided for a time. He preceded me in school by a decade. I related that my paternal grandfather in 1904 had built the house in which he lived and that my Dad, at 10 years old, helped with construction by hauling building and roofing materials to the carpenters. The future president reminisced about school life and how he walked the two blocks from the house to class every day along Fremont Street. He told me that Nancy's step-grandparents, now deceased, had lived in Galesburg. I was aware of that, since I had childhood friends who'd played with her. Reagan said we would talk to her after lunch.

Reagan and I talked some baseball. I told him I sometimes listened to him broadcast Chicago Cubs games over WOC radio transmitting from Des Moines and Davenport in Iowa before he became a movie actor. At WOC he would recreate the games from a ticker tape out of Wrigley Field in Chicago. It was on a trip to California to cover a Cubs spring training camp that he took a screen test. Then, with lunch finished, the whole group got into the Q and A session, where politics and his future were discussed.

When I met Nancy Reagan, she recalled summers in Galesburg as a little girl with her step-grandparents, Albert and Laura Davis, over on Mulberry Street. In 1929, Nancy's mother, Edith Luckett, a stage actress, had married Dr. Loyal Davis, the noted Chicago neurosurgeon. Both were divorced. They met earlier that year on a voyage to England. Nancy was eight years old. Dr. Davis, who adopted Nancy when she was 14, was born (1896) and reared in Galesburg, where his father was an engineer on the Burlington railroad for 33 years. During World War I, Albert Davis piloted an engine that ran ahead of a troop train en route to Chicago. West of Chicago, he encountered saboteurs who had stretched a chain across the track at a Fox River bridge. He broke the chain with his engine and slowly crossed the bridge without incident.*

Both Loyal Davis and Nancy were staunch Republicans and each played a part in Reagan's conversion from liberal Democrat to the GOP. Reagan claimed the Democratic Party had left him and not the other way around. He cast his first Republican ballot in 1952 for Eisenhower and Nixon.

Bobby Kennedy's agonizing over a presidential run, so on display at the Sperling breakfast, ended in March, 1968, when he declared his candidacy. I immediately asked Maxwell by teletype about coverage saying that "Bobby will have a press plane operating out of Washington for his campaign. The first trip is tomorrow (March 20th), when he makes a rather interesting swing into George Wallace country in Alabama and

---

*David G. Stuart, Find a Grave *website member*

then on to Tennessee, where the Demo kingpin is Gov. Buford Ellington, a confidant of LBJ. Do you want us to cover?"

Maxwell's reply was direct: "Coverage of Kennedy not deemed necessary."

I was disappointed. I thought Maxwell's attitude, once again, showed a disconnection with a changing world. He seemed unable to put aside partisan or ideological considerations, even for one of the big stories of the day. A paper of the Tribune's size, prestige, resources, and geographical importance surely should have covered a campaign of historical significance.

A year or so after I became executive director, Larry Spivak, moderator of *Meet the Press*, asked me to be a panelist on the TV program. But after two appearances, Kirk told me not to go on again. He said Walter had objected to Maxwell over my presence.

It's an unhealthy development when a retiring bureau chief tries to discredit his successor. It damages the soul. Once appointed executive director, I wanted to run bureau operations my way. I certainly knew Trohan's shortcomings. There were things I thought needed to be done better.

I never tried to embarrass Trohan publicly, although I knew that I had a public relations project to remake the bureau's image as a more active participant in the everyday political and social life of the capital. There were a lot of cobwebs that had to be swept away. When a fellow has a job to do he should be allowed do it in his own way. That was my belief. I told Kirk that I didn't think I was appointed to maintain the status quo. I was surprised at Chicago's edict and disappointed.

The *Meet the Press* imbroglio highlighted differences between Trohan and me on the use of TV to promote the paper and bureau members. I knew that being seen on TV increased a journalist's prestige among politicians. The same applied to the paper's name being seen and heard. Trohan argued that programs like *Meet the Press* should be boycotted by print journalists. He claimed that we were being used to help TV grow. Of course, that battle had been over long ago. The intermingling of print journalists and TV programs was an established practice by the time I was executive director of the bureau. It certainly had become a matter of "if you can't beat them, join them." I remained unhappy with Chicago's decision and I continued to argue my case but the ban stood. Although the move was shortsighted, it helped me gain insight into the insular nature of the management in Chicago. I already knew Trohan's irascible intransigency. I began to suspect that he also suffered isolation from reality.

I'm a panelist on *Meet The Press* in 1970 (third from left)

Meanwhile, I received an invitation to the annual dinner of the Chowder and Marching Society. The society had been founded by Nixon after he arrived in Congress in 1946. He got together a dozen or so young backbench Republican lawmakers like himself in hopes they, as a group, could carry some weight in a House chamber where old-timers pulled the strings of power. Close friendships developed among the newcomers. In time, the society included Gerald Ford and George H. W. Bush as they became members of Congress. Add Nixon to their names, and three presidents were members of the society.

Sally and I were invited to the annual apple festival picnic that Sen. Harry Byrd, Jr. of Virginia threw annually on a Sunday afternoon at his home in the Shenandoah Valley during the harvest. We sat next to Arthur Krock, the legendary *New York Times* newsman, during the picnic lunch. I felt that we were stepping in high cotton. He inquired how I was getting along with Trohan, whom he had known for years. Krock laughed hardily at some of my replies. Of course, Trohan, was somewhat of a legend himself. He was also among the last of the big metropolitan newspaper bureau chiefs whose byline made them famous in the days before television when newspapers were the media kings.

I enjoyed appearing on *Meet the Press,* but it required homework. The format in my day was to have four panelists plus Spivak ask questions of the guest. That meant a panelist got to ask two, maybe three questions at most, as each panelist asked a question in turn. Since the program was on NBC, the lead panelist was an NBC reporter. I was told by colleagues to have at least 20 to 25 questions ready in advance of air time. How right they were. It is amazing how many subjects a guest eliminates in his responses.

Sandy Vanocur was the NBC reporter the second time I appeared. The guest was Larry O'Brien, longtime aide to President Kennedy and chairman of the Democratic National Committee. I was in the second seat next to Sandy. After my third question, I relaxed thinking it was my last one for the day. But, the next two questions were answered quickly and Spivak called on Sandy again. He startled everyone by replying he had nothing more to ask. I gulped. No one does that! I hoped Spivak would ask a question himself. Fortunately, I came up with a question when Spivak moved on to me. Part of O'Brien's answer even became controversial when he implied the Republican Party supported apartheid.

Trohan and I had little contact after I began running the bureau. He stayed in his office to write his column, answer his mail, and to prepare for his weekly radio broadcast on WGN, the Tribune's station in Chicago. His office was just a few square feet short of the bureau's entire newsroom. I asked Willard Edwards once why Trohan had such a large office. He said it was to match the size of the editor's office in Tribune Tower in Chicago. When I became bureau chief, I turned half of his office into a conference room to use for interviews of VIPs by bureau members. I turned the other half into two smaller offices — mine and one for Jean McGuinness, the new office manager/secretary, whom I hired a month before I became bureau chief to succeed Helen Young, who retired when Trohan did.

Jeannie was one of those persons people think about when they refer to someone as being born outside the mold. She was unique and pleasantly Irish through and through. She often referred to me as "himself." Jeannie had worked for several lobbyists after coming to Washington from Quincy, Massachusetts and she knew the capital and its ways. She also knew many of the town's politicians and their aides. Jeannie was a story by herself. Everyone liked her. She fit right in with the new face I wanted to put on the bureau.

CHAPTER THIRTY

LBJ'S DOWNFALL

L yndon Johnson was majority leader of the Senate when I came to Washington. Once I'd received my passes to the Senate and House press galleries I spent several of my days off familiarizing myself with Capitol Hill. Johnson was on the floor on my initial visit to the press seats above the Senate chamber. I'd never seen him before. Until he became president, I had no direct contact with him. I was struck by his tall physique as he stood moving some routine Senate business along. So, this is the man who knocks heads together and gets things done, I mused as I studied him. It has baffled me for decades how this astute man, who could move political mountains, became embroiled in war in Vietnam.

I thought in those days that the United States Congress was the greatest deliberative body in the world, not the dysfunctional disgrace it became decades later. In mid-century, members of Congress did not have the travel allowances they had later. Democrats and Republicans stayed in the capital, socialized, and became friends. Intimate dinner parties marked their calendars. No one felt obligated to rush home to their states and congressional districts every weekend to politic and raise money for the next election. That treadmill of endless money raising and vote getting hadn't been built yet.

With his presidential election victory in 1964 I concluded that Johnson had become the master of his own fate. He had his own administration; he was no longer caretaker of the last year of Kennedy's term. Also, Bobby Kennedy was out of the way after resigning as attorney general the preceding September and being elected the new junior senator from New

York State. Besides his own landslide victory, Johnson reaped another victory. The House of Representatives that convened in January, 1965, was the most liberal since the heyday of Franklin Roosevelt's New Deal. Everything was in readiness for LBJ's Great Society.

Johnson had outlined the main themes of his Great Society—end poverty and racial injustice—the preceding May on the campus of the University of Michigan in Ann Arbor. I thought that with his powers of persuasion, and intimate knowledge of government operations he would succeed in much the same way FDR did with his New Deal. In early 1965, his voting rights bill was passed, followed by his war against poverty. The war in Vietnam, which would be his downfall, was just a speck on the horizon.

I had little to do with the Tribune's LBJ coverage in the first year or so of his new term. That began to change dramatically for me as events unfolded within the Tribune itself.

It was during the Vietnam years that I had my closest contact with Johnson. I saw his downfall first hand. By the time I became executive director of the bureau in 1967, his triumphs with desegregation and voting rights legislation were being smothered by his increased involvement in the conflict in faraway Southeast Asia. Even before his election to the White House in his own right in the fall of 1964 he expanded the American military role in Vietnam, Cambodia, and Laos. Eisenhower and Kennedy had sent several thousand military advisors to South Vietnam, as well as millions of dollars in military equipment and economic aid. Still, the South was unable to stand alone.

The Gulf of Tonkin resolution passed by Congress on August 7, 1964, gave Johnson the power he needed to widen the war. The reported attack on two American destroyers in the gulf by North Vietnam gun boats remains a murky episode. It is questionable the attack happened but the incident resulted in the first air strikes against North Vietnam. The Johnson administration decided only direct military intervention could turn the tide in favor of the South. It was a fateful conclusion that bedeviled LBJ to the end of his presidency and beyond.

Escalation in America's involvement in Vietnam was gradual through two decades following the end of WWII. During the Eisenhower Administration years in the White House the "domino effect" theory became popular. It surmised that if one nation fell to communism in the Cold War, neighboring nations would also topple. So, if anti-communist South Vietnam fell, all of Southeast Asia that had been part of French Indo-China would go communist as well in a chain reaction. The French collapse in Indo-China had been long and agonizing. By 1955, French military forces had been defeated and Vietnam was divided into North and South, and South Vietnam was in serious danger of falling to a communist-led insurgency from North Vietnam.

The domino theory certainly played a part when LBJ began heavy bombing of North Vietnam in early 1965 and introduced the first U.S. ground troops in March of that year. LBJ was a restless soul. He was interesting to cover because he was a man of many moods and facets. His determination to win the war in Southeast Asia and bring about an honorable peace never faltered. If there was one failing of the man in carrying on the war, I thought it was his deep involvement in the day-to-day fighting. He should have left the battlefield to the military. Instead, early every morning he received a summary of the fighting and casualties. As the war dragged on, it became clear that the only way out was de-escalation and compromise. This was especially true after Hanoi's Tet offensive in late January 1968 when North Vietnamese and Viet Cong forces struck with a series of coordinated attacks on more than 100 cities and villages that included the South Vietnamese capital of Saigon. Although American forces beat back the communist attack, the deep penetration achieved by the enemy was a psychological blow to American public opinion.

The latter subject arose at regular Friday afternoon get-togethers with Secretary of State Dean Rusk. There were 10 or so reporters, including me. John Scali of the Associated Press asked Rusk one Friday why U.S. intelligence had not detected the attack in advance. The question angered Rusk. He insisted American intelligence was not at fault. He pointed out that American forces had routed the enemy eventually. Rusk had held the weekly gatherings for several months and they continued on indefinitely. We sat in a semicircle around the secretary. A small table by his chair held a glass tumbler which contained a shot or two of bourbon which he sipped as the discussions went on. Rusk was reluctant to accept growing disillusion with the war. When I told him there was dissension in the military, he challenged my observation.

"Show me," he said.

I cited two examples. One was an army major whose son was a Boy Scout with my son. He openly criticized administration wartime policies in my presence. The other was a neighbor, a light colonel and West Point graduate, who had just resigned his commission over Vietnam.

I wish I had jotted down a summary of my thoughts and observations of Rusk's performances each week. But I was more interested in them as background for breaking stories. I wish I had done the same on walks around the south lawn of the White House with Johnson and other White House reporters. His physician told him he needed more exercise so we talked as we walked. Looking back, the same would be true of an informal discussion with LBJ at the ranch one birthday celebration. The president sat in a big easy chair in the ranch living room while we reporters sat on the floor around him. His present of a new pair of leather cowboy boots with the presidential seal on the outside of each boot was easy to see. He commented that he was very proud of them and that they felt great on his feet. I should have taken notes.

LBJ was never at a loss for topics. He absorbed news and current events like a blotter. He had Associated Press and United Press teletypes in the Oval Office and he watched them closely. One day he held an impromptu press conference at his desk. The then pressroom, off of the public entrance to the West Wing Lobby, was small, and there wasn't space for everybody. The United Press's telephone was in a phone booth just inside the lobby entrance door. I watched with fascination as LBJ strode through the lobby to the booth within minutes after the press conference was over. He rapped his knuckles on the folding glass door to get the attention of Al Spivak as he dictated to his office.

"You've got the wrong lead, Al." the president shouted. "Your lead is all wrong."

Obviously, he'd seen the first few paragraphs of Spivak's copy move on the United Press wire and disagreed with its emphasis. Spivak turned his head away and continued his dictation. When he finished, Spivak unfolded the booth door and spoke:

"Yes, Mr. President?"

"Never Mind," Johnson replied.

The president was calm again. He retreated across the lobby into the Roosevelt Room on his way back to the Oval Office. As a vivid follower of the news, LBJ listened to as many radio newscasts as he could and he watched the newscasts of the national television networks.

By February 1968, LBJ began having very tough days. The news was dreary. First, there was the Tet offense in Vietnam. Then he ran poorly in the New Hampshire presidential primary of the Democratic Party, the first popular test of his Vietnam policy. He worried about a possible coup within the government of South Vietnam that would have put the White House in a bad predicament. Nascent Paris peace talks had stalled. There were signs, however, that North Vietnam was slowing down its military operations and that it was ready to concentrate on bringing the fighting to an end. Americans, too, were war weary. Anti-war protesters were taking to the streets increasingly and college campuses had become sites of anti-draft demonstrations. Against this backdrop President Johnson announced on March 31, a Sunday, that he would make a television address to the nation that night. That meant that Washington bureaus were manned by skeleton staffs, if at all.

Most of the president's speech was devoted to Vietnam. He announced a lull in the bombing of the North. He named W. Averell Harriman his personal envoy who would go "anywhere, anytime" to make peace. Then came the dramatic surprise. LBJ told his fellow countrymen that he would not run for re-election. As his speech ended, he added the line, "I shall not seek, and I will not accept, the nomination of my party for another term as president."

Douglas Brinkley tells in his biography *Cronkite* how Johnson's announcement caught CBS and its legendary television news anchor flatfooted. The same was true of the other TV networks and major newspapers. This has always puzzled me. George Christian, LBJ's press secretary, told me earlier in the day that the president would have an addendum to his prepared talk. With a wink, he suggested that I be prepared. I took him seriously. I'm sure Christian gave bureau chiefs of other news organizations the same heads up. My memory is that the UP city wire also carried a note to editors that Johnson would have a few additional words to say.

I figured that there was more than a 50-50 chance Johnson would say he was not running again.

I beefed up our coverage for that possibility. In addition to Bob Young, our regular White House correspondent, I sent Bill Kling to the White House to write a feature story on what went on behind the scenes if LBJ said he wouldn't run. Young would write the main story. I had Jim Yuenger and Aldo Beckman ready back at the bureau office to get reaction from both Democratic and Republican officials. I wrote what in those days we called a news analysis.

Cronkite, meanwhile, according to Brinkley, was at home relaxing with his wife, Betsy, and missed reporting the story. Roger Mudd, a

LBJ, sitting on Air Force One in Chicago, reads about his decision
not to run in the Tribune

long-time friend, covered the speech for CBS. Brinkley quotes him as
saying the announcement left him "shocked, disbelieving and babbling."
Not so for me. I climbed into bed satisfied that I had called the shot.

Young was given a $250 bonus for what Kirk called "an extraor-
dinarily fine job." John Zornek, our teletype operator that night, was
awarded a $50 bonus for "outstanding work" on sending the stories of
the president's announcement. Kirk wrote him that "it was a very big
file and you handled it well." The four teletype operators employed by
the Tribune in Washington were certainly an integral part of the bureau.
They caught misspellings and challenged clumsy copy as they moved
it along to Chicago. I wonder how many, if any, teletype operators are
still at work in the world. If there are any, please text me their locations.

The president gave a speech in Chicago the next day. I have a White
House photo of him on Air Force One reading the bureau's coverage
as he flew back to the capital. An eight column headline on the paper
he is holding says in bold, black type **"LBJ: Won't Run."** The photo
was by Yoichi Okamoto, LBJ's photographer.

CHAPTER THIRTY-ONE

JAMES GARRISON AND JFK'S MURDER

Four years after the assassination of John Kennedy I was drawn into a conspiracy theory about the murder that was being pursued by James "Jim" Garrison, District Attorney of Orleans Parish, including New Orleans, in Louisiana. My story was not about the alleged plot, but about Garrison himself and his mental stability.

I've always liked New Orleans, the hum of the French Quarter, the bustle of Jackson Square. It had a special touch that made it different from other American cities. In pre-WWII years, the sound of the city's radio station, WWL used to sneak up the Mississippi River valley into Illinois late at night. I'd drop off to sleep listening to a mahogany-finished Philco sitting atop a bedside table. Often Johnny Long's band was playing from the Blue Room in the Roosevelt Hotel. I floated in a dreamy world with the music.

Later, I visited New Orleans on a three-day pass during WWII. When Robert Penn Warren's novel about Louisiana politics, *All The Kings Men,* was published in 1946, I devoured it. Sally and I spent a week there one fall absorbing the atmosphere of the French Quarter and the old homes along St. Charles Avenue. The state's colorful politicians, past and present, intrigued us, some of them deliciously corrupt.

I've never been into conspiracy theories. To me, they seem to be mind games that twist and turn over nebulous ideas that will never become reality. Seasoned investigators work to make $2 + 2 = 4$. Conspiracy theorists try continually to make $2 + 2 = 5$. There are people who spend a lifetime pursuing conspiracies, playing with the truth, and trying to make something real out of conjecture and supposition. The pursuit is so dogmatic it becomes an obsession; to some even a religion.

Garrison was teetering between the latter two when I became involved. Flamboyant and determined, he played a rough and tumble game. A lot of people thought he was playing fast and loose with the truth. Some thought fantasy had overcome him, that he was reckless. His critics claimed he abused his power as an officer of the law. In some ways it is hard to classify Garrison. Many thought he was a crackpot, others thought he was a standup guy.

In early winter of 1967, I was told that Garrison had been dismissed from the National Guard with a medical discharge that hinged upon mental disability. By that time, he was a national figure with his investigation tying a group from New Orleans to Kennedy's death. The information about Garrison came from a lawyer friend of mine. I took the information seriously because the lawyer was close to Washington officials, both in and out of the Johnson administration. I sensed a "leak" but, at the same time, I wondered how I could possibly get access to private medical records.

Several times I saw the lawyer at Christmas season parties and each time he mentioned the Garrison information.

"I'm working on it," I always told him.

I had made some discreet inquiries at the Veterans Administration but nothing turned up. I thought I might be on a wild goose chase. I decided to end my hunt. This is what happened. As the year wound down, I decided there was only one thing to do: go to the National Guard Bureau in the Pentagon and ask for Garrison's file. I settled on Christmas Eve morning in the belief the bureau office would have a skeleton staff because of the holiday season. Perhaps they would be in a relaxed mood. When I walked in one man was on duty.

"Good morning. I'm Russ Freeburg of the Chicago Tribune," I said, introducing myself. "I'm interested in looking at the personnel file of a James C. Garrison."

"I'm sure I saw that file just the other day in a room across the hall," he replied without hesitation, as he motioned for me to follow him.

My God, I thought, they've been waiting for me. In the office across the hall, he walked directly to a file folder atop a table, handed it to me, and left. The folder held Garrison's military records. As I sat down at the table and began to read the papers in the folder, I realized it would take several hours to make notes on the information. I returned to the office across the hall folder in hand.

"There's a lot here," I said. "Does your office have a copier?"

Again, without hesitation, he pointed to a Xerox machine in a corner of the room. With an occasional comment or two, he watched as I copied pertinent pages. When I handed the folder back to him, I wished him a Merry Christmas and left.

Garrison's medical records disclosed that when he was relieved of active duty in 1952 at Brooke Army Hospital in Texas, he suffered from a "severe and disabling psychoneurosis of long duration" which "interfered with his social and professional adjustment to a marked degree." The evaluation further said that Garrison "is considered totally incapacitated from the standpoint of military duty, and moderately incapacitated in civilian adaptability." Long-term psychotherapy was recommended. His records said he was under the care of a psychiatrist for 4½ years from the fall of 1950 to the spring of 1955. The treatment continued in later years. Even as district attorney, Garrison usually spent only half the day in his office.

The question to me was whether his behavior was affected by his disability.

My story appeared in the Tribune of December 29, 1967. Tribune lawyers saw no legal ramifications in publishing the information. I never saw a story travel around the world as fast as this one. A number of papers printed my story in total with my byline, including the *Los Angeles Times* and the *Washington Post*. Anything connected with Kennedy's murder was always news, but the revelation about Garrison's medical history was upsetting and provocative. Everyone also concluded that now that Garrison's medical history was public no other journalist was going to be allowed to see his records. Privacy advocates condemned the story. Radio talk shows discussed the pro and cons of releasing the information. Several letters appeared in the *Washington Post* from government workers saying I had no right to Garrison's records.

Garrison wouldn't talk to a Tribune reporter sent to interview him in New Orleans. I never pursued how the information was so readily available for me but Garrison, by bringing up once again JFK's murder, had peeved various Washington power centers including the White House, the Kennedy family, and the Warren Commission that concluded Harvey Lee Oswald had acted alone. The Inspector General of the Pentagon asked to interview me, but I refused and he did not pursue me further.

Garrison was the only one to hold a trial in connection with Kennedy's murder. It included bizarre charges of involvement by the CIA and Russia's KGB. It took a jury less than an hour to acquit Clay Shaw, director of the New Orleans Trade Mart, who Garrison charged was a kingpin in the plot. Conspiracy buffs clung to Garrison, however. Oliver Stone in his 1991 movie *JFK* (an appalling travesty of history) was based on Garrison's theory and portrayed Garrison as a hero. The movie included Garrison in a cameo part as a trial judge.

Several months after my story appeared, the Pentagon announced it had been unable to track down the "leak" of Garrison's medical records.

"The investigation did not develop evidence that the information was obtained from any individual within the Department of Defense," reported Col. John F. Wilhelmy, Jr. in a press release "nor did it develop evidence that the release had been made by persons outside of the department."

Make of it what you will. My conclusion is that a person, or persons, very high in Washington wanted the information out in public.

CHAPTER THIRTY-TWO

I MEET JOHN MITCHELL

After his 1962 defeat to Democrat Pat Brown for governor of California, Nixon decamped to New York City to soothe his political wounds, and remake his image. It was there he met John Mitchell in early 1967 when their law firms merged. Mitchell was an expert in municipal and state bonds and as such had a wide acquaintance among mayors and governors. The two men were a good political fit with Mitchell soon becoming a Nixon confidante and close adviser.

I was covering a convention of Young Republicans in the spring of 1968, when Bill Timmons approached me in the lobby of the Washington Hilton, the meeting site. Bill was a Congressional aide and active in the YRs, those members of the GOP 40 years of age and younger. He said John Mitchell was in a suite upstairs and would like to meet me. I wasn't about to pass up an opportunity to meet someone in Nixon's inner circle, and I told Timmons to lead the way.

I found Mitchell to be an engaging man, friendly and relaxed in his shirtsleeves. I liked him immediately. After a few minutes of get acquainted talk he got down to business saying that he was interested in the Republican gubernatorial primary in Illinois.

"What do you know about it?" he asked me. "Who do you think is going to win?"

He said Nixon had his eye on the votes of the Illinois delegation to the Republican national nominating convention in August. Nixon thought the winner of the governor's race would control the delegation, and he wanted to align himself with the victor.

Illinois was a populous state and its delegation was large. Corralling its delegates early would be a big step for Nixon who once again sought the Republican nomination for president eight years after his defeat to John Kennedy in 1960.

I followed the primary contest but from afar. Still, I thought I had a good feel about how the race was taking shape and I didn't hesitate to express my opinion. The Tribune tracked developments daily and I mixed the information I read in our stories with intuition of my own. Illinois politics were second nature to me. I grew up with an inside look. My parents were active in politics. As a young boy, I attended precinct meetings with them, where I sat quietly and listened as local and state politics and politicians were discussed. I learned early the nitty-gritty of selecting candidates.

"Richard Ogilvie will win." I told Mitchell.

The race was between him and John Altorfer in a classic Cook County versus downstate battle that I understood so well. Ogilvie was a highly popular lawyer in Cook County, where he'd been sheriff and chairman of the county's board of commissioners. Everyone knew of the Democrat's powerful Chicago machine. But in those days, suburbs surrounding the city were Republican, and I was sure Ogilvie would be the beneficiary of their largess. He was their guy.

Altorfer was a banker from downstate Peoria along the commercially important Illinois River. Always, the question in statewide races is whether the Cook County candidate would build a large enough plurality in Chicago and its suburbs to offset the expected large vote the downstate candidate would receive from voters outside Cook County.

Peoria has been forever the quintessential American town. For any national conundrum it is asked: Will it play in Peoria? Going for Ogilvie was his reputation as a crime fighting sheriff with the unique twist of being an Ivy Leaguer. Once, at the American Enterprise Institute, I was on a panel on freedom of the press with historian Arthur Schlesinger, Jr. and others. At a pre-panel dinner, we got to talking about politics. I mentioned that Ogilvie was probably the only Yale man who was ever a sheriff. Schlesinger, being a Harvard man, was fittingly amused.

Ogilvie won the primary, and the Illinois delegation backed Nixon. As I suspected, Ogilvie's big vote in Cook County was enough to bring him victory. In the general election he beat the incumbent Democrat, Sam Shapiro. I first met Ogilvie at the convention in Miami, when

Mitchell took us to dinner. We were picked up by a speedboat and whisked across North Biscayne Bay to a restaurant.

"I understand I have you to thank for Nixon's support in the primary," Ogilvie said, as the three of us talked.

Mitchell nodded. "He coached me well."

Mitchell always called me "Coach" thereafter, both during the campaign, and as attorney general.

It's too bad that Mitchell did not seek my counsel about the episode that became known as the Watergate scandal, which led to jail time for him. I would have coached him not to take part. I talked to Mitchell the morning after the White House-directed burglars were caught in their infamous break-in at Democratic Party headquarters in the Watergate office complex. I asked him what happened.

"Damned if I know," he replied.

Of course, he did know and it crushed me when he was implicated. He was a good friend. I was closer to him than other high officials in Washington. He helped me on stories and Sally and I saw him and his wife, Martha, on social occasions. Ironically, they lived in the apartment complex of the Watergate building.

Mitchell handed me the best story of the convention: written plans for opponents to gang up on Nixon in a floor fight to stop his nomination. However, Don Maxwell, the Tribune's editor, balked at printing the details laid out in the acquired papers, saying that years before at a nominating convention in Philadelphia, the Tribune had been burned in a similar situation that turned out to be a hoax. Senior staffers in Miami, who had been in Philadelphia, were called, along with me, to Maxwell's hotel suite to discuss what to do. The senior staffers recommended skipping the story. But, when I said I intended to ask those allegedly involved, elementary really, Maxwell gave me the go ahead.

It turned out the scheme was true. Nelson Rockefeller and Ronald Reagan, both pursuing the nomination (Reagan from the right, Rockefeller from the left) admitted they were cooperating with each other in a one-two punch against Nixon. It was indeed a political odd couple. They thought that if they could block Nixon from a first ballot victory one of them would go on to win the nomination. They couldn't agree on which one, they would battle that out on the floor of the convention. The story caused a stir and brought excitement to a gathering that pundits had written off as cut and dried. It took the steam out of the plan, however, and Nixon coasted to his easy first ballot nomination.

I never understood Mitchell's participation in Watergate. By the time it happened, he had resigned as the nation's top law enforcement officer, and was again campaign manager for Nixon's run for a second term. I've often asked myself why he and Nixon risked so much in a clumsy adventure for iffy information at best. The operation was the work of fertile minds, perhaps, but not mature ones. As a journalist, I probably have a desire to know more than other people. But even I know that there are things best left alone. Certainly, it's a waste of time to chase after information that will turn out to be of little or no value. Trying to know everything is a fool's game. Believe me when I say that the Watergate burglars would have found no earthshaking secrets valuable to the Nixon campaign. Top covert strategies are not lying openly around headquarters of political parties. The latter are bureaucracies set up to run party infrastructure, year in, and year out. They have no other purpose, except maybe gossip.

The year before Watergate, Mitchell, still attorney general, became involved with the Pentagon Papers, a secret study of the United States military and political involvement in Vietnam from 1945 through 1967. I had returned to Chicago as managing editor when the story broke in early June, 1971. When the *New York Times* began publication of the papers, Mitchell asked it to stop voluntarily. I called Mitchell to ask him why, since I thought the decision conflicted with a free press. I also inquired why he even cared, since the papers involved the Kennedy and Johnson administrations and not Nixon's. I said publication was of no embarrassment to the Nixon administration so why not let it proceed. He said Nixon had thought the same way, but Henry Kissinger had convinced him otherwise, arguing that not challenging the *Times* would set a precedent.

The next day, Mitchell, as attorney general, asked a federal court for an injunction on behalf of the government to halt further publication on grounds of national security, which was granted.

The Pentagon review was completed in early 1969, just days before Nixon's inauguration. It had been created by Robert McNamara, secretary of defense in both the Kennedy and Johnson administrations. It concluded that both JFK and LBJ had deceived the American people in their conduct of the conflict. First, Kennedy had planned to assassinate the president of the Southeast Asian country. Then Johnson widened the war without saying so. Four days after the Times halted its printing of the papers, the *Washington Post* began a series of articles on its own of the study. Once again, Mitchell filed for an injunction, this time against the *Post*, which he lost. Within days, the case was before the Supreme Court of the United States, which ruled in a 6 to 3 decision that the government had failed to meet the burden of prior restraint. Both the *Times* and *Post* resumed publication of the papers.

In the court's decision, its majority concluded that protection of freedom of the press in the Bill of Rights trumped the government's attempt to maintain secrecy. The majority said that the government couldn't enforce prior restraint on newspaper articles on findings the government itself had made. Justice Hugo Black said in his opinion that "Only a free and unrestrained press can effectively expose deception in government." He wrote that the press was protected so it could bare the secrets of government and inform the people and that paramount among the responsibilities of a free press is the duty to prevent any government from deceiving the people and sending them off to distant lands to die of foreign fever and foreign shot and shell.

Those are sweet words for a journalist to hear. I was delighted. Nixon's decision, on the other hand, embroiled him voluntarily in controversy that he should have avoided. It put him on even footing with his predecessors when he could have been distancing himself from them by letting the papers be published. He should have left the papers to scholars and historians to peruse and draw conclusions. Instead, he tied the papers to the politics of his own administration, when they had nothing to do with him. There seemed to be an extraordinary yearning in Nixon for control. But, control is illusive and attempts at absolute control lead to tragedy. I called Mitchell after the decision. He was gracious in defeat and our friendship continued.

During the 1968 campaign, Nixon's headquarters were in New York City so I saw little of Mitchell in the months leading up to Election Day. I relied on inside information from Bob Ellsworth, a Nixon operative in the capital. Bob, tall, slim and authoritative, was a former congressman from Kansas and upon Nixon's election he became ambassador to NATO in Europe. I often had breakfast with Ellsworth in the dining room of a small hotel near the Tribune offices, beginning with Nixon's declaration of his candidacy in February. He was a good backroom source. Late in the campaign, Bob Finch, Nixon's campaign manager in the Nixon-Kennedy1960 race, came aboard. He sometimes briefed me and other reporters privately on broad policy aspects of a Nixon presidency. I saw more of him after the election at pre-inaugural parties to which Sally and I were invited.

Finch was lieutenant governor of California during Reagan's first term as governor. He resigned after two years to join Nixon's cabinet in Washington as secretary of Health, Education and Welfare. But he was always more than that. He and Nixon were close going back to Nixon's first years in politics and the Alger Hiss case. Nixon wanted Finch as his vice presidential running mate in 1968 but Finch declined. Lyn Nofziger told me Finch was never good in a crisis when he and Finch were with Reagan on the west coast. He said Finch was often a bundle of nerves and seemed always to end up in the men's room, away from the action. Those traits didn't lend themselves to running a sprawling, unwieldy department like HEW. Management difficulties were routine at HEW. In all honesty, I stumbled onto Finch's difficulties at HEW in an intriguing way. I first got a whiff of them from Anita Glover, who had been on Nixon's campaign staff and had gone to work at HEW after the election. Anita called me one Friday afternoon to ask if I'd heard anything about a personnel upheaval underway at HEW. She told me that a lot of whispering was going on and that Finch's private secretary, Anita's good friend, had been asked to dinner by Finch that evening. Rather casually, Anita slipped in our conversation that she and her friend were going to meet afterwards for a drink. That's when my journalist's instinct kicked in. I asked Anita to give me a call at home if anything definitive was taking place.

Our phone rang just past nine o'clock. Anita told me that Finch was leaving his job at HEW to become Nixon's top staff aid and that the announcement was to be made by the White House the next morning. I could break the story ahead of the White House since it was only 8:30 p.m. Central time in Chicago and several hours before my next deadline. The Saturday edition of the Tribune carried my article on the front page and other news organizations, especially radio networks and wire services, picked it up, quoting me.

Nixon and Finch had agreed to make the change about 10 days to two weeks earlier. This was about the time Finch left Walter Reed Hospital in Washington following a mysterious numbness in his left arm. Finch had been taken to the hospital several days earlier just as he was prepared to speak before a meeting of HEW employees upset over Nixon's Cambodian military operation.

At his Saturday press briefing, where he made my information official, Ron Ziegler, the White House press secretary, asked me how I got the story, but I sidestepped his query.

"The change was very closely held," he said with a cocked eyebrow.

Yes, I thought, Nixon and Finch probably thought it was safe between them alone.

CHAPTER THIRTY-THREE

HUMPHREY'S CHICAGO: CHAOS AND RAGE

Sixteen days after I left Miami, I was in Chicago to cover Vice President Humphrey at the Democratic National Convention. I'd dawdled in the Florida city a couple of days after the Republican meeting to close our makeshift pressrooms in the Fontainebleau basement and the convention center. Sally flew in to join me. We swam in the surf and enjoyed stone crabs. In Chicago I had no managerial duties. The Tribune city desk had taken over the chore of getting the paper's facilities ready, including walkie-talkies as back-ups in communications because a strike by Illinois Bell telephone employees made telephone use questionable.

The venerable Conrad Hilton Hotel, sitting majestically on Michigan Avenue overlooking Grant Park, was Democratic headquarters and the International Amphitheater in the city's famous stockyards on the near west side was the site of the meeting itself. Both were familiar from my days in Chicago and they sparked a bit of nostalgia.

But the week turned into a nasty affair and I left the city riven by the turmoil unleashed.

Tensions were high already when my plane touched down at O'Hare from Washington. Anti-war and civil rights protesters had gathered in force. So had Chicago's police, the Illinois National Guard, and the Secret Service. I hoped there wouldn't be rough and angry days ahead. But protest leaders made clear that they were hell-bent to engage in confrontation politics and Richard J. Daley, the city's tough minded-mayor, was equally determined to stop them. Daley said he wasn't going to let an unruly mob besmirch the name of the city he loved.

I checked into my room at the Hilton, a definite downgrade from the luxurious suite with its gold plated bathroom fixtures that Kirk and I had shared at the Fontainebleau in Miami Beach. Now I was in a cramped little space with hardly enough width to get out of the bed. It was no fault of the Democrats. When it opened in 1927 as the Stevens Hotel, the Hilton had been one of world's most opulent, and certainly the largest, with 3,000 rooms that were customary in size for that time. It had been built, and then lost to foreclosure in the Great Depression, by the family of a later Supreme Court of the United States justice, John Paul Stevens. Newer hotels were more spacious for guests and in the next decade, the Hilton's interior was gutted and redesigned with 1,456 fewer, but larger rooms to keep it competitive in the tough world of hoteliers.

With the convention in the Tribune's hometown, I had nothing to do with coverage of the protesters. That task fell to the city desk. By dusk on the eve of the convention our reporters found several thousand dissenters gathered in Lincoln Park, three miles north of the Hilton. Blue-helmeted police were there to contain them. There was no permit for the gathering. Daley had denied all requests for meetings and marches, and he'd set an eleven o'clock curfew for people being in parks. A skirmish took place when police dispersed the crowd at curfew hour. The stage was set. The days ahead would determine whether the city teetered on a razor's edge of conflict or routine convention days.

Humphrey was bedded down in the Hilton and he would conduct his business from there. I gathered with other reporters in a large foyer between his suite and the elevators, where Secret Service agents stood checking credentials of everyone alighting. One of his first visitors was Daley, making a courtesy call of welcome. Daley was not a Humphrey supporter. He wanted the party's nod to go to Ted Kennedy. The mayor, Irish Catholic to the core, wanted to reignite the magic of John Kennedy's 1960 triumph for his brother. The vice president sent word to us that he was unconcerned. Although he hadn't run in any primaries, Humphrey felt he would win a first ballot nomination. He thought he had 100 to 200 more delegates in his corner than he needed with solid support among blacks, labor unions and Southern Democrats. Still, Humphrey had a large negative. Because he refused to disavow the president's wartime policies he was seen as LBJ's man. Johnson's unpopularity sat heavy on his vice president's shoulders.

Peace activists continued to gather in Lincoln Park. Their attempts to march to the International Amphitheater were thwarted, and the streets between the loop hotels and the stockyards were kept open for delegates traveling back and forth. To me the amphitheater resembled a concentration camp with a newly installed chain link fence topped off with barbed wire surrounding it. Security was there in force. The scene wasn't pretty. Yet, convention business took place inside as scheduled even though outside "the city that works" was being turned upside down.

As twilight came on Wednesday, the peace activists left Lincoln Park en route south to the Hilton. The first marchers reached the hotel as night fell, a slow-moving mass that stretched back into the far distance northward on Michigan Avenue. I stood in front of the Hilton watching them. Some carried sawed off broomsticks. A ball of adhesive tape, with a dozen big nails sticking out of it, rolled to a stop at my feet. Suddenly, the police line along the sidewalk broke and a melee began. The police charged into the marchers, swinging billies and activating chemical mace canisters. Soon tear gas from National Guard troops choked the air. The action was brutish. Buried in my mind still are images of cracked heads of protesters, police clubs poked into protesters' kidneys, eyes burning with pain from the mace. Blood ran down the faces of some protesters. The battle spilled over into Grant Park as paddy wagons rolled in among the crowd to haul those arrested off to jail.

On television, a startled world watched.

Above the skirmish in his Hilton suite, Humphrey watched his name placed in nomination at the stockyards. At the convention podium, Sen. Abraham Ribicoff of Connecticut looked down at Mayor Daley on the floor and denounced "the Gestapo tactics on the streets of Chicago" as he nominated Sen. George McGovern of South Dakota as a peace candidate. The name of Sen. Eugene McCarthy of Minnesota, who led the so-called "Children's Crusade," that toppled LBJ in early party primaries, was also placed in nomination. But Humphrey, as he anticipated, won on the first ballot. His victory seemed hollow compared to the street fighting in front of the Hilton. The Democratic Party was in shatters, and it would be up to him to glue it back together before the general election.

I tried to make sense of the chaotic drama taking place as I walked back into the Hilton's grand lobby that night, the lingering stench of tear gas and stink bombs souring the air. I knew I had witnessed an event with political and social implications. I found no comfort. I had a growing dislike of the war. I had begun to question its purpose. But

I felt no sympathy for the protesters and I disliked the police action. There was little for me to be upbeat about. Politically and emotionally my country was in a mess.

With his nomination won, Humphrey chose his vice presidential running mate the next afternoon. He set the announcement for 3:00 p.m., right on the Tribune's deadline for its first edition. We decided to use our walkie-talkies. I took one into the conference room where the announcement would be made.

"It's Muskie," I whispered into the walkie-talkie when Humphrey walked in with Sen. Edmund Muskie of Maine on his arm.

"I've got it," answered Bill Anderson, our city editor, stationed in the Tribune's work space in the hotel basement.

Muskie's biography was already in type in the composing room as a possible nominee. All that was required was a few quick lead-in paragraphs to have the story on the streets in time for homeward-bound commuters. Humphrey and Muskie made their acceptance speeches to the convention that night. But the police battle with protesters made enthusiasm difficult. Instead of coming together, the Democrats would leave Chicago split apart, worse than ever.

After half a century, I remain unsure of how I feel about what I witnessed in Chicago. The protesters weren't innocents, but they were young. I did not see any provocation that caused the police to charge into the marchers. I think Mayor Daley made a mistake by disallowing permits to parade but allowing protesters to stay in the parks overnight. Those moves by Daley overheated the situation from the start. Humphrey defended the actions of Daley and the police during the convention and again back at his home in Waverly, Minnesota two days after accepting his party's nomination. He said Daley did nothing wrong in protecting convention delegates and party officials. Violence breeds counter-violence, he said. To me, it was the old chicken and egg argument. Which came first? In Chicago, who provoked whom? Humphrey said protesters incited the violence. He claimed he had little time for those who rejected normal political processes and who thought that all they had to do was riot and they would get their way. A commission that investigated what happened that night concluded otherwise.

It called the happening a "police riot."

Chicago's image was tarnished. It's too bad, because Chicago is a great city. Our political system was stained. The country seemed emotionally drained by an increasingly unpopular war that defied an honorable end. Humphrey knew full well the challenges that faced him as his campaign got underway. In Boston that September, he acknowledged the odds, proclaiming that regardless of the election's outcome, he wanted it to be said of him that in an "important and tough" moment in his life, he stood for what he believed in, and would not be shouted down by anti-war protestors and assorted hecklers.

CHAPTER THIRTY-FOUR

CAMPAIGNING WITH HUMPHREY

I decided to travel with Humphrey early in his campaign and then with Nixon at the close of his. In between, I would remain in Washington as other bureau members took over. I wanted as many bureau reporters as possible to travel with the candidates so I broke assignments down into 10- to 12-day swings. This arrangement would give them a chance to be with both Humphrey and Nixon and hobnob with their top advisers and aides. Whoever won, we would have contacts within a new administration.

After his nomination as his party's presidential candidate, Humphrey met with a small group of reporters in his vice presidential office on Capitol Hill to outline his campaign. He would begin in the Northeast and wind his way west on his first swing across the country.

"How about Cadillac Square?" I interrupted. "Won't you go there first?"

"Well, Walter has talked to me about this" he replied, referring to Walter Reuther, head of the United Auto Workers Union. "He told me his members aren't interested in Cadillac Square anymore. They've got cottages and boats on Michigan lakes, and they wanted to be there on the holiday with their families instead of attending a political rally."

For many elections going back to New Deal days, it had been traditional for the Democratic nominee to kick off his run for the White House with a large and colorful union rally in Detroit's Cadillac Square on Labor Day. That was to be no longer. The change was a grand reminder of rising wages and benefits in a booming American economy. There was no thought then that higher wages would lead several decades later to

American jobs lost overseas, or to the decline of Detroit into an impoverished city.

I boarded the press plane accompanying Humphrey early the morning of September 19 for the flight to Boston and a noontime rally with Ted Kennedy and 10,000 of Bean Town's Democratic Party faithful. Some 1,000 booing and yelling anti-war protestors were there, too, and this prompted "the Humph," as his detractors nicknamed him, to pledge defiantly that he would not be shouted down by them. I felt buoyed to be back on the campaign trail again with all its hoopla and noise: the stages wrapped in red, white and blue bunting, the waving flags, the high school bands, and the homemade signs lofted high in the crowds. All this against a backdrop of sunny, warm fall days, splashed with the gold and red colors of turning leaves. Autumn has always been my favorite season. Mixing campaign stops in with it was the height of satisfaction.

For Humphrey, this was a time for mending fences and little by little trying to stitch a badly splintered party back together. From Boston, leaving Ted Kennedy behind, we flew westward to Sioux Falls, South Dakota, where Humphrey joined another convention foe, Sen. George McGovern. They made a show of public unity since even a fractured party needed to show a semblance of healing among its leaders. Even Eugene McCarthy, Humphrey's fellow senator from Minnesota, eventually endorsed the vice president.

Image making was also at work on this swing. Humphrey had to re-establish himself as someone worthy of the presidency. After a quick stop in Kentucky the next morning, we flew to Springfield, Illinois and a noontime rally with Humphrey speaking from the steps of Lincoln's home. How can a man go wrong attaching himself to the memory of our greatest president? Here in the state of the famous Lincoln-Douglas debates of 1858, Humphrey chastised Nixon for avoiding face-to-face debates of their own.

I listened to the speech with half an ear. My dad, a widower now, and I took advantage of the stop for a visit with each other. He and my Aunt Millie drove down to the capital from Galesburg earlier in the day, and they were waiting as I stepped from the press bus. My dad had stayed with us in Virginia for some months after my mother died two summers earlier but after a while he became anxious to return home to his church activities and his weekly pinochle games. We stood on the edge of the crowd and talked. We walked back to the bus as Humphrey finished and lingered there until I had to board. I told my dad I would file a quick story at the airport about the Springfield stop for the Tribune's early edition but that I would top it later with the main event of the day: Humphrey's visit with former president Harry Truman.

From the Illinois capital, we flew to Kansas City, and bussed over to the Truman's home on a shady street in Independence. Humphrey arrived in Missouri still resisting the call from party doves, including McGovern, that he break with Johnson on Vietnam policy, and even resign as his vice president. But he stood firm even though polls showed him running far behind Nixon. We arrived at Truman's home in the late afternoon. Muskie and his wife had joined Humphrey. There was little doubt about the symbolism of the visit. If ever there was an underdog it was Humphrey. Why not recall Truman's come-from-behind win over Thomas Dewey in 1948 and plant the seed that he can do it, too. Maybe a little of the old political warrior's stardust would rub off on Humphrey as they stood shoulder to shoulder.

As twilight settled in over the Midwest, I and the rest of the traveling press corps waited outside Truman's home. After a 45-minute meeting inside the white clapboard house, Humphrey emerged onto its large front porch with Truman, who was steadied by a cane but otherwise chipper. Gathered around them were Truman's wife, Bess, and the Muskies. Photographers snapped pictures of the folksy scene. I thought it was ready-made for a Norman Rockwell painting. For a moment or two, the war in Vietnam was forgotten, a brief respite from the anger and hatred the conflict had inflicted upon our country. Truman told us he had no special formula for political victory. "See as many people as possible and always tell the truth, even if it hurts," he said. So far, Humphrey had spoken to sparse crowds. Truman had, too, in the beginning of his 1948 campaign. But as he lambasted what he called "a do-nothing Congress," his crowds grew. Humphrey could only hope his would also but maybe he needed a new message. That's what I was beginning to think.

From Independence, we flew to Ohio to complete another day of hopscotching across the country. As we flew east, I thought of the long distrust the Tribune and Truman had for each other. I knew Truman hated Tribune editorial writers referring to him as a failed haberdasher. I thought it was a cheap shot. A lot of businesses closed shop in the Great Depression years. On the other hand, Truman said he had to read the

Tribune to keep up with things going on in his own Democratic Party, for it wasn't uncommon in those days for feuds within one's party to be leaked first to opposition newspapers. Of course, Truman savored the famous "Dewey Defeats Truman" Tribune headline in an early edition on election night in 1948. Did that give Truman the last laugh? Maybe!

It was in the Buckeye State that I sensed a slight shift in Humphrey's view of Johnson's Vietnam policy. In Toledo, during a hookup with European journalists from London at a local TV station, he vowed, if elected, to reassess the war. During a stop in his hometown of Minneapolis the next day, Humphrey asserted during a press conference that his bid for the presidency was gaining ground. I doubted that and when we flew into Los Angeles from the Midwest, there was more of the same: small crowds, and little money. Humphrey in a talk at Pepperdine University proposed that he, Nixon, and George Wallace, the third party, segregationist candidate, crisscross the country together, sharing costs as they went to the same towns and discussed the issues before the same audiences. Born of desperation, it was a helpless call that went nowhere.

As we moved north along the California coast, Humphrey began appearing on local radio and TV newscasts as a way to reach voters. He was broke and the broadcasts were free. He still backed United States involvement in the war in the face of protesters but he said once again, as he had in Ohio, that he would reassess the war if elected. This time he added that he would do it with new advisers, not LBJ holdovers. His promise didn't stop the protesters. At a daytime rally in San Francisco's Market Square, Humphrey was booed and heckled. But he looked protesters in the eye and told them they were akin to Hitler's storm troopers.

That same day, George Ball resigned as the administration's ambassador to the United Nations as he publicly turned against the war.

The next night in Portland, Oregon, Humphrey had the first big rally of his west coast swing. Supporters filled the city's Civic Auditorium. Several hundred protesters sneaked in with them and interrupted his speech with calls of "end the war." Partisan Democrats chanted "We want Humphrey" in response. Shouted down, the hecklers marched from the hall. Two hours behind Chicago in time, I left the rally early to return to my room in the campaign hotel to call in a new lead for the late editions. As I walked through a downtown park nearby, I saw a car pull up in front of the hotel. Two men stepped out and hurried inside. One of the arrivals was George Ball. I didn't recognize the other man. I stepped up my pace in hopes of talking to them but just as I reached the lobby the elevator doors glided shut with them inside.

Later, when a group of us gathered for a late dinner, I kept what I had seen to myself. For the first time ever, I had poached salmon. In 1968, there were still regional foods in the United States: lobsters in Maine, oysters and crabmeat along Chesapeake Bay, beef in the Midwest, grits and fried green tomatoes in the South, gumbo in Louisiana. As we ate, I was sure that the arrival of Ball signified change for the campaign. Just what, I couldn't foresee. But I clocked his arrival as the appearance of emergency aid, for it was more obvious every day that Humphrey was getting nowhere in overcoming the apathy towards him by voters.

Ball kept out of sight the next day. He didn't accompany Humphrey as the vice president flew up the Columbia River from Portland to The Dalles, and then motored farther upstream to dedicate the new John Day Dam. The routines of daily campaigning were absent on this occasion. The first excitement came when we arrived at the airport to find an ancient DC-3 aircraft waiting for us. What fun to be taken back to the first days of modern commercial flights in the 1930s and the early post-WWII years when the DC-3 was king of the sky. In December, 1946, I flew out of St. Louis in a DC-3 on my way to Sally's and my wedding. How small the old plane looked standing on the tarmac near the big jet in which we had been traveling. It had a mere 21 seats and the aisle, when we boarded, ascended at a steep angle to the cockpit from the cabin door near the tail. But there were no landing fields large enough for our jet at The Dalles, or elsewhere up the valley. We flew along the side of Mount Hood on our way. It was the same with Mount Rainier on the flight from The Dalles to Seattle that afternoon. We were below the peaks of both mountains. It was a beautiful, sunny day and I could see smoke twirl lazily skyward here and there among the endless forests below.

And to think that for doing this I got paid.

Humphrey was more vice president than a presidential candidate in dedication of the dam. He never mentioned the campaign, though it was certainly on everyone's mind, including two United States senators and the governors of Washington State, Oregon and Idaho, all part of the Columbia River's watershed. The premier event of the day came when Humphrey pushed a button which raised the spillway gate and sent the river's waters on their way to the Pacific Ocean far away. In the Seattle Center Arena that night, Humphrey was again greeted by several hundred hecklers trying to shout him down. But he fought back saying "I shall not be driven from this platform by a handful of people who believe in nothing." It was clear, however, that the constant appearance of protesters dispirited the candidate and his staff. The next day, Sunday, September 29, all events were canceled, and Humphrey secluded himself in his suite in the Olympic Hotel with Ball and Larry O'Brien, his campaign manager, who'd flown in from the East.

I wandered into the pressroom in late morning, empty except for Ted Van Dyk, a Humphrey aide. He had little to say. A Gallup poll released overnight had Humphrey far behind Nixon 44 to 29%. I decided to exit the hotel. The weather was bright and sunny outside. I boarded a monorail to the city's iconic Space Needle. When I had free time I often went sightseeing. In late afternoon we headed to the airport for our flight to Salt Lake City, where Humphrey was scheduled to speak at noon in the famed Mormon Tabernacle.

In the past 10 days, the Humphrey campaign had almost come to a complete stop several times because of anti-war protesters and a lack of money. The campaign reached absolute bottom in Seattle. The political decision that had to be made was obvious. Humphrey, in some way, had to disconnect himself from Johnson administration war policy. We were told that Humphrey would make a televised speech to the nation from Salt Lake City in addition to his already scheduled activities. The speech was an absolute necessity. His campaign had to change its direction. When he went on TV, the vice presidential seal was missing from the podium in front of him, a symbolic gesture telling the nation that he was speaking as his own man and no longer as President Johnson's surrogate. Humphrey proposed a halt to the bombing of Vietnam and called for a cease-fire. He said that both were an acceptable risk for peace.

Behind the scenes, Humphrey campaign personnel made contacts with anti-war leaders, especially the younger ones, to ask them to curb the dissent. The pitch was that Humphrey, rather than Nixon, was more like them. The patience of the anti-war people was sought for the duration of the campaign. This worked. After Salt Lake City, Humphrey never encountered a major anti-war demonstration again. Money began coming in to keep the campaign going. Within hours after the Salt Lake City speech, as we flew to Nashville, the mood and psychological atmosphere of the campaign changed. It was a mood of "we finally got it off our chest, and now things will get better." They did. The momentum of the Humphrey campaign picked up, and from that day forward, he began to gain on Nixon.

CHAPTER THIRTY-FIVE

CAMPAIGNING WITH NIXON

I joined Nixon in New York City on October 20 and remained with him through the election on November 5. I'll tell you right now, it was one hell of an exciting finish. But there were still 15 days of campaigning when I checked into the Waldorf Astoria Hotel, Nixon's headquarters, that Sunday afternoon. On the way to my room, I ran into Bud Wilkinson and his wife in the elevator. Now a Nixon aide, Bud had won fame as coach of national champion University of Oklahoma football teams. His record of 47 straight victories still stands.

"Bud, how's the campaign going?" I asked, as we whizzed upward.

"We're going to win, Russ," he replied with a smile, as though he was ahead of Nebraska with less than a minute to play. "We're going to win."

After I dumped my luggage on the bed, I headed for the pressroom. There wasn't any point in unpacking since we were flying to Cincinnati the next morning. Talk in the pressroom was about George Wallace, who was running as a third party segregationist candidate for the presidency. Nixon was somewhat concerned about Wallace. Polls showed the Alabama governor drawing a constant 20% of the vote. Nixon, meanwhile, had slipped a little since I left Humphrey.

But, the big news wasn't politics. It was the wedding of Jacqueline Kennedy. In a tiny chapel on the island of Skorpios, the widow of the late president a few hours earlier had married Aristotle Onassis, the Greek shipping magnate, and one of the world's wealthiest men.

Nixon still felt the sting of his narrow loss to Kennedy in 1960. I thought Wilkinson was too upbeat, some anti-war Democrats had come home since Humphrey's Salt Lake City speech. Certainly, there would be more. There were also undecided voters. Nixon's hope was to pick up the undecided and to cut into Wallace backers to climb above 50%. He wanted to avoid, if possible, being elected as a minority president.

So it was apparent that in addition to covering his daily campaign events, I should track the polls. A dramatic finish could be possible, after all, if the spread between Nixon and Humphrey continued to narrow. I hoped to get my first feel of the Nixon campaign in Cincinnati. A nighttime rally there was big and boisterous. The next morning we left by train on a whistle-stop tour that traveled northward across the state toward Toledo. His crowds along the way were good.

In mid-afternoon, we chugged into the little town of Deshler, the hub of a prairie area of farms as far as the eye could see. It was here that a 13-year-old eighth grader, Vicki Lynne Cole, carried a sign that became a poignant moment in the presidential race. There were few placards in the crowd, so this one stood out. I remember it as three lines of black block letters on white art board. I was about 50 feet away when I spotted it. It said, "Bring Us Together." Simple words, but somehow they were breathtaking and emotional. Those few words expressed it all: reunite a bitterly divided country.

With nascent peace talks underway in Paris, Nixon didn't mention divisive Vietnam much in his stump speeches. But he assailed Humphrey for doing so. He said Humphrey had the fastest, loosest tongue in America, and that the vice president was unable to keep his mouth shut, despite the negotiations. He charged Humphrey couldn't make up his mind on whether the bombing of North Vietnam should, or should not, be stopped. Nixon charged that one day Humphrey was for stopping the bombing unconditionally, and on the next, that there should be conditions.

Despite Nixon's attacks on Humphrey, the race tightened. Gallup reported that Nixon's lead in the 12-state region of the northeastern United States had been cut from 13 points to five. Nixon aides were tight-lipped as we left Ohio and went north into Michigan. After a rally in Grand Rapids, Nixon returned to the east to campaign outside of New York City with short trips into Pennsylvania and northern New Jersey. We stayed in the Waldorf Astoria for four days, returning each night. The stop was a good time to send out laundry and it made mealtime easier. I loved the Eggs Benedict at the Waldorf and I had them every morning for breakfast during our stay there. I remember the price was $3.50. Maybe a little high but it was the Waldorf after all. Compared to current prices the dish was a steal.

On our last night in New York, Nixon made a nationwide radio address. I soon understood that Nixon was frequently using nationwide radio hookups to reach voters. It was an inexpensive way to campaign. He had done so in Cincinnati and he would continue to do so at other rallies until Election Day. This time he did talk about Vietnam, saying that forcing a coalition on South Vietnam in the Paris peace talks would constitute a thinly disguised surrender.

The next morning, we embarked on a flying tour through the more populous states in the run-up to the election, now eight days away. As we took off from LaGuardia for the state capital in Albany in upstate New York, Nixon engaged in an informal discussion about polls after the *New York Daily News*, a Tribune Company paper, gave Humphrey a 4.2% lead over him in New York State. He released a statement in which he asked voters to give him not merely a plurality in a three-man race, but an overwhelming victory that would constitute a mandate to govern.

He also continued to use radio and television. The Soviet Union became the subject of his talks. At a rally in Bloomfield, New Jersey, which was carried by radio nationwide, he pledged to seek a meaningful arms control agreement with the Russians, and he pushed for ratification of a treaty to halt the spread of nuclear weapons, big issues of the era. Two days earlier near Pittsburgh, in Hazleton, Pennsylvania, again on radio nationwide, he took a harder line, pledging he would build a "clear cut" American military superiority over the Soviets. In between the two rallies, he spent a night in New York doing a one-hour live TV panel session beamed into New York State, Ohio, Maryland, Pennsylvania, and Massachusetts.

In Syracuse, New York, I saw my only organized protest against Nixon. But it wasn't exactly anti-war. Nixon was confronted there by a chorus of Syracuse University students as he spoke in the War Memorial Auditorium. The group of 1,000 sang the Simon & Garfunkel song *The Sounds of Silence,* as they entered, to protest Nixon's refusal to debate Humphrey. Nixon took the interruption in stride. He gave them the floor, saying he was delighted to hear their views. They charged he was a creature of Madison Avenue ad men, with no stance on issues. He sat quietly on the stage. When the audience, estimated at 12,000, began to chant "We want Nixon" he silenced them. Later, he answered the students' complaints as he spoke.

The next night we were in Cleveland, Ohio. Nixon made no pretense that he still held a comfortable lead over Humphrey. He understood that the race for the presidency had tightened since Humphrey's Salt Lake City speech, and he challenged his Democratic foe to pledge support for the candidate with the most popular votes in the election, now five days away. If Humphrey failed to do so, said Nixon, it proved that his opponent had lost all hope of winning except through the House of Representatives.

"I stand ready to accept the decision of the electorate," Nixon said. "Does Humphrey?"

In my view, the odds for the House of Representatives deciding the election were small to none. Only two presidents in American history were picked by the House—Thomas Jefferson in 1800 and John Quincy Adams in 1824. Nixon now raised the possibility of a third. Under the Constitution, the House selects the president if no candidate wins a majority of the 270 Electoral College votes. In 1968, each state delegation in the House would cast one vote with a majority of 26 needed to win. But within 24 hours all this was forgotten, as one of the wildest finishes in a presidential race in history was underway.

LBJ entered the fray, announcing that he had ordered a stop to the United States bombing of North Vietnam, and that Hanoi, in return, had agreed to let the South Vietnamese take part in the Paris peace talks. Johnson said his order applied to all air, naval, and artillery bombardment of the North. That same night (October 31), Nixon had one of his biggest rallies of his campaign when 19,000 supporters packed Madison Square Garden in New York City to hear him speak. It wasn't lost on anyone that it was also Halloween. Was it a political trick or treat by President Johnson?

Nixon addressed a colorful and enthusiastic crowd in the Garden, but he said little about Johnson's move other than he also wanted peace. He said he had to be cautious about commenting for fear something he said might upset the talks. Nixon aides told me that LBJ had called the GOP candidate at his New York City apartment with details of his speech about four hours before addressing the nation. They cautioned that the reaction of the South Vietnamese government, in far-away Saigon, was subdued, and it had issued a communiqué saying Johnson had acted unilaterally.

But Nixon appeared to be sticking to a pledge he made to the GOP nominating convention back in August, where he said, "We all hope in this room that there's a chance that current negotiations may bring an honorable end to the war. We will say nothing during the campaign that might destroy that chance."

The next night in San Antonio, Texas, Nixon stayed away from public comment on the peace talks, but there was no lack of conversation behind the scenes on LBJ's dramatic action. It wasn't possible to determine yet if the president's move would affect the election, but there was worry it could. Nixon attacked Humphrey as one of those "fuzzy thinkers and fake prophets" who profess to believe that keeping America strong was somehow against peace. Then, Nixon turned his criticism on LBJ, and charged the president had permitted a security gap to develop in the nation's military strength in the Cold War against the Soviets.

We flew westward toward California from San Antonio the next morning to spend the weekend before the election in Los Angeles. Along the way we stopped in El Paso, where Nixon returned to his theme of law and order in another radio address and rally. Then, it was on to Long Beach, in the Golden State, for another rally before checking into the plush Century Plaza Hotel on the site of the old 20th Century Fox movie studios. I could see the old backlot, with its make-believe props and street fronts from the window of my room.

On Sunday, November 3, Nixon awoke to bad news. A Gallup poll disclosed that his lead over Humphrey had fallen to two percentage points: 42 to 40. The final days of the campaign were obviously not going to end with a sputter. It was now a contest that could go either way, with the peace talks at its center. Publicly, the situation was delicate. Voters had lost faith in the war. Nixon told them he would be willing to go to either Paris or Saigon to get talks off of dead center. It was easy to cover Nixon's public appearances, but his action, or actions on his behalf, out of public view were difficult to ascertain. Rumors abounded. In the center of them was the South Vietnamese government. Would it, or wouldn't it, accept the invitation to join the talks? I was in the same position I had been in during the Cuban missile crisis; I knew something was going on, but I didn't know any details. I could sense tenseness among Nixon and his top advisors, but any actions by them were not revealed.

Much is known now about what took place in those final hours leading up to the election. In passing years, audiotapes of Johnson's telephone conversations have become public, and Nixon's contacts with the South

Vietnamese government have been disclosed. Slowly, a history of what happened in that crucial weekend before the voters went to the polls has fallen into place. It's too bad that a play-by-play account wasn't available at the time for the public, for what went on had all the espionage elements of a dark spy thriller: a brainy, beautiful woman of the Orient, furtive intelligence operations, and secretive politicians.

On the evening of November 2, as Nixon arrived in California, President Johnson received an FBI message from Washington at his ranch in Texas. The report detailed a just-completed telephone conversation between the South Vietnamese ambassador in Washington, Bui Diem, and Anna Chennault, a well-known Chinese-American active in Republican politics. Chennault told Diem she had received a message from "her boss." She said the message was "To hold on. We are going to win. Hold on. He understands all of it."

Chennault wasn't a stranger to Johnson administration officials. They were monitoring her activities in Washington. They knew she had visited the South Vietnam embassy three days earlier. Although Saigon was an ally, American intelligence agencies were following the activities of its officials closely. The National Security Agency was reading their diplomatic cables. The FBI had listening devices and a telephone wiretap in the embassy, and the CIA was tracking activities in the South Vietnamese capital.

Chennault was especially intriguing. Sometimes referred to as "the dragon lady," and at other times as "little flower," she was the widow of Lt. Gen. Claire Chennault, a WWII hero, who commanded American air operations in China. His Flying Tigers were famed for the ferocious animal paintings covering the front of their fighter planes. She was popular in Washington social circles, especially among Republicans, and she had contacts throughout Asia. When Diem visited Nixon in the Hotel Pierre in New York City in July, she was present along with John Mitchell. Nixon told Diem that Anna would be in touch with him. From then on, she was Nixon's go-between.

After Anna told Diem to "hold on," President Thieu announced in Saigon that South Vietnam would not send a delegation to Paris, a move that stalled the peace talks, and deflated both LBJ's halt in the bombing of the North, and the positive charge his action had put into Humphrey's campaign. Johnson was furious, but he was hamstrung in going public because of his use of wiretaps and bugs to learn of Nixon's actions. Johnson insisted Nixon had violated the Logan Act, a federal law that forbids unauthorized citizens from negotiating with foreign governments that have a dispute with the United States. The law, established in 1799, is almost as old as the Republic itself, but no one has ever been prosecuted under it. Johnson worked himself up into a huff, and accused Nixon of "treason," but no one else went that far. In siding with Nixon, the South Vietnamese feared that Humphrey, if elected, would quickly withdraw from the war. They saw Nixon taking a harder stance, and they hoped their actions would tip the election in his favor.

Johnson called Nixon and he asked Nixon to back off, citing the Logan Act. Nixon waffled in reply, so LBJ turned over his information to Humphrey, and urged the Democratic candidate to go public with it. Humphrey declined, but he had second thoughts when he wrote a memoir years later.

"I wonder if I should have blown the whistle on Anna Chennault and Nixon," he wrote. "He must have known about her call. I wish I could have been sure. Damn Thieu. Dragging his feet this last weekend hurt us. I wonder if that call did it? If Nixon knew? Maybe I should have blasted them away."[8]

Nixon stayed out of the public view on Sunday, but turmoil prevailed behind the scenes in fear that Humphrey would overtake him. Lou Harris, a nationally-known Democratic pollster, thought Humphrey actually surged ahead of Nixon for a few hours that afternoon. On Monday, with Election Day 24 hours away, Nixon paid a visit to his party headquarters in Los Angeles, where he made a late appeal to get out the vote. That night, he held a four-hour telethon from NBC studios, in which he took questions from voters. The first two hours were devoted to Eastern and Midwest time zones, and the last two hours to Rocky Mountain and Western time zones. With his old friend Bud Wilkinson as moderator, Nixon appeared relaxed and eager to engage his audience in their call-in questions.

The next morning we were up early to fly to New York City. The flight put us in the air most of the day, arriving in NYC about five o'clock eastern time. The plane trip was a great way to while away the hours while the nation voted. By the time we landed, polls along the east coast would soon close; the ballot count would begin, and slowly move westward though the night. The Waldorf Astoria was again Nixon's headquarters. It was evident that the race was now close.

Humphrey had closed strong from his hapless early days as he plodded along with no money and little support.

Midnight came and went. Humphrey won New York State and Pennsylvania. Nixon took Florida, Ohio, and Illinois. The race was too close to call as other, smaller states reported their results. Then, Texas went to Humphrey. Nixon sent word that he would make no comment until California's result was known. I took advantage of the blackout to grab a few hours of sleep. Then, I had my usual Waldorf breakfast of Eggs Benedict. About midmorning Wednesday it became clear that Nixon would win California. Victory was declared, but Nixon had won by the slimmest of margins. The final count of the popular vote gave him 43.4% to Humphrey's 42.5%. Nixon had practically the same percentage he had at the start of his campaign, when polls gave him 44% of the vote. Wallace ended with 13.5% of the vote by taking five southern states.

After a victory appearance with his wife, Pat, and daughters, the president-elect took off for his retreat in Key Biscayne, Florida. En route, we stopped in Washington, where he visited briefly with former president Eisenhower in Ike's suite in Walter Reed Army Hospital. I got off the plane while it waited at Andrews Air Force base and called Sally. I told her I would travel on to Florida, but not for long. I returned home after a few days, and she and I left for a planned two-week vacation on St. Croix in the Virgin Islands. We had a wonderful time dining, swimming, and sailing to the nearby island of St. John, where we snorkeled in an underwater national park. We rented a Volkswagen Beetle, which we drove around St. Croix and high into the island's rain forest.

I thought I was through with the campaign after that. But during Christmas week in 1969, former president Johnson, in a television interview on CBS, said that Humphrey lost the 1968 election with his speech in Salt Lake City. I disagreed publicly with LBJ in a column, saying Humphrey's speech almost won the election for him. I also disagreed with Johnson's assumption that he would have been re-elected if he had run in 1968. I think he would have been slaughtered at the polls. It is questionable whether he could even have campaigned personally around the country, the anti-war sentiment being what it was.

I wrote in the column that Humphrey's Salt Lake City speech was adroit since it muddied up the water as to his position. It was subject to widespread interpretation of just what he meant. He didn't break entirely from Johnson and become an all-out dove. On the other hand, by implication, he indicated his approach to the war would be quite different from Johnson's. It was what the anti-war movement wanted to hear to make them believers. It was a speech designed to placate the doves and keep the hawks in the Democratic Party. In retrospect, contrary to Johnson's position, I think it succeeded.

It is estimated that Humphrey picked up eight million votes between his Salt Lake City speech and Election Day. There is no way this could have been done in the few days left after LBJ's bombing halt. Humphrey, like a steady drip of water on a stone, slowly eroded Nixon's lead. It is hard to determine if war was the one issue that brought Humphrey to the edge of victory. Other factors seemed to be involved, such as the pocketbook, and Democrats in the Deep South staying loyal to Humphrey. The byplay was much stronger between Humphrey and Wallace than Nixon and Wallace. This indicated to me that more traditional voting factors were involved. But without quieting the war dissent at Salt Lake City, Humphrey may never have gained the time, and money, to develop those factors.

CHAPTER THIRTY-SIX

I'M WASHINGTON BUREAU CHIEF: AFTERNOON NEWSPAPERS FADE AWAY

The year 1969 began with a new president. I took the title bureau chief, as planned, on January 1. Back in Chicago, Kirk became the Tribune's editor the same day. I was sure I'd landed the best position in journalism: directing coverage of news for a major newspaper in a global power center. I had the job of my dreams. I expected it to be a challenge. No one can predict when and what kind of news will break in a world in which people's interactions are mostly concealed in a veneer of invisibility. I expected the days ahead to be exciting for me.

I reflected on my life. I decided I was somewhat a risk-taker, unafraid to enter uncharted territory, to move ahead when the end result was yet unseen. I wasn't careless. I weighed outcomes to the best of my ability. I wasn't blind to possible failure. Remember the adage that it is better to love and lose than never to love at all? I felt that way about my life. It's worth the chance to veer off on less-traveled roads, to take the gamble, to experience the passion of the journey itself. It was just an introspective peek. I didn't weigh in to become a full-time philosopher; a world of reality waited me.

That included a weakening newspaper industry. For the first time in Tribune history, a budget had to be prepared for the bureau. The same situation was underway in Chicago. The bureau had always been run with a revolving fund kept solvent in Riggs Bank. When the cash ran low, Chicago replenished it. The bureau spent what it had to for coverage. No one worried about the cost. But the shadow of the newspaper industry's decline was falling over us. Afternoon newspapers were disappearing altogether. Evenings spent reading newspapers, thrown on family porches at twilight, were now devoted to television. Advertising revenues were shifting away from newspapers to TV, especially national advertising involving industries like automobiles and home appliances.

In time, the cash cow of newspapers—want ads—would be taken away by the internet.

Nixon took White House press conferences a step beyond Kennedy's live afternoon sessions. He made them nighttime affairs, moving them into prime time TV to bring in even more viewers. Even though the networks rebelled because of revenues lost from cancelled shows, TV was now clearly the dominant media of the day.

Perks remained for me, however. I was given a car, a Buick LeSabre, for my personal use, a Tribune tradition for its bureau chiefs around the world. Along with it came payments for gasoline, and the monthly fee to park in the garage of our office building. The paper also took over payment of my monthly dues to the University Club. This was more than personal. It gave the bureau a place for business dining and entertainment functions. There had never been any of the latter. But I thought it was time to do more socializing as an adjunct to our news-gathering. It was my aim to end the bureau as a fiefdom for its chief and include its members as a whole on social occasions when possible.

I was curious about how Nixon would grapple with Vietnam. He said during the campaign that he had a plan. I was skeptical. Ron Ziegler, the president's press secretary, asked me what I thought of Henry Kissinger and slipped me word that Nixon would name the political scientist his national security adviser. Kissinger was on the Harvard faculty and well-known as a consultant on foreign affairs outside of academia. I was hopeful Nixon wouldn't make Johnson's mistake of running the war out of the White House. FDR had left the battlefield to his generals in WWII. Military victories come by taking land and holding it. Vietnam was a hellhole of guerrilla combat, with both sides moving back and forth across the same territory. The situation wasn't all that different from the trench warfare of WWI with land taken and then relinquished time after time. That war ended in an armistice. Vietnam was moving in that direction with the inchoate Paris peace talks. Johnson thought saturation bombing of North Vietnam and Viet Cong positions would bring Hanoi to its knees. But air power alone can never win a war.

Nixon's foreign policy was yet to take shape as he entered office. I took the kids to his inauguration. Sally declined to come along, the freezing and snowy ceremonies of the Kennedy inaugural still lingered with her. The weather was nippy for Nixon's inauguration, so the children and I went to the offices of Congressional friends on Capitol Hill to warm up. Nixon's inaugural address was thematic, rather than specific. Vietnam wasn't mentioned by name, nor was the Cold War with the Soviet Union—two big issues he faced.

Still, it was an easy speech to write about. His Quaker background sprung to life. *"The greatest honor history can bestow is the title of peacemaker,"* Nixon said. *"This honor now beckons America."* The words forecast his later foreign policy—détente with Russia, an opening to Communist China, and the Paris Peace Accords. One of two Bibles on which he placed his hand to take the oath of office was open to Isaiah 2:4—*And he shall judge among the nations, and shall rebuke many people: and they shall beat their swords into plowshares and their spears into pruning hooks: nation shall not lift up sword against nation, neither shall they learn war anymore.*

Nixon shortly began to reshape LBJ's Vietnam policy. He first used the term "Vietnamization" in March. He ended Johnson's search and destroy strategy, which lessened the use of Agent Orange and napalm, and replaced it with a gradual and phased withdrawal of American troops from the Southeast Asia battleground. This was coupled with increased training and supplying of South Vietnam troops so the South Vietnam government, in turn, could slowly take control of its own destiny.

In early June, I accompanied Nixon as he flew west to meet President Thieu of South Vietnam on the Pacific Ocean island of Midway, so named for its location half-way between the west coast of the United States and Mainland Asia. It was 27 years since the battle of Midway in WWII, a key turning point in America's fight with Japan. As dawn broke on June 4, 1942, the Japanese fleet steaming near Midway ruled the Pacific. When the sun set that day, its exulted carrier force had been destroyed by United States planes. The Japanese would never regain the offensive again.

After a two-day rest stop in San Clemente, California, Nixon's west coast residence, and overnight in Honolulu, Hawaii, we landed on Midway on June 8. I expected a tropical paradise. Instead, I was greeted with a cold wind and a 63 degree temperature as I stepped off the press

Nixon greets President Thieu of South Vietnam on Midway Island in the Pacific during the Vietnam War to discuss American troop withdrawals

plane. The airstrip landscape was bleak and barren. Only the island's military headquarters and the commandant's home, where Nixon and Thieu met, were surrounded by trees and flowers.

Nixon, with Thieu standing beside him, announced his first withdrawal of American forces, 26,000 troops, from Southeast Asia. I was a long way in time and distance, from Chicago and communication from Midway for the press was extremely limited, but I was determined to get the story to Chicago for the Tribune's late editions. Soon we would be airborne for home and once on the plane there would be no way to move copy. I left the other reporters listening to the two presidents, and hurried to a building in which space had been allotted to the press. No one was there. In an empty office I spotted a telephone. When I picked up the mouthpiece an operator answered. I gave her the telephone number of the Tribune telegraph desk in Chicago and was immediately put through. I quickly dictated my story. I found out later that the telephone belonged to CBS.

Nixon was a master at global politics. But he forever undermined himself with nasty traits. I never knew another politician with such a split personality as Nixon. An evil twin seemed to lurk within him. He was the walking example of a man who conquered his world but lost his soul in the process. I never understood why he couldn't be more forgiving of enemies after finally winning the presidency. I never witnessed personally in Nixon the vindictive and hate-filled man who came to light on the Watergate tapes. He always seemed upbeat and pleasant around me. I regretted the time I missed having a private lunch with him and Mrs. Nixon in the White House. But Watergate was so outrageous to me that I lost my pride in knowing him.

The missed luncheon was a tangle of unintended cross-purposes. Once a year Jack Sutherland, the *U.S. News and World Report* White House man, and I would take a day off and sneak away for a round of golf at a course we liked in southern Pennsylvania. In midmorning, Herb Klein, The White House communications director, called the bureau seeking me. Told that I was out for the day, he said he had to reach me because the Nixons wanted me and bureau member Louise Hutchinson, who covered Mrs. Nixon, to come to lunch. The chase began. Sally told the bureau I was golfing somewhere around Gettysburg. A call was made to the Gettysburg Golf Club. No luck there, but a pro at a nearby course said we were at his course. He said it had begun to rain after we'd played a few holes and that Jack and I had driven to the nearby town for lunch, and we'd be back if the rain stopped. He gave the bureau the names of a couple of restaurants to call but we hadn't gone to them, instead we'd stopped at a roadside tavern. It continued to rain after lunch so we headed back to Washington. The sun was out there so we finished our round of golf at Jack's club in Maryland. Herb never found me, and Louise and I never had lunch with the Nixons.

Such was life in the days before cell phones. It's always intrigued me that a person can go days, even weeks, with nothing happening then—BANG—there is a conflict of gigantic proportions. Why, of all days, would the president choose the time of Jack's and my once-a-year golf outing to invite me to lunch? Even if found I doubt I could have returned to Washington in time. I was two hours away, and the bureau's frantic effort to reach me was always a step behind. It would have been so interesting to break bread with them in such an informal way. Sally and the children first met the Nixons on a weekend in Florida. Ron Ziegler came to the press plane when we landed at Homestead Air Force Base and took us over to the president and first lady coming down the steps of Air Force One. We talked there on the tarmac. I had a high regard for Mrs. Nixon. She suffered through some hard times.

Sutherland and I often palled around together on presidential trips. Years earlier, in Los Angeles, I decide to walk down two floors in the Beverly Hilton to Jack's room. Behold, the door to his floor was locked for security purposes as were all the other doors in the stairwell. My only escape was to trudge up to the penthouse were President Kennedy was staying. There the Secret Service, with a security desk in the hall, heard my knocks and opened the door for my escape.

Although Vietnam dominated, other newsworthy events happened in my first year as bureau chief. In July, two American astronauts landed on the moon, the first earthlings ever to do so. The bureau covered that historic mission from liftoff to landing. As the world watched the moon shot, the word "Chappaquiddick" entered my lexicon. On the night of July 18, Ted Kennedy drove a car off a small wooden bridge into a pond on a lonely road on the island by that name drowning Mary Jo Kopechne. Somehow, the senator escaped from the auto. I sent Jim Yuenger to Massachusetts to cover the story. But I also had to see the scene myself. A few days after the incident, I flew to Martha's Vineyard to meet Yuenger. We took the ferry across to Chappaquiddick late in the day and waited for nightfall. We then walked the same route Kennedy had walked in the darkness from the accident scene. He passed several houses without stopping at the cottage a mile or more away where he and Kopechne had been partying with friends. It was hard to believe that Kennedy had missed seeing the Dike house, as he claimed. The Dike house stood right on the road within a stone's throw of the bridge. Or that he missed seeing, as he passed, the island firehouse with a red light glowing above its doors. My conclusion: the fate of his political career and a cover story to save it was paramount in his mind and not Mary Jo Kopechne.

Nixon's Vietnamization policy moved forward slowly in 1969 but it did not lessen massive protests against the war. I was in Chicago on May 4 meeting with Larry Fein, the telegraph editor, when four youths were shot by national guardsmen on the campus of Kent State University in Ohio. We were sitting at the telegraph copy desk talking when the first Associated Press bulletin came through on the wires. I spent most of the month in Chicago with Larry working to modernize the Chicago-Washington relationship. On May 9, I was back in Washington and witnessed a massive anti-war demonstration. Thousands of protestors, their flags waving, filled Pennsylvania Avenue from the Treasury Building to Capitol Hill. It was a colorful sight. Even more impressive was the demonstration on November 15 that drew a half million protestors to the mall for a daylong rally. On both occasions, the Treasury Building and the White House were ringed by empty buses; some so old and rusty I wondered where they'd been found.

That same month I spent an evening at the White House that was far different from covering the anti-war protestors. It began with a telegram to my home from the Executive Mansion's social secretary requesting the pleasure of my company at a dinner honoring Prince Philip, Duke of Edinburgh (and husband of Queen Elizabeth of Great Britain) on November 4 at eight o'clock. The telegram went on to say black tie, stag, formal invitation follows. The tuxedo would be far different from the old clothes I wore at the anti-war demonstrations.

Prince Philip flew into Washington the day of the dinner, piloting his own plane. He'd just come from a weekend with friends in Sheridan, Wyoming, and before that a tour of Canada. I was among 107 guests seated at an E-shaped table in the state dining room. Earlier in a receiving line we individually shook hands with the prince. It had been announced that his son, Charles, the Prince of Wales, would soon visit the United States, and I told his father that Chicago would be honored to be part of his tour. Philip responded with a delighted laugh and "we'll see."

Not that time, but later, Prince Charles did visit Chicago and the Midwest.

In his after-dinner remarks, Prince Philip recalled that he'd seen Washington for the first time as a young naval officer in WWII. He told us that while on shore leave, as his ship was being resupplied at the big United States Navy base in Norfolk, Virginia, he and some shipmates hitchhiked to the nation's capital because "that's where the girls were." It was a reference to the large wartime women's workforce. Of course, he and President Nixon both talked about the close relationship between their two countries. Secretary of State William Rogers and two of his predecessors—Dean Rusk and Dean Acheson—were there along with Sen. William Fulbright, chairman of the Senate Foreign Relations committee. After the dinner, it was more fun to talk to Bob Hope, also a guest.

Nixon was now entering his 10th month in office. The world's two communist giants, Russia and China, were feuding with each other. Nixon decided, as a result of this, that he was not going to allow one communist state, Russia, to speak for all of the communist countries. Since February, he'd covertly sought rapprochement with Beijing through third-party nations. The long used term "Red China" was quietly dropped by the White House, and substituted with "People's Republic of China." Secretary of State William Rogers announced that the United States favored cultural and scientific exchanges with the People's Republic. Slowly, vestiges of former policies and the diplomatic debris of the last 25 years were being cleared away. In time, policies of détente, and an opening to China, would be in full bloom.

As 1969 ended, I thought the bureau had improved its coverage and become more active in the social fabric of the capital. We had expanded dramatically our list of guests for the annual White House Correspondents' Association dinner. We held a private reception for them in an upstairs suite before going down to the hotel ballroom. An even bigger social step was taken in September, 1970, when Louise Hutchinson was elected president of the Women's National Press Club. It was an honor both for her and the Tribune. After her inauguration and a club reception, Sally and I hosted a buffet supper for 200 guests at the University Club to salute the occasion. In a thank you letter to us, Louise wrote that "from a number of people, I heard how welcome and comfortable you made everyone feel. In truth, of course, the matter goes much deeper than this. Nothing very much would be possible at all had not the mood and goals of the bureau changed so dramatically that the staff at last is able to function creatively and with zest. Please know that I am deeply appreciative to you both."

But, we still weren't where I wanted to be. When I expressed some unhappiness to Kirk, he replied by letter that it was all right to feel discouraged once or twice a week but not every day. Well, such feelings certainly didn't linger. I began traveling to Chicago more, at Kirk's request, to plan with him a daily op-ed page which would include outside writers. It was to be called *Perspective*. Our editorial writers didn't like the idea. But more and more papers did. When it became inevitable to the editorial writers that there would be an op-ed page, they asked if there could be a page between them and the op-ed writers. Really, now! But there was a problem with the page across from theirs. Marshall Field, the famous Chicago department store, had run a two-column ad on that page every morning for decades. It didn't want to move it. After some tough negotiating by the Tribune advertising department, Field agreed to give up its space. So, one more step in modernizing the editorial department took place.

My best story in 1970 was a scoop in the fall when I reported that the United States had forced the Soviet Union, in a series of "quiet and tough" diplomatic talks, to dismantle a base for missile-class submarines that it was building in Cuba. After American aerial photography disclosed the base under construction and U.S. and Soviet diplomats met secretly three times in Washington and once in Moscow, an agreement was reached to stop work and dismantle. The discussions started two days before Nixon went on a European trip in late September and they ended in mid-October in an exchange of messages through news media in what amounted to code.

My story disclosed the background of what took place.

Tass, the Russian News Agency, in a release four days before my story said that the Russians where not building a submarine base in Cuba. It said such reports were a falsification. The U.S. government took this to mean the base was gone, a view that jibed with photos taken by American overflights. American officials noted that in the English language translation of the *Tass* story, the news agency used the phrase "its military base" not "a military base."

Robert McCloskey, spokesman for the State Department, told reporters that United States officials had "noted the *Tass* statement and considered it to be 'positive.'" He wouldn't elaborate on why a statement accusing the American government of "falsification" was positive. My story said McCloskey's response was a signal to the Soviets, telling them in effect that the United States understood what the *Tass* message meant: the crisis was over.

The base, near the town of Cienfuegos on the southern cost of Cuba, was near completion when the United States first announced its discovery. No Soviet submarines ever entered the base, although a sub tender was spotted there. Chalmers Roberts, the veteran foreign affairs writer for the *Washington Post* at the time, speculated that my story had to be given to me by either Nixon or Secretary of State William Rogers. My source was Nixon, who had Herb Klein brief me.

In early November, 1970, I flew to Chicago to cover the midterm Congressional elections. My presence was in the long tradition of the Tribune for the Washington bureau chief to be in the city room on election night to write the main overall story. This followed a day later by an analysis of what had happened. The Democrats swept to a big victory and I wrote my analysis from that point of view.

I received a letter from Kirk upon my return to Washington which said, "Your analysis of the election, needless to say, caused quite a stir around here. My own feeling is that, while it was in conflict with our editorial and with Trohan, whose analysis was widely admired, it was a very useful operation and should be helpful in our effort to reduce the credibility gap."

Kirk went on to say that a recent letter of mine suggested to him "that our thinking follows similar channels as far as coverage of a big news event is concerned." He said that he had the same feeling that I had about our treatment of the space shot. "We can only change these things by telling staff members exactly what we want and by giving them direction." Kirk, like me, was not doctrinaire about politics. He told me once that he voted for Adlai Stevenson, not Eisenhower, when Ike ran for a second term in 1956. Upon becoming bureau chief, I visited members of the Illinois Democratic delegation and Democratic Congressional leaders. I told them that I could do nothing about Tribune editorials but that the bureau under me would be fair in our news coverage of them.

In late November, Kirk told me he wanted me to return to Chicago as managing editor at the beginning of next year, 1971. I was appalled. That was the last thing in the world I wanted to do. I told him no. I think he was surprised. But, my family and I had carved out a life in Washington, and across the Potomac River in Virginia where we lived, that we loved. Our lifestyle was pleasant. The Fairfax County school system was excellent. The winters were mild. Events and friends were stimulating. We had arrived in the area a decade earlier seeking new adventures and never looked back.

Kirk continued to push the issue, however. Sally told me years later that he flew to Washington and over lunch had asked for her help to persuade me. She told him it was my decision to make and that she would not interfere. This was our introduction to demands a corporation can make on the personal lives of families that are a part of management. It was a dilemma for us. How much do you owe the employer that feeds you? Finally, Kirk told me that I would have to leave the Tribune if I did not accede to its wishes.

CHAPTER THIRTY-SEVEN

CONFRONTING McCORMICK'S GHOST

I flew into Chicago on January 1, 1971, New Year's Day. My plane landed in a snowstorm. The weather was cold. I'd been managing editor for 14 hours. Kirk was waiting for me. I was surprised to see him considering how hard it was snowing. As we left O'Hare and drove into the city I saw snow drifts from previous snows that hadn't melted. Now more snow was falling on top of them. Visibility was low and driving was slow. Our windshield wipers moved back and forth at a quick pace as they battled to push the snow away.

I would have to get used to Midwest winters again. Days with temperatures below zero were certain to come along. Sidewalks would be icy at times. Heavy coats, hat and gloves would become the norm. For a few minutes, my thoughts went back in time. When I'd arrived in Washington 11 years earlier, almost to the day, I traveled in a reverse weather pattern. I moved to warmer weather. It was a new wintertime experience for me and I relished it. Often in late winter afternoons the bureau windows were open. I knew in Chicago the windows would be closed and often covered with a foreboding white frost.

Since it was a holiday, there was little traffic on Michigan Avenue as we pulled up in front of the Chicago Athletic Club, where I'd chosen to stay. Kirk had agreed to let Sally and my daughters stay behind in Virginia until the end of the school year. Jon was already in the Midwest as a freshman at Beloit College in nearby Wisconsin. The Club was across the Chicago River and down a half dozen blocks from Tribune Tower. It was in easy walking distance of my new job. The Club had a dining room and athletic facilities that included an Olympic-sized swimming pool, a sauna, and exercise room. I used the dining and athletic facilities regularly in the six months I was alone in Chicago. I became acquainted with employees of the Club and they were forthright in their opinions of the Tribune. They favored change.

During the ride from O'Hare, Kirk inquired if Frank Starr had arrived in Washington before I left. I said he had. Kirk and I differed on Starr as bureau chief. I was against him succeeding me and fought to prevent it. Kirk said he deserved the assignment as a reward for the time he spent as the Tribune's Moscow correspondent. I argued that you can't parachute a man into Washington and expect him to know what is going on. But I told Kirk that Sally and I had arranged a reception in mid-January at the University Club in the capital to introduce him and his wife, Hanalorie, to journalists and politicians.

I didn't have a high opinion of Starr as a newsman. His uncle, Don Starr, had been the paper's longtime editor of the cable desk before his retirement. As such, he handled foreign wire copy and stories from our correspondents overseas, including those of his nephew. Don Starr and Maxwell were close friends. I thought that relationship was more important than ability in determining my replacement. Frank Starr did not work out in Washington. In two years or so he was gone.

The snow showed no sign of abating as I walked into the Athletic Club. Kirk pulled away from the curb and headed for home. The unpleasant weather let up at nightfall and I headed up Michigan Avenue to the tower. John Wagner, one of my assistant editors who worked weekends, joined me for dinner. We continued a discussion begun several weeks earlier in Washington on style changes in make-up that would bring a livelier look to Tribune pages.

Change was the watchword as I began my tenure as managing editor.

Before I left Washington, City Editor David Halverson and I had discussed his idea to create a full-time investigative task force. I told him to have it ready to go when I arrived in Chicago. He set up a four-reporter team to whom we gave autonomy to work on investigations of their choice. They did not disappoint us. Their work included exposure of a real estate practice involving minorities known as redlining and also the use of skid row alcoholics and drug users to fulfill blood bank quotas. I was put out when the Associated Press Managing Editors organization chose an investigation of prison abuses in Florida as the best of the year. That subject seemed a shopworn old hat to me.

Throughout its history, the Tribune had functioned on a 24-hour news cycle. Once the day's paper was put to bed all unused stories and carbons of the day's copy were put into big barrels by copy desks to be thrown out and a new cycle began. It was a formula newspaper. Day in and day out an eight column headline heralded the story the managing editor picked as most important. An eight column sub-line topped the story chosen as second most eventful. This worked well before the five-day workweek. But, the five-day workweek (Monday through Friday) wrought havoc with the Sunday Tribune. No longer was there enough interesting spot news to fill news holes with meaningful copy. I thought we had to do more planning.

The Sunday Tribune wedded to breaking news had become a very bad paper. Near the end of my first week as managing editor, I called a meeting of all editorial department heads—finance, sports, city side, cable, telegraph, etc., plus assistant editors such as make-up to discuss how to improve the Sunday paper, especially, and also the Monday paper, a smaller version of our Sunday problems. I outlined some of my broader goals for transferring from a 24-hour cycle to a more holistic operation. I told them that we would keep doing things that work but we would drop things that were no longer meaningful or I thought were counter-productive to developing a more update product, a product that catered to the thoughts and desires of readers of the day.

Those words might sound presumptuous. After all, the Tribune was a highly innovative newspaper from its beginning in 1847, but now it seemed increasingly out of touch with the post-WWII world. I understood the loyalty of the old-timers. McCormick had given them employment during the Great Depression. He had built a publishing empire that ran with fine precision from timberlands owned in Canada for newsprint to the finished product for sale at the corner newsstand. But complacency had set in. I sometimes wondered if I had a right to change the Tribune's persona. But no one should try to second-guess a dead man, and this had become a Tribune problem. There were editors who felt nothing should change after Colonel McCormick's death in 1955. When presented a problem they asked themselves: "What would the colonel do?"

In 1966, when Martin Luther King, Jr. campaigned for racial justice in Chicago, Maxwell refused to see him. He seemed oblivious to the national drama unfolding.

"I don't think Colonel McCormick would have received him, and I didn't see why I should," Maxwell explained later in an interview with the *Wall Street Journal*. "You can't talk to everyone who comes to town and has a press agent who asks you to see him."

McCormick was dead. Who knows what position he would have taken on King or whether he would have been hawkish or dovish on America's involvement in Vietnam? Who knows what his reaction would have been to the Nixon tapes and Watergate? I felt it was time to let the colonel rest in peace and go where the news is. No one can run a living, breathing organization from the grave.

A year earlier, I attended a meeting of executives where Harold Grumhaus, who had become publisher, explained his credo: "Tell it like it is." He said this could mean much in getting away from "sacred cows and protecting politicians." Kirk echoed Grumhaus, saying that letting facts speak for themselves was paramount to a good newspaper. I thought that one of the most interesting things Kirk said was that he didn't believe it was any longer possible to create circulation by arousing passions. He said William Randolph Hearst rode to glory on that formula but in the end, because he rode it too long, it also caused his destruction. I thought the implication was clear. Changes, big and small, had to come to the Tribune.

Surveys by the Tribune showed that readers desired a reasoned and rational approach in coverage and that a staunch, uncompromising political slant was frowned upon. The latter would be up to Kirk and Grumhaus to end, not me. My job was to manage the day-to-day operations of the reportorial staff. In that regard, I did want to keep the paper's news pages politically neutral.

Circulation figures were discussed in the meeting. In the inner city at the time, the Tribune and its rival morning paper, the *Sun-Times*, were about the same, and that included African-American readership. It was a myth that the Tribune lacked readership among African-Americans. But, at the same time, the Tribune's greatest area of potential growth was in the suburbs. The Tribune circulation when I became managing editor was around 780,000. That was 220,000 below the paper's peak at the end of WWII.

Looking back, it's clear that no one in the newspaper industry really had an answer to what was happening. The destiny of newspapers was no longer in control of print journalists, no matter how good they were. A massive shift in the living habits of the American populace was beginning. Newspapers were in a holding action. No matter how valiantly we fought we were going to lose our dominance. In retrospect, TV was merely the harbinger of what was to come in new and competitive technologies that would change forever how people get their news. The business model that served newspapers for centuries became hopelessly inadequate but that sad truth for print journalists wouldn't became obvious until the first decade of the 21st century when creative destruction within the communications industry reached full bloom.

I've lived long enough to witness the change. But in 1971 I considered other newspapers my main competition. It was important for the Tribune's changing management, of which I was a part, to understand the mood of the era as we tried to build a new readership. Kirk took a hands-off attitude toward my day-to-day management of the newsroom. We had many dinners together during which we discussed broad issues. Dining with him was convenient for me since I was alone in Chicago.

In early spring, every two or three days I began to remove the color political cartoon that had been a fixture in the middle of the front page for as long as I could remember. I didn't want to stop the tradition cold for I knew the move would be controversial both inside and outside Tribune Tower. I understood the power of political cartoons. But having one on the front page among the top news stories every day sent a mixed message to readers. The political cartoon belonged on the editorial page. It would be just as powerful there in black and white as on the front page in color and the separation of news from editorial positions would be clear.

The front page political cartoon had been a potent weapon for Colonel McCormick in his long and bitter fight with President Roosevelt over FDR's New Deal. It was a symbol of McCormick's deep disdain for his antagonist. But both had been dead now for many years. The country was five presidents beyond FDR. After 40 years the entertainment value of a front page rollicking political brawl cartoon was gone. The country had moved on and so should the Tribune. I never understood why "old guard" Tribune officials had to be dragged kicking and screaming into the last half of the 20th century.

It is interesting to note that two Tribune political cartoonists of later years, Jeff MacNelly and Dick Locher, won Pulitzer Prizes for their work in black and white that appeared on the editorial page.

The Tribune without a doubt had excellent, even famous, political cartoonists through the years. John T. McCutcheon, Carey Orr, and Joe Parrish were household names. McCutcheon and Orr won Pulitzer Prizes. McCutcheon, who was with the Tribune from 1903 to 1946, was before my time. He was known as the "dean of political cartoonists." Even Orr and Parrish were only names to me. They had no personal connection with the newsroom. I did not know them. I never knew how they felt when I dropped the cartoon completely from the front page. Kirk never said a word to me about the change. Those above me just let it happen.

Without the political cartoon we now had space for photographs on the front page in addition to the printed word. Any hint of political indoctrination was gone. We had more flexibility in make-up of the page. The front page is the managing editor's page. I determined what stories would be on it, and where they would be placed. As far back as I could remember, the front page format of the Tribune looked the same day after day. It had become a formula newspaper. I believed otherwise. I thought a paper's front page should roll with the news. When big news broke let the reader know its importance with an eight column banner. On days when the news was soft, forego the banner headline and make-up the page with lesser headlines. Earmark the main story with the biggest headline but not an automatic eight column line.

One afternoon when I was a city room reporter, Maxwell called me to the center desk near the deadline for first edition copy. He told me he did not have a story to justify an eight column line but a robbery that might fill the bill had just been reported in a luxury apartment building along Lake Shore Drive a mile or so north of Tribune Tower. He told me to get up there, find what information I could, and dictate it to rewrite for the first edition. I figured I had at most a half hour to reach the crime scene, find police, and call in what they said happened. It wasn't much of a robbery, just several hundred dollars. The woman victim said she'd been struck by the robber as he fled. The only occurrence that saved the story at all was the police telling me that in escaping the robber had jumped over a gangway to the roof of a building next door.

My point is this. We needed a story to fit a long-used formula. The headline was great, in the usual big, bold type, about a robbery on the "Gold Coast" as this exclusive part of Chicago was and still is called. The leap over a gangway allowed us to call the thief a "cat robber" to add drama. The story, while true, was essentially manufactured for the headline. In later editions, when a better story turned up for the eight column line, the robbery was far back in the paper. A more flexible make-up that day would have eliminated the necessity to scramble for a story to fit a long held rule.

The incident made a big impression on me. The whole exercise seemed archaic. When I became managing editor, I discussed with Kirk the idea of a more flexible approach to front page make-up. I thought I'd taken the first step toward that goal with the switch of the front page political cartoon to the editorial page. I recalled for Kirk his comment about Hearst: he waited too long to stop playing on readers' emotions to sell papers. I said daily eight column headlines were in that same category. Kirk told me that I could go without the eight column line some day when the news was soft.

That day did come. It passed without incident and I continued to drop the eight column line as I saw fit. But one weekend Kirk called me at home and said he would like to come over. It was early fall and nights were cool. When he arrived I had a blaze going in the living room fireplace of the home Sally and I had bought in suburban Hinsdale that summer. After we settled in, Kirk said I was going without the eight column line too often.

"We need to talk about this," he said. "The eight column headline is a Tribune tradition. Old time readers expect to see it. There has to be a limit on going without it."

Oh boy, I thought, a new formula. From the day of my birth until I became managing editor, the Tribune had used the same front page make-up day in and day out.

"Our old time readers are dwindling away," I told Kirk. "Why can't we just roll with the news? That way, we have flexibility on make-up. You know my philosophy."

"You're not going to be shut out completely," he countered. "You can still go without the line eleven days a month."

"How do I pick those eleven days?" I asked. "It might be difficult to space out eleven days evenly."

But I was making progress. I said I would do has he directed.

I had no choice, of course. A week or so later I poked my head into Kirk's office to seek a minute of his time. But, I withdrew when I saw Dr. Theodore Van Dellen, a friend of Colonel McCormick's widow who for many years had written a health column for the Tribune, seated before Kirk and deep in conversation. Later, Kirk informed me that Van Dellen told him I was ruining the paper. I don't know why I was singled out as though I were a thing unto myself. All of the present management seemed to be together in the changes going on.

I will say that each of us seemed to have a great deal of autonomy. We did have weekly meetings chaired by Grumhaus but I didn't think we discussed anything substantive. I pointed out several times, along with Charley Corcoran, our circulation manager, that the presses sometimes were breaking down during their nightly runs with deliveries being delayed, or canceled. The only answer was that the presses were old. The apathy seemed especially strange to me since Grumhaus had come up through the production department. The presses were his babies.

One day Kirk stopped by my office off of the newsroom to ask me if I had noticed anything different in the masthead. I picked up a copy of that morning's paper on my desk. "I'll be damned," I exclaimed. With a quick glance I saw that the Tribune's longtime slogan "The World's Greatest Newspaper" was gone. The slogan had been controversial for many years. Political opponents of the paper often made fun of it. The phrase went back to an era when American businesses had watchwords for their products, including newspapers. The *New York Times* said it contained "All the News That's Fit to Print." The *Atlanta Journal* claimed it "Covered Dixie Like the Dew." The *Denver Post* said it was "The Voice of the Rocky Mountain Empire." The *Baltimore Sun* said it was "The Light for All." In February, Grumhaus had told the *Wall Street Journal* in an interview that "in a journalistic sense we definitely are the world's greatest newspaper." In the same article Kirk said, "of course we aren't. It's not a literal statement. It's a poetic phrase that attempts to set some objectives."

However it was interpreted, now it was gone. A few months earlier the motto "An American Paper for Americans" placed under an imprint of the American flag in the masthead was withdrawn. I pushed for the flag to be dropped also, replaced by the weather forecast in a box. But the flag remained. I was leery about pushing patriotism as a tenet of the paper. Patriotism is not a self-proclaimed commodity. It is an honor bestowed. I didn't believe that many readers were attracted to the Tribune because of the Stars and Stripes. Readers bought the paper for its news content and giving them a good news package every day was my job. The weather seemed more attuned to news than the flag.

I never liked the phrase "An American Paper for Americans." It didn't fit a country of immigrants. There was an uppity tone to it. I didn't mind "The World's Greatest Newspaper." I could take it or leave it. I think most readers recognized it for what it was: a harmless holdover from the circulation wars in the heyday of print journalism. Now that it was gone, the decision was fine with me. No newspaper was ever going to be great again with the changes underway in the media. In the technologically dominated world of many voices that was to come, the long-held newspaper role of principle opinion maker would be stripped away. Newspapers, including the Tribune, would fight to stay alive and relevant. Most would become skeletons of their former selves.

But at the end of 1971 the Tribune remained a highly profitable organization. Circulation had stayed steady throughout the year. Still, when an institution tries to change its image to adjust to changing cultures and lifestyles, the move is bound to meet resistance from some executives, stockholders, and old-time employees who were happy with a formula that had worked for a half a century. One of the factors that led to my resignation on December 29, just short of a year as managing editor, was a feeling I sensed in corporate management that I was moving too fast, that I was different. Nothing sinister was involved and there was nothing I was bitter about. It was just a matter of a difference of opinion. I knew that eventually the Tribune would accomplish what I wanted to accomplish. But my timetable was disputed. I felt that as long as our changes weren't meeting resistance from readers we might as well go for more. My family's unhappiness in the Chicago area was another factor. Our daughters, Holly and Allison, had lived virtually their entire lives in the Washington area, and were anxious to go back. Sally and I had discussed returning to our old neighborhood in Virginia outside of Washington as early as October.

We had been through a lot together with the Tribune, sometimes good, sometimes bad. In the end, my leaving tipped toward the latter. When I called Sally to tell her I'd resigned, her first words were "Thank God, at last." So, once again, like the time we left St. Louis years earlier, we entered a world with our future unknown.

Two days after I left, Kirk posted a staff memo which listed 27 innovations made at the Tribune since 1965. He noted that 12 of them, almost half, had taken place while I was managing editor. The *Chicago Journalism Review* listed some: no more mandatory eight column line, the success of the task force in investigative reporting, removal of the political cartoon from the front page, "*Accion Rapida*," a Spanish language version of a reader service column, "Action Express," and noticeable strides in removing the "pompousness and innuendo" that appeared in some Tribune stories in the past. Also, the Sunday paper had been turned into an interesting, readable package with one million copies sold each week.

That night, Kirk and I had a long dinner together. He acknowledged that I had carried a heavy load for several years going back to Trohan's initial conflicts with me in Washington. We discussed the changes that had been made in the paper. But I told him I did not believe more change would ever be enough to ward off further declines in the circulation and advertising revenues. The Tribune was still in excellent financial shape. It had been the wealthiest Chicago paper for more than a century. It was still the dominant paper in mid-America. But we agreed that the newspaper business was a beleaguered industry. New technologies were ripping apart and changing the media world. Within a few years both remaining Chicago afternoon newspapers were gone. The Tribune's daily circulation is now about evenly divided between paper and digital subscribers. The printed paper is a skeleton of its former self. Tribune Tower has been sold to a real estate developer. Gone are the Canadian timberlands and paper mills and the Tribune-owned Great Lakes freighters that carried newsprint to Chicago

Then on June 8, 2018, after 93 years, the Tribune staff vacated its newsroom in Tribune Tower and moved a few blocks south across the Chicago River to the Prudential building. Everything that had connected me physically to the Tribune was now gone. The move was truly the end of a once dominating newspaper empire.

I was shocked. I always had such a wonderful feeling inside me about working in Tribune Tower; there was a certain nobility of purpose about the structure itself. It was so iconic. The paper and the tower were one in the same to me. I always had a feeling of grandeur as I walked in and out of the tower daily.

But those days are gone. Like other remaining newspapers, the Tribune struggles to stay afloat. I never thought the Tribune would change as it has. But that is what happens when hedge funds and realtors become involved. Each new owner weakens the enterprise in some way. Take the money and run until there is nothing left.

Chou Ein Lai, former premier of China, was asked once if he thought the French Revolution had been a success. He reportedly replied that it was too early to say. It is also too early to say if the digital revolution will be a success, not technically, but in positive ethical and moral ways. With the change to online editions of newspapers, along with social media platforms and cable, news is updated minute by minute throughout the day. As a result, news comes at the public with lightning speed. There is no longer time to digest news in a systemic fashion, to have a contemplative lag to absorb in one's mind what has just been reported. Chaos, disruption, even anxiety, occur daily. It isn't a healthy development, either physically or mentally. I've lived through historic change in communications. A look at the list of names which are accredited now to the various Congressional press galleries on Capitol Hill shows that Radio and Television gallery personnel outnumber those in the Newspaper gallery by around two to one, a startling reversal from my first days in Washington. Newspapers were supreme when I was born. They only hit the street once every 24 hours. There was time for reflection before reaction. The world was orderly in receiving news. That orderliness is gone.

I hope newspapers continue in some fashion. It is important to have a robust marketplace with as many outlets as possible. Print reporters will always be needed to walk the halls of governments if there is to be a check on corruption and political skullduggery. They are inherently better at this than electronic media reporters.

Trohan lived to be 100 years old. I always said that he was around for so long because God didn't know what to do with him. As I move into my mid-nineties, I'm beginning to think that I might be in the same situation myself.

NOTES

1. Hubert Humphrey, *The Education of a Public Man: My Life and Politics* (Garden City, NY: Doubleday & Company, 1976).

2. Kurt Vonnegut, Jr., *Slaughterhouse-Five* (New York: Delacorte Press/Seymour Lawrence, Bantam Doubleday/Dell Publishing, 1969).

3. Anatoly Dobrynin, *In Confidence* (New York: Times Books, a division of Random House, 1995).

4. Dobrynin, *In Confidence.*

5. Dobrynin, *In Confidence.*

6. Gary Zukav, *The Seat of the Soul* (New York: Simon & Shuster, 2014).

7. Evan Thomas, *Ike's Bluff* (New York: Little, Brown and Company/ Hachette Book Group, 2012).

8. William Manchester, *American Caesar* (Boston: Little, Brown and Company, 1978).

PHOTOGRAPHS

INDEX